The Economics of Climate-Resilient Development

The Economics of Climate-Resilient Development

Edited by

Sam Fankhauser

Grantham Research Institute on Climate Change and the Environment, London School of Economics, UK

Thomas K.J. McDermott

School of Economics, University College Cork, Ireland

Edward Elgar
PUBLISHING

Cheltenham, UK • Northampton, MA, USA

Published by
Edward Elgar Publishing Limited
The Lypiatts
15 Lansdown Road
Cheltenham
Glos GL50 2JA
UK

Edward Elgar Publishing, Inc.
William Pratt House
9 Dewey Court
Northampton
Massachusetts 01060
USA

A catalogue record for this book
is available from the British Library

Library of Congress Control Number: 2016931793

This book is available electronically in the **Elgar**online
Economics subject collection
DOI 10.4337/9781785360312

ISBN   978 1 78536 030 5 (cased)
ISBN   978 1 78536 031 2 (eBook)

Typeset by Servis Filmsetting Ltd, Stockport, Cheshire
Printed and bound in Great Britain by TJ International Ltd, Padstow

Contents

Figures

Tables

Boxes

Contributors

EDITORS

Sam Fankhauser, Grantham Research Institute on Climate Change and the Environment and Centre for Climate Change Economics and Policy, London School of Economics, London

Thomas K.J. McDermott, School of Economics, University College Cork, Cork, and Grantham Research Institute on Climate Change and the Environment, London School of Economics, London

CONTRIBUTING AUTHORS

Mook Bangalore, Climate Change Group, World Bank, Washington, DC

Mintewab Bezabih, Grantham Research Institute on Climate Change and the Environment and Centre for Climate Change Economics and Policy, London School of Economics, London

Laura Bonzanigo, Climate Change Group, World Bank, Washington, DC

David Castells-Quintana, IREA, Universitat de Barcelona, Barcelona

Hélia Costa, LSE Cities, Grantham Research Institute on Climate Change and the Environment and Centre for Climate Change Economics and Policy, London School of Economics, London

Simon Dietz, Centre for Climate Change Economics and Policy, Grantham Research Institute on Climate Change and the Environment, and Department of Geography and Environment, London School of Economics, London

Charlie Dixon, Vivid Economics, London

Marianne Fay, Sustainable Development Vice-Presidency, World Bank, Washington, DC

Jared Finnegan, Department of Government, Grantham Research Institute on Climate Change and the Environment and Centre for Climate Change Economics and Policy, London School of Economics, London

Graham Floater, LSE Cities, London School of Economics, and Centre for Trade and Economic Integration, The Graduate Institute, Geneva

Stephane Hallegatte, Climate Change Group, World Bank, Washington, DC

Alistair Hunt, Department of Economics, University of Bath, Bath

Tamaro Kane, Climate Change Group, World Bank, Washington, DC

Maria del Pilar Lopez-Uribe, Department of Economics, London School of Economics, London

Stefania Lovo, Grantham Research Institute on Climate Change and the Environment and Centre for Climate Change Economics and Policy, London School of Economics, London

Courtney McLaren, Grantham Research Institute on Climate Change and the Environment and Centre for Climate Change Economics and Policy, London School of Economics, London

Ulf Narloch, Sustainable Development Vice-Presidency, World Bank, Washington, DC

Julie Rozenberg, Sustainable Development Vice-Presidency, World Bank, Washington, DC

Gregor Singer, Grantham Research Institute on Climate Change and the Environment and Centre for Climate Change Economics and Policy, London School of Economics, London

Swenja Surminski, Grantham Research Institute on Climate Change and the Environment and Centre for Climate Change Economics and Policy, London School of Economics, London

David Treguer, Agriculture Global Practice, World Bank, Washington, DC

Adrien Vogt-Schilb, Climate Change Group, World Bank, Washington, DC

Maria Waldinger, Grantham Research Institute on Climate Change and the Environment and Centre for Climate Change Economics and Policy, London School of Economics, London

John Ward, Vivid Economics, London

Paul Watkiss, Paul Watkiss Associates, Oxford

Acknowledgements

The production of this book was supported by the International Development Research Centre (IDRC) under the project *The Economics of Adaptation and Climate-Resilient Development*. Chapters 1, 6, 7 and 11 are direct outputs of the project, while Chapters 8 and 9 received partial support. We also acknowledge the University College Cork Strategic Research Fund, the Grantham Foundation for the Protection of the Environment and the UK Economic and Social Research Council (ESRC) through its support of the Centre for Climate Change Economics and Policy.

The book also brings together research and analysis from several other projects. Chapters 2, 4, 9 and 10 stem from another IDRC-sponsored initiative, *Pathways to Climate-Resilience in Semi-Arid Economies* (PRISE). Chapter 3 summarizes the recent World Bank report, *Shock Waves: Managing the Impacts of Climate Change on Poverty*, which received funding from the Global Facility for Disaster Reduction and Recovery (GFDRR) and the UK Department for International Development (DFID). Chapter 5 is derived from work that was also commissioned by DFID.

In addition to support from IDRC, Chapters 6 and 7 further draw on research undertaken as part of the ECONADAPT project, funded by the European Union's Seventh Framework Programme (Grant Agreement No. 603906) and work commissioned by DFID on early value-for-money adaptation. Chapters 8 and 10 also draw on research carried out under two EU Framework Programme 7 projects, *RAMSES* (Grant Agreement No. 308497) and *ENHANCE* (Grant Agreement No. 308438).

The chapter authors would like to acknowledge the comments and feedback from fellow authors as well as the following individuals: Guy Jobbins (Chapters 2, 4, 9, 10); Annika Olsson (Chapters 2, 4, 5); Declan Conway and Estelle Rouhaud (Chapters 2, 4, 11); Florence Crick, Hayley Leck and Helen Parker (Chapters 2, 4); Malcolm Smart (Chapter 5); Lisa Mackie and Philipp Rode (Chapter 8); Bhim Adhikari, Chris Duffy, Ara Jo, Anna Okatenko and Catherine Simonet (Chapter 11). Rossi Abi Rafeh, Veda Narasimhan and Monir Shaikh provided research assistance for Chapters 2 and 4.

The views expressed in this book, and any remaining errors, are the sole responsibility of the authors.

1. Climate-resilient development: an introduction

Sam Fankhauser and Thomas K.J. McDermott

1.1 INTRODUCTION

This book is about the link between economic development and adaptation to climate change from an economics perspective. Stern (2015) has called climate change and poverty alleviation the two biggest societal challenges of the twenty-first century. They are linked, Stern observes, and failing in one means failing in the other. The notion of climate-resilient development acknowledges this complementarity.

Low-income countries will be among the most affected by climate change, to the point where development progress might be at risk. At the same time, the rapid development these countries are undergoing – in terms of economic growth, capital accumulation and demographics – is changing fundamentally their vulnerability to climate change, for better or for ill. The combination of rapid population growth with ongoing urbanization, for example, is expected to lead to a large-scale expansion of urban areas, a trend that is most pronounced in locations that are vulnerable to climate extremes.

The pace and scale of changes underway means that the greatest opportunities for achieving climate resilience lie in guiding current development trends. This is reinforced by the danger – if climate risks are ignored – of locking in long-term risks, for example, through haphazard urban development in risky locations. There is a window of opportunity to act now to reduce future vulnerability.

The dynamic interaction of development trends with climate exposure and vulnerability is at the heart of climate-resilient development, and in contrast to traditional adaptation analysis. Much of the economic literature still treats adaptation to climate change as a set of self-standing activities that are assessed at the micro-level, for example, through cost-benefit analyses of specific response options. This often includes a fairly sophisticated treatment of climate scenarios and uncertainties, but little discussion of macro-level trends such as urbanization, economic diversification and openness to trade.

Climate-resilient development is just one aspect of the broader notion of climate-smart development, which puts equal weight on reducing greenhouse gas emissions and managing residual climate risks. Even broader are the concepts of green growth – defined as growth that preserves aggregate natural capital (Bowen and Hepburn, 2014) – and sustainable development, which has an economic, social and environmental dimension (for an early definition see Pearce et al., 1989). It is important to take a holistic approach to development that encompasses all these concerns. However, there is also value in exploring in more depth the narrower challenge of climate-resilient development. That is the purpose of this book.

1.2   FROM ADAPTATION TO CLIMATE-RESILIENT DEVELOPMENT

Climate-resilient development both builds on and departs from traditional adaptation economics. To understand how it is worth reviewing how the economic analysis of adaptation has evolved over time.

Initially, the main objective of economic adaptation studies was to refine the understanding of climate change impacts. It was recognized that, to be accurate, climate change impact assessments had to factor in people's response to that change. As it was put at the time, farmers were not dumb (Schneider et al., 2000). They would adjust farming practices in response to new climate conditions. Similarly, coastal planners would adjust sea defences and households would increase air conditioning demand, all of which would alter the profile of climate change impacts. The insight was brought to its logical conclusion in the Ricardian approach to impact assessment (the pioneering paper is Mendelsohn et al., 1994). Ricardian studies compare the economic performance of well-adapted societies with different climates. That is, they assume a level of near-perfect adaptation. In reality, of course, farmers are neither dumb nor capable of adapting perfectly overnight. Adaptation requires forethought and effort.

The recognition that adaptation requires forethought turned it into an interesting economic problem in its own right. Researchers began to explore in normative terms how good adaptation decisions should look, particularly when dealing with climate uncertainty (Ranger et al., 2010; Hallegatte et al., 2011), and they developed prescriptions about who should do what and when (Fankhauser et al., 1999; Hallegatte et al., 2010).

Positive analysis explored why adaptation may be sub-optimal as a consequence of market, policy or behavioural barriers (Repetto, 2008; Cimato and Mullan, 2010) or more generally a lack in adaptive capacity (Brooks et al., 2005). Classifications were developed to better understand

and describe the various forms of adaptation (Füssel, 2007). There was a suspicion, later corroborated by empirical evidence (for example, Tol and Yohe, 2007), that adaptation constraints were particularly prevalent in developing countries. This became known as the adaptation gap and effort went into understanding its causes (Fankhauser and McDermott, 2014).

An important question throughout was how much adaptation might cost (Fankhauser, 2010) and how the incremental cost of adaptation might be disentangled from baseline costs (Callaway et al., 2006). This was because developed countries had promised to support the adaptation efforts of poor countries under the United Nations Framework Convention on Climate Change. Negotiators wanted to know the size of the bill.

In all these research efforts, adaptation to climate change was treated as a distinct new challenge, a problem that had not existed before. Yet, adaptation to climatic risks is not a new problem. It is intricately linked to long-standing challenges, such as disaster risk management, water management, coastal zone planning, crop choices and infrastructure design. The climate context has always been crucial to these decisions. It is more useful therefore to think of climate change as adding further complexity to existing problems, instead of treating adaptation as a field in its own right.

One of the strongest links to existing challenges is between climate change and economic development. Adaptation and development are so heavily intertwined that in most practical cases it is not possible to ascertain where development interventions end and adaptation to climate change begins (McGray et al., 2007). Education, sanitation, good institutions and access to credit are core concerns of economic development. They are also important determinants of people's ability to deal with climate risks (Kahn, 2005; Tol and Yohe, 2007; McDermott et al., 2014).

This then is the basic tenet of climate-resilient development: to treat development and adaptation as heavily interrelated problems and to pursue poverty alleviation and climate resilience in an integrated way.

1.3 THE LINKS BETWEEN CLIMATE AND DEVELOPMENT

How does climate-resilient development differ from conventional development? Schelling (1992, 1997) famously claimed that economic development was the best form of adaptation, implying that conventional and climate-resilient development is one and the same. Yet not all forms of development have the same outcome in terms of climate resilience. There are important differences (Bowen et al., 2012). To identify them it is useful to revisit the main inter-linkages between climate and development.

For many linkages the causality runs from climate to development. The main impacts of climate change on development are summarized by David Castells-Quintana, Maria Lopez-Uribe and Thomas K.J. McDermott in Chapter 2 and reviewed in more detail by the Intergovernmental Panel on Climate Change (IPCC, 2014). Climatic factors have a direct impact on development through agriculture and labour productivity, through the prevalence of disease and through the impact of weather extremes on physical and human capital. Less tangibly, and less well understood, climate factors may also affect development indirectly through their effect on institutions. In Chapter 3, Stephane Hallegatte, Mook Bangalore and co-authors outline the implications of climate change for poverty alleviation.

Most impact studies concentrate on level effects, such as a climate change-induced reduction in agricultural output, but these static effects have dynamic repercussions. There is evidence that, at least in developing countries, climate extremes are associated not just with lower economic output, but also with lower rates of growth (Dell et al., 2012). Growth rates are affected in a number of ways (Fankhauser and Tol, 2005). A reduction in economic output will translate into lower levels of investment, in absolute terms, and therefore slower capital accumulation and growth. Forward-looking agents may also change their savings behaviour if future returns on investment are at risk from climate change. In a world where growth is endogenous, these two effects may be exacerbated through changes in labour productivity and the rate of technical progress.

For other linkages the causality runs the other way round, from development trends to climate vulnerability. Many development choices have the potential to fundamentally alter the vulnerability profile of countries to climate change. Contrary to Schelling's (1992, 1997) conjecture, not all of these changes are necessarily positive.

As countries develop, many things change. The structure of their economy evolves, typically away from agriculture into industry and ultimately services. Across the economy, sectors become more productive as firms invest in modern technology and adopt new production techniques. The location of economic activity also shifts. This is often associated with migration away from rural areas and into the urban centres (Vivid Economics, 2015). Finally, income per capita rises. With higher incomes, the demand for climate protection also goes up. People invest more in adaptation (Fankhauser and McDermott, 2014).

Of these changes, only the increased demand for adaptation unequivocally reduces climate change risks. The net effect of the other trends is unclear. Although agriculture is highly sensitive to climate change, a structural shift into services and industry is beneficial only if those sectors are not themselves subject to climate risks. They may well be, for example, if production facilities are located in hazard zones, if water-intensive industries add to water stress or if firms are linked to vulnerable sectors through their supply chain (ASC, 2014). A similar story holds for structural shifts from outdoor activity (for example, agriculture, construction) to indoor occupations (manufacturing, services) and for rural-urban migration. The growth of coastal cities in Asia, for example, is associated with a massive increase in flood risk exposure (Hanson et al., 2011).

The impact of development trends on climate resilience is therefore ambiguous and context-specific. However, this means that it can at least in part be managed. By incorporating climate change concerns explicitly into development strategies, spatial plans and infrastructure decisions it is possible to anticipate and reduce future climate risks. This integrated, proactive approach to adaptation is the essence of climate-resilient development. There is much uncertainty about the specific nature of climate change impacts at the local level, but this does not imply a wait-and-see approach to adaptation planning, as discussed in the next section.

1.4 ENSURING CLIMATE-RESILIENT DEVELOPMENT

Climate-resilient development requires intervention on a number of fronts. Much of it will be carried out by private agents, but some of it must be spearheaded by government. In Chapter 4 David Castells-Quintana, Maria Lopez-Uribe and Thomas K.J. McDermott review the basic response strategies available to decision makers. The chapter distinguishes between *in situ* adaptation, which aims to make existing locations, livelihoods and forms of production less vulnerable, and *transformational* adaptation, which involves the movement of people and economic activity across sectors and across space.

Not all measures need to be implemented at once. In Chapter 7, Paul Watkiss identifies three generic priority areas, where adaptation action is required now: (1) strategic decisions with a long time horizon, such as spatial or urban settlement planning, which lock in vulnerability profiles for the long term; (2) low-regrets measures that have an immediate development impact as well as climate-resilience benefits; and (3) measures with long lead-times, such as research and development, which take time to come to fruition. The three priorities go back to a theoretical framework developed in Fankhauser et al. (1999), which recognizes the long-term, sequential nature of climate-resilient development (Box 1.1).

It makes sense to address climate change concerns in lockstep with conventional development planning. Development strategies typically have a

BOX 1.1 SETTING PRIORITIES FOR CLIMATE-RESILIENT DEVELOPMENT

Ensuring climate resilience is a long process that will span over decades as climatic changes become increasingly evident. This raises the question of how response measures should be sequenced and timed.

From an economic point of view, an adaptation response should be fast-tracked if the net present value of implementing the measure now is greater than the net present value of implementing it later.

In simple mathematical notation, the net present value (NPV) of implementing a measure now can be written as follows:

$$NPV^{now} = -Cost^{now} + ST\_Benefit^{now} + \delta \cdot LT\_Benefit^{now}$$

The net present value is the discounted sum of capital costs (which occur now), short-term benefits (also occurring now) and long-term benefits (which occur later and are therefore discounted at rate σ). For simplicity, we assume there are only two time periods, 'now' and 'later'.

We can compare this net present value to the NPV of implementing the same measure at a later date:

$$NPV^{later} = -\delta \cdot Cost^{later} + \delta \cdot LT\_Benefit^{later}$$

Capital costs now occur in the later period and therefore have to be discounted. Although the proposed measure is the same, future costs may differ, for example, because retrofitting a measure into existing structures is more expensive than doing so at the outset. Long-term benefits may also differ, for example, if they ramp up slowly over time. Since implementation is delayed there are no short-term benefits.

Bringing the response measure forward makes sense if NPV^{now} is greater than NPV^{later}. That is, if $NPV^{now} - NPV^{later}$ is greater than zero. So we subtract the second equation from the first and find:

$$(\delta \cdot Cost^{later} - Cost^{now}) + ST\_Benefit^{now} + (\delta \cdot LT_{Benefit}{}^{now} - \delta \cdot LT_{Benefit}{}^{later}) > 0$$

This gives us three generic factors that justify bringing resilience measures forward:

- If the capital cost of implementing the measure later is higher than doing so today, that is, if we risk *lock-in* into a costly development path.
- If a measure has substantial short-term benefits that would otherwise be forgone, that is, if it is a *low-regret option*.
- If a delay would reduce future benefits, for example, because they would not materialize in time due to *long lead-times*.

time horizon of perhaps five to ten years, although they influence development paths and climate vulnerability over several decades. Over a five- to ten-year time horizon, there are numerous development, investment and planning decisions that meet one of the above criteria for priority adaptation.

In terms of low-regrets options, interventions that yield both development and climate-resilience benefits relate, for example, to human development, environmental protection and rural development. There is an urgent need to improve agricultural productivity and reform the institutional environment in terms of land titling, water abstraction and water management, as Mintewab Bezabih, Stefania Lovo and co-authors discuss in Chapter 9. Another promising option with immediate benefits is risk sharing and insurance, reviewed by Swenja Surminski in Chapter 10. There is a long tradition of managing risks by spreading them across larger population groups, and a lack of post-disaster finance for reconstruction is known to aggravate and prolong a crisis (World Bank, 2010). However, formal insurance schemes in developing countries are still rare.

There is also a large number of development interventions that have long-term consequences for climate resilience. Much of the basic infrastructure in developing countries is yet to be built. There is a huge need to invest in roads, railway lines, ports, airports, electric power systems and water supply networks. Urban areas are also developing rapidly. The point in time when new urban centres are planned and large-scale infrastructure is built is a natural 'entry point' for adaptation. In Chapter 5 Simon Dietz, Charlie Dixon and John Ward review the infrastructure deficits and plans in sub-Saharan Africa with a view to identify future adaptation hot spots. In Chapter 8, Hélia Costa, Graham Floater and Jared Finnegan discuss the particular challenges of climate-resilient urban development.

The identification of generic adaptation priorities and 'hot spots' for intervention does not obviate the need for careful project appraisal. Resilience measures can easily be mis-specified. In Chapter 6, Paul Watkiss and Alistair Hunt discuss the analytical challenges that this may raise, in particular in dealing with climate uncertainty. While the basic processes that drive climate change are well understood, the exact nature of future climatic changes at particular locations remains highly uncertain. In designing adaptation responses, the right combination between robustness and flexibility must therefore be found to prepare for different possible climate outcomes.

It is worth emphasizing that climate uncertainty does not imply a wait-and-see approach to climate resilience. For one thing, the prospects for improvements in our ability to forecast climate changes at a fine spatial resolution appear dim (Stainforth et al., 2007; Heal and Millner, 2014), which limit the value of waiting for new information. Moreover, in the case where adaptation policy might avoid locking in long-term exposure to climate risk the presence of uncertainty favours the early adoption of adaptation measures, under a precautionary principle (McDermott, 2016).

1.5 TRANSFORMATIONAL CHANGE

As Paul Watkiss observes in Chapter 6, most climate-resilient development plans currently aim to protect existing locations and activities through *in situ* adaptation, perhaps because their primary concern is moderate climate change. There is an argument that more attention should perhaps be paid to transformational adaptation.

Current adaptation strategies tend to be overly static (Kocornik-Mina and Fankhauser, 2015). They are geared at preserving current economic structures, for example, by putting a heavy emphasis on maintaining agricultural output, even though rural economies are evolving fast. After an extreme event, there is a temptation to rebuild the economy 'just as it was before', rather than factoring in manifest climate risks. Even analytically, climate change impact assessments often impose climate change on today's economy, rather than the socio-economic structures of the future.

Climate-resilient development is inherently more dynamic. It recognizes that even before climate change many developing countries are undergoing a process of deep socio-economic change. Factors like economic growth, population growth, technological innovation, globalization and urbanization are combining to alter the fabric of developing economies. Strategies for climate resilience have to recognize and leverage these trends, rather than trying to stem them. In other words, adaptation to climate change has to become more transformational.

Resilience measures are considered to be transformational if at least one of three conditions holds: (1) the measures are pursued at a large scale; (2) they rely on novel approaches and tools; or (3) they involve deep structural changes to economic activity and/or location (Kates et al., 2012). The classification makes it clear that transformational adaptation is not without friction. Even if it leverages existing trends, there may be rigidities and path dependencies that are hard to overcome. The successful implementation of transformational change is therefore as much about the political economy as it is about development planning.

The transformational adaptation response where this is most manifest is relocation. Migration away from hazard zones is a well-established and common coping strategy in many countries, as Maria Waldinger shows in Chapter 11. However, such migration is often temporary and in most cases domestic. International migration caused directly by climate shocks is rare. Even so, Chapter 11 makes clear the large degree of institutional safeguards that are needed, both in the sending and the receiving jurisdiction, to make migration an effective adaptation tool. Unplanned and unco-ordinated migration, quite possibly from one hazard zone into another, is more likely to be a sign of adaptation failure.

1.6 CONCLUSIONS

Climate-resilient development integrates development policy with adaptation to climate change. The integration is sensible, given the multiple links between the two concerns. A certain amount of climate change is now unavoidable and developing countries are likely to be most affected by it. But there is also an opportunity to reduce future vulnerability by guiding growth and development in a climate-resilient direction.

Policy makers must become aware of the consequences for climate vulnerability of development choices, and identify 'entry points' for adaptation action; that is, opportunities to incorporate climate resilience into long-term development, infrastructure and spatial planning decisions. This is likely to reveal trade-offs – for example, between urban growth and climate vulnerability – but well-designed projects will also be able to exploit synergies between climate resilience, growth and poverty alleviation.

Pursuing climate-resilient development has implications for both adaptation and development policy (Kocornik-Mina and Fankhauser, 2015). It forces development planners and adaptation planners to work more closely together. In the process, economic development plans will become more climate-aware and acknowledge future climate risks. In turn, adaptation plans may begin to reflect better the dynamism and evolving nature of modern economies, perhaps leading to more transformative forms of adaptation.

There are also institutional consequences. Climate-resilient development shifts the responsibility for adaptation from environment departments and hydro-meteorological offices to planning and economic ministries. These tend to be more powerful and better able to instigate the necessary reforms. It is an important and sometimes overlooked side-effect of moving from adaptation to climate-resilient development.

REFERENCES

ASC, 2014. *Managing Climate Risks to Wellbeing and the Economy. Progress Report 2014*. London: UK Adaptation Sub-Committee.

Bowen, A. and Hepburn, C., 2014. 'Green growth: an assessment', *Oxford Review of Economic Policy*, **30**(3), 407–22.

Bowen, A., Cochrane, S. and Fankhauser, S., 2012. 'Climate change, adaptation and growth', *Climatic Change*, **113**(2), 95–106.

Brooks, N., Adger, W.N. and Kelly, P.M., 2005. 'The determinants of vulnerability and adaptive capacity at the national level and the implications for adaptation', *Global Environmental Change*, **15**(2), 151–63.

Callaway, J.M., Louw, D.B., Nkomo, J.C., Hellmuth, M.E. and Sparks, D.A., 2006. 'The Berg river dynamic spatial equilibrium model: a new tool for assessing the benefits and costs of alternatives for coping with water demand growth, climate variability, and climate change in the Western Cape', Document de travail de l'AIACC No. 31, 41.

Cimato, F. and M. Mullan, 2010. 'Adapting to climate change: analysing the role of government', Defra Evidence and Analysis Series, Paper 1, UK Department for the Environment, Food and Rural Affairs, London.

Dell, M., Jones, B. and Olken, B., 2012. 'Temperature shocks and economic growth: evidence from the last half a century', *American Economic Journal: Macroeconomics*, **4**(3), 66–95.

Fankhauser, S., 2010. 'The costs of adaptation', *Wiley Interdisciplinary Review Climate Change*, **1**(1), 23–30.

Fankhauser, S. and McDermott, T.K.J., 2014. 'Understanding the adaptation deficit: why are poor countries more vulnerable to climate events than rich countries?', *Global Environmental Change*, **27**, 9–18.

Fankhauser, S. and Tol, R.S.J., 2005. 'On climate change and economic growth', *Resource and Energy Economics*, **27**(1), 1–17.

Fankhauser, S., Smith, J.B. and Tol, R., 1999. 'Weathering climate change. some simple rules to guide adaptation investments', *Ecological Economics*, **30**(1), 67–78.

Füssel, H.M. 2007. 'Adaptation planning for climate change: concepts, assessment approaches, and key lessons', *Sustainability Science*, **2**(2), 265–75.

Hallegatte, S., Lecocq, F. and de Perthuis, C. 2011. 'Designing climate change adaptation policies. an economic framework', Policy Research Working Paper No. 5568, World Bank, Washington, DC.

Hallegatte, S., Shah, A., Brown, C., Lempert, R. and Gill, S., 2012. 'Investment decision making under deep uncertainty – application to climate change', Policy Research Working Paper No. 6193, World Bank, Washington, DC.

Hanson, S., Nicholls, R., Ranger, N. et al., 2011. 'A global ranking of port cities with high exposure to climate extremes', *Climatic Change*, **104**(1), 89–111.

Heal, G. and Millner, A., 2014. 'Uncertainty and decision making in climate change economics', *Review of Environmental Economics and Policy*, **8**(1), 120–37.

IPCC, 2014. *Climate Change 2014: Impacts, Adaptation, and Vulnerability. Contribution of Working Group II to the Fifth Assessment Report of the Intergovernmental Panel on Climate Change*. Cambridge: Cambridge University Press.

Kahn, M., 2005. 'The death toll from natural disasters: the role of income, geography, and institutions', *Review of Economics and Statistics*, **87**(2), 271–84.

Kates, R.W., Travis, W.R. and Wilbanks, T.J., 2012. 'Transformational adaptation when incremental adaptations to climate change are insufficient', *Proceedings of the National Academy of Sciences*, **109**(19), 7156–61.

Kocornik-Mina. A. and Fankhauser, S., 2015. 'Climate change adaptation in dynamic economies', Policy Brief, Grantham Research Institute on Climate Change, London School of Economics.

McDermott, T.K.J., 2016. 'Investing in disaster risk management in an uncertain climate', World Bank Policy Research Working Paper, No WPS7631. World Bank: Washington DC.

McDermott, T.K.J., Barry, F. and Tol, R.S.J., 2014. 'Disasters and development: natural disasters, credit constraints and economic growth', *Oxford Economic Papers*, **66**(3), 750–73.

McGray, H., Hamill, A., Bradley, R., Schipper, E.L. and Parry, J.-O., 2007. *Weathering the Storm. Options for Framing Adaptation and Development*. Washington, DC: World Resources Institute.

Mendelsohn, R., Nordhaus, W. and Shaw, D., 1994. 'The impact of global warming on agriculture: a Ricardian analysis', *American Economic Review*, **84**(4), 753–71.

Pearce, D., Markandya, A. and Barbier, E., 1989. *Blueprint for a Green Economy*. London: Earthscan.

Ranger, N., Millner, A., Dietz, S., Fankhauser, S., Lopez, A. and Ruta, G., 2010. 'Adaptation in the UK: a decision-making process', Policy Brief, Grantham Research Institute on Climate Change and the Environment, London School of Economics.

Repetto, R., 2008. 'The climate crisis and the adaptation myth', Working Paper No. 13, Yale School of Forestry and Environmental Studies.

Schelling, T., 1992. 'Some economics of global warming', *American Economic Review*, **82**(1), 1–14.

Schelling, T., 1997. 'The cost of combating global warming: facing the tradeoffs', *Foreign Affairs*, **76**(6), 8–14.

Schneider, S.H., Easterling, W.E., and Mearns, L.O., 2000. 'Adaptation: sensitivity to natural variability, agent assumptions and dynamic climate changes', *Climatic Change*, **45**(1), 203–21.

Stainforth, D., Allen, M., Tredger, E. and Smith, L., 2007. 'Confidence, uncertainty and decision-support relevance in climate predictions', *Philosophical Transactions of the Royal Society A: Mathematical, Physical and Engineering Sciences*, **365**(1857), 2145–61.

Stern, N., 2015. *Why are We Waiting? The Logic, Urgency and Promise of Tackling Climate Change*. Cambridge, MA: MIT Press.

Tol, R. and Yohe, G., 2007. 'The weakest link hypothesis for adaptive capacity: an empirical test', *Global Environmental Change*, **17**, 218–27.

Vivid Economics, 2015. *Understanding Patterns of Climate-resilient Economic Development: Synthesis Report*, Report for the UK Department for International Development, London.

World Bank, 2010. *World Development Report 2010: Development and Climate Change*. Washington, DC: World Bank Group.

PART I

Concepts

2. The role of climate in development

David Castells-Quintana,
Maria del Pilar Lopez-Uribe and
Thomas K.J. McDermott

2.1 INTRODUCTION

The links between climate change, economic development and poverty reduction have gained increasing attention over recent years in both the academic and policy literature. Climate change can affect the processes of poverty reduction and economic development directly, by modifying relevant environmental conditions, with impacts, for example, on agricultural and labour productivity, disease environments and via the effects of extreme weather events on capital formation. These mechanisms are now increasingly recognized in the literature, albeit the evidence base in some cases remains relatively thin, given the relative novelty of this area of study.

Climate change might also affect development paths indirectly by altering the socio-political environment within which poverty reduction and development take place. We discuss two specific channels through which climate change might affect development: institutions and conflict (and their interaction). Both institutions and conflict matter hugely for development outcomes. Each might be affected by climate change, for example, through its effects on poverty, inequality and the distribution of economic or political power, on the availability of resources and on the movement of people. The potential for indirect effects from climate change to development is less well established in the literature. While there is a growing literature on climate and conflict, it tends to be largely empirical and lacking specific mechanisms for identifying causal effects.

Understanding both the direct as well as the indirect effects of climate change is not only fundamental for the design of mitigation and adaptation strategies but also in the design of broader strategies for poverty reduction and economic development.

The rest of this chapter proceeds as follows. In Section 2.2 we discuss the direct effects (both immediate and longer term) of climate change on economic development; in Section 2.3 we discuss indirect effects, via both institutions and conflict (and their interaction); and Section 2.4 concludes.

2.2   DIRECT EFFECTS

The direct effects of climate on economic development can be divided between the effect of geography as a fundamental determinant of long-term development and the more immediate effects of climatic variability and shocks.

2.2.1   Geography and Economic Development

Geography clearly matters for development. The spatial distribution of economic activity (globally and within regions and countries) is not random. Instead, human settlements and economic activity tend to cluster in particular locations. Some of the earliest towns and cities emerged on flood plains, benefitting from the available fertile soils and favourable climate. Roman and medieval settlements tended to be based at strategic sites of military or economic importance (Michaels and Rauch, 2013). Modern-day economic activity is heavily concentrated on coasts and near (ocean-navigable) rivers, to avail of the gains from trade (Gallup et al., 1999).

The effects of geography on development can be traced back to the beginnings of civilization; certain regions where conditions were favourable (for example, those with a greater availability of crops and domesticable animals) were the first to develop sedentary agriculture, enabling the Neolithic Revolution to take place, and therefore gained a head-start in the emergence of non-food producing classes, specialization and the accumulation of knowledge and wealth (Diamond, 1997). Differences in initial conditions still matter today, it is argued, as they persisted over time through urban agglomeration effects and the colonial dominance of the European nations (see, for instance, Acemoglu and Robinson, 2012).

The observed relationship between geography and development derives at least partly from differences relating to the fundamental characteristics of locations. For example, high transport costs, due to remoteness from markets, difficult mountainous terrains or the fact of being land-locked can significantly reduce the growth potential of countries by reducing trade opportunities (Gallup et al., 1999), investment and technology absorption (Henderson et al., 2001). Many of these factors are fixed (that is, unchanging over time) and therefore will be unaffected by climate change. It may also be that some historically important characteristics of locations may be less relevant in a modern economy. However, climate change is likely to result in changing risk profiles. This might have particularly important implications for economic development given the concentration of economic activity in specific locations, particularly on coasts, creating the potential for climate change to have costly impacts.

Spatial differences in economic development, whether between countries, between regions within countries or between rural and urban locations, can be explained not just by natural geographic factors (inherent conditions of locations) but also by the process of circular causation reinforcing agglomeration and development in initially favoured locations (Henderson et al., 2001). Geography gives some places a head-start that magnifies over time and which helps us explain the vast spatial differences we see today. This implies that small differences in terms of geographic characteristics can have long-lasting consequences and create *natural* patterns of divergence between different locations that are difficult to reverse. However, the relationship between geography and economic development is not deterministic, but rather is mediated via socio-economic and institutional factors, for example, urbanization, trade, colonization, political regimes and war (Findlay and O'Rourke, 2007).

On the one hand, it seems then that climate should matter a lot given the importance of differences in inherent productivity of locations and the possibility of these being reinforced by agglomeration effects. On the other hand, those same agglomeration effects might mean that future climate changes are unlikely to alter the *relative* spatial distribution of development. However, this has important implications for adaptation (and development planning generally). The historical lock-in of spatial development patterns might create excessive exposure to natural hazards. For example, the fact that the earliest towns and cities emerged on flood plains obviously leaves them vulnerable to flooding. In the past, that risk may have been worthwhile to avail of the economic benefits inherent to those locations (in this case soil fertility). However, such location benefits may no longer be economically relevant, creating an excessive or unwarranted exposure to flood risk. The difficulty of reversing patterns of spatial development therefore reinforces the need to consider future climate risk for development planning. Moreover, as those particular geographic characteristics more suitable for economic development are likely to change over time (for instance, as transportation and communication technologies evolve or as economic structure changes) it also implies that sound interventions to foster specific advantages of locations can generate magnified benefits.

2.2.2   Temperature and Rainfall Fluctuations

Climate change represents a change in the distribution of future weather. These changes are anticipated to exacerbate existing environmental challenges in poorer countries that already face hotter and more variable weather conditions (World Bank, 2010; IPCC, 2014), to which they struggle to adapt (for example, Brooks et al., 2005; Barr et al., 2010).

It has often been observed that hotter countries tend also to be poorer (for example, Gallup et al., 1999). Several recent studies have attempted to identify a causal effect from temperature (changes) to economic growth (for example, Bansal and Ochoa, 2009; Jones and Olken, 2010; Dell et al., 2012; Heal and Park, 2013; Deryugina and Hsiang, 2014; Burke et al., 2015). They generally find significant effects on growth in poor countries, but not in rich. They also find that the effects are not confined to agriculture, but are also observed in other sectors including manufacturing exports and industrial output. These effects might operate, for example, via the effect of temperature on productivity (see Martin et al., 2011; Advaryu et al., 2014), in line with arguments emphasising that factory workers are less productive when it is hot.

Several other papers focus on the economic impacts of (changes in) rainfall patterns (for example, Brown and Lall, 2006; Barrios et al., 2010; Brown et al., 2013). Again this literature has found evidence of negative impacts from changes in rainfall patterns on economic activity, predominantly in poorer countries. In Africa, a significant decrease in rainfall levels has been observed since the 1960s. According to Barrios et al. (2010), this decline in rainfall might have accounted for between 15 and 40 per cent of the observed gap in gross domestic product (GDP) per capita between countries in sub-Saharan Africa and developing countries in other regions.

One constraint on estimates of the economic impacts of climate change is that they are based on observations of relatively modest climatic changes that have occurred in the (recent) past. A further caveat with respect to most of this empirical literature is that it tests 'reduced form' relationships – that is, looks directly at the relationship between climate variables (for example, temperature or rainfall shocks) and economic growth (or output), without formally testing the causal mechanisms connecting climate and the economy. In what follows we discuss some of the most likely mechanisms.

2.2.3   Potential Mechanisms Linking Climate Change and Economic Performance

2.2.3.1   Agriculture and labour productivity
Several channels allow for climate change directly to affect economic performance. In particular, deteriorating climatic conditions can reduce

agricultural productivity (Deschenes and Greenstone, 2007; Schlenker and Lobell, 2010) as well as labour productivity in industrial sectors (Martin et al., 2011; Advaryu et al., 2014). Low agricultural productivity, for instance, due to poor soil quality, lack of fresh water, prevalence of pests, and in general less suitable conditions for the spread and improvement of agriculture, not only reduces agricultural output but it can also retard industrial development (for example, Diamond, 1997).

2.2.3.2 Disease environments and population dynamics
Changing weather patterns might also have longer-term development effects by altering disease environments, both via changes in environmental conditions and via the effects of weather patterns on migration/urbanization patterns. Particularly harsh disease environments, for instance, characterized by a high prevalence of malaria, can significantly reduce productivity in several ways (see Masters and McMillan, 2001). A harsh environment affects health (Deschenes and Greenstone, 2011) and reduces work capacity and productivity (Seppanen et al., 2006; Sudarshan and Tewari, 2014). Diseases also increase child mortality and lower life expectancy, which in turn increases fertility and harms incentives to acquire and accumulate human capital, creating regional-specific patterns of demographic transition, leading ultimately to slower development of regions with unfavourable environmental conditions (Strulik, 2008).

Climatic conditions can also affect population dynamics and migration patterns (see Waldinger, Chapter 11, this volume), in turn affecting the pace and form of structural change and urbanization processes (for example, Barrios et al., 2006; Henderson et al., 2014). One risk of the concentration of population in urban areas is that urban agglomerations are particularly susceptible to flooding and heat stress, and allow more rapid spreading of diseases such as cholera – especially where basic services such as access to water and sanitation facilities are underprovided.

2.2.3.3 Frequency/intensity of extreme weather events
Climate-related shocks, such as extreme weather events, can also depreciate the stock of physical, human and environmental capital (Hochrainer, 2009), and damage key infrastructures (Heltberg et al., 2008). Likewise, climate-related shocks also modify saving and investment decisions, not just of domestic agents (Hallegate, 2014) but also of potential foreign investors (Escaleras and Register, 2011), affecting both physical as well as human capital accumulation. Several papers find that natural disasters represent setbacks for economic growth (for example, Hsiang, 2010; Hsiang and Narita, 2012; Hsiang and Jina, 2014; McDermott et al., 2014). According to Loayza et al. (2012), different disasters have differentiated

effects on growth depending on the economic sector; droughts and storms are found to have the strongest negative effects for agricultural productivity. Given that the elasticity of poverty to growth generated in the agricultural sector is higher than for other sectors of the economy, these disasters can be expected to affect the poor disproportionately (see also the evidence presented in Hallegatte et al., Chapter 3, this volume).

2.2.4 Poverty and Vulnerability to Shocks

The evidence reviewed so far appears to indicate that geography (including locational fundamentals and climate) matters a lot for economic development, particularly in its early stages, but perhaps less so as modern economic growth 'takes off'. This is also reflected in the empirical evidence on the impacts of climate shocks and disasters, which appear to have important macroeconomic (and growth) impacts in poorer countries, whereas similar events tend not to disrupt the economies of relatively wealthy developed nations. There is thus, perhaps, some threshold of development (in terms of income and institutional quality) below which climate will continue to exert a significant direct influence on economic development.

The difficulty faced by many poorer countries in escaping from poverty results from a combination of factors. A lack of basic economic, financial and physical infrastructure is often compounded by weak institutions and patterns of governance that restrict the opportunities for economic development (see, for example, Collier et al., 2008; Dercon, 2012). These same factors explain the relatively low adaptive capacity of many poorer countries (see, for example, Fankhauser and McDermott, 2014) and their subsequent economic vulnerability to climate shocks.

In the preceding sections we have focused on the direct impacts of climate change on development. In the next section we turn our attention to indirect impacts.

2.3 INDIRECT MECHANISMS: CLIMATE CHANGE AND INSTITUTIONAL DEVELOPMENT

Beyond its direct effects, geography (broadly defined) can also affect the possibilities for development by affecting the socio-political environment in which development takes place. For example, geographic factors can significantly influence institutional development (Engerman and Sokoloff, 1997; Acemoglu et al., 2001, 2002) and the likelihood of conflict (Miguel et al., 2004; Hsiang et al., 2011; Dell et al., 2014). These effects might be particularly relevant in 'fragile' or 'failed' states – characterized by weak policies, institutions and governance – that are unable to perform minimum functions expected from modern sovereign states (Zartman, 1995; Torres and Anderson, 2004).

The 'fragility' of the state, including weak governance and deficient institutions, is relevant in the analysis of the effects of climate change on development for at least two main reasons. On the one hand, as outlined above, poor countries with weak institutions are more vulnerable to climate shocks (see, for example, Fankhauser and McDermott, 2014). On the other hand, climate might have an effect on state fragility itself, for example, as a catalyst of conflict or as a factor increasing the extent and intensity of existing conflicts.

In this section we analyse the role of geography in the socio-political environment to better understand potential indirect effects of climate change in the process of economic development and poverty reduction.

2.3.1 How 'Good' Institutions Evolve

Good institutions and economic development go hand in hand. The relevance of institutions in the prosperity of nations has been highlighted since the beginnings of modern economic thought (for example, Smith, 1776). However, defining institutions is not straightforward and has become a topic of extensive research and debate. According to many authors, institutions develop differently according to initial conditions, and what can be considered 'good' institutions is likely to be context-specific (for example, Grindle, 2004; Rodrik et al., 2004; Rodrik, 2008). Societies face a set of 'institutional opportunities' that improves as countries emerge from poverty and accumulate human, social and physical capital (North, 1990; Djankov et al., 2003; Glaeser et al., 2004). But these institutional opportunities also depend on the opportunities and challenges that the environmental context poses. Similarly, North (1990) has suggested population and technological change, as well as changes in the costs of information, as important determinants of institutional change.

Institutions clearly matter greatly for economic development. However, our understanding of how institutional arrangements evolve over time and what factors contribute to successful institutional reform remains somewhat limited. It appears that geography, broadly defined to include climate, physical geography and resource endowments, may have played an important role in the emergence of modern institutions and the apparently crucial distinction between locations that evolved *extractive* versus *inclusive* institutions. For example, Acemoglu et al. (2001) famously used variation in disease environments to explain the emergence of extractive institutions in some locations (for example, Africa) and inclusive institutions in others (for example, North America).

It does not automatically follow, however, that climate change should have any great influence on the future development of economic and political institutions. It seems unlikely, barring catastrophic scenarios, that climate change will have any major bearing on institutional arrangements in places with established stable and inclusive regimes.[1] However, in locations where power, institutions and the rule of law are more contested – that is, in fragile states – subtle changes to political incentives resulting from changes in environmental conditions, changes in the value of natural assets or disputes over resources could generate non-negligible effects on institutional quality. For less developed regions generally, their greater vulnerability to climate change and relatively weak existing institutions could make the threat of climate change more relevant for institutional development.

Other potential mechanisms from climate (change) to institutional change, discussed in more detail below, include the reinforcement of existing social and economic inequalities due to the unequal distribution of anticipated impacts from climate change; disruptions to long-run investments, including the provision of public goods and services, and human capital investments following weather shocks that reduce output or destroy assets; and disruptions to political stability, in the form of the (at times violent) contesting of power following income shocks.

Conflict, and political instability more generally, have been found to significantly hamper growth and economic development (Barro, 1991; Knack and Keefer, 1995; Easterly and Levine, 1997; Rodrik, 1999; Sala-i-Martin et al., 2004). Less developed countries are in turn more prone to conflict and instability. Indeed, countries in conflict are among the worst Millennium Development Goals (MDGs) performers, frequently regressing on key indicators, with the direct impacts of warfare usually accompanied by a weakened economy and government capacity, leading to lower development prospects, in some cases pushing countries into a downward spiral (UNDP, 2011).

2.3.2   The (Potential) Role of Climate Change

There appears to be some correlation between weather conditions and conflict globally. For instance, drylands are among the most conflict-prone regions of the world. In 2007, 80 per cent of major armed conflicts worldwide occurred in drylands (UNDP, 2011). Although such correlations tell us nothing about causation, there is now a growing empirical literature that finds evidence of climatic stress as a contributing factor in conflict (see Dell et al., 2014).

Looking at global patterns, Hsiang et al. (2011) find evidence that civil conflicts may indeed be associated with climatic variation, while a number of papers link periods of drought with increased conflict (for example, Couttenier and Soubeyran, 2013; Maystadt and Ecker, 2014). Similarly, Burke et al. (2009) find that hotter years are associated with increased incidence of civil war in Africa in the late twentieth century. It has even been argued that changing climatic conditions can lead to the collapse of societies, as a result of increased conflict associated with environmental stress (Diamond, 2005).

Burke and Leigh (2010) and Brückner and Ciccone (2011) are among the first to test empirically the relationship between climate and *institutional* change. Although these studies use changes in climatic conditions as an exogenous shock to output, their conclusions seem to support the idea that weather shocks may lead to institutional change; in this case democratization. In both papers, the mechanism proposed is via output: negative rainfall shocks open a 'window of opportunity' for democratic improvement because it translates into a transitory negative GDP shock and a lower opportunity cost of contesting power. Dell et al. (2012) also show that adverse temperature shocks might increase the probability of irregular leader transitions such as coups. They support their results on the previous empirical evidence that riots and protests are more likely in warmer weather (Boyanowsky, 1999).

These somewhat contrasting results illustrate the need for a greater understanding of the mechanisms that potentially link climatic conditions to institutional change. The authors cited above emphasize the effects of weather shocks on income, leading to changes in the opportunity cost of contesting power. However, such a mechanism potentially represents a double-edged sword for institutional development. On the one hand, the opportunity to contest power offers a possible 'window of opportunity' for institutional improvement (for example, through removal of an autocratic regime). On the other hand, contesting power might involve (violent) conflict, with no guarantee of an improved outcome. A low opportunity cost of fighting, usually associated with low levels of income per capita, has often been identified as one of the main determinants of the probability of conflict (Collier and Hoeffler, 1998, 2004; Miguel et al., 2004; Besley and Persson, 2008; Collier et al., 2009).[2]

According to Chassang and Padro-i-Miquel (2008), the likelihood of conflict increases after negative shocks while it decreases with the expectations of higher incomes. Hence, lower and volatile growth can lead to higher risk of conflict. As climate-induced income shocks hit the poor in a disproportionate way, climate change might affect the likelihood (and severity) of conflict by reinforcing existing poverty dynamics.

However, income shocks are not the only mechanism that potentially links climate change to institutional change and conflict. In the rest of this section, we discuss other potential mechanisms, relying mainly on theoretical arguments, given the relative lack of empirical work in this area to date.

2.3.2.1 Inequalities
Different institutional forms are partly the result of conflict of interests and the distribution of power within societies (for example, Acemoglu and Robinson, 2001, 2009; Besley and Persson, 2011). Improved economic opportunities for the majority of the population and political empowerment of the poor can play a fundamental role in fostering institutional change (for example, Grindle, 2004; Rodrik, 2008). Conversely, 'bad institutions' are the consequence of unequal structures of production and social organization (for example, Engerman and Sokoloff, 1997, 2000). Theoretical models predict a high likelihood of conflict in divided societies – either by class, geography, religion or ethnicity (Ray, 2009) and when there is a high probability of a shifting distribution of power (Garfinkel and Skaperdas, 2000).[3] Thus, where climate change is expected to reinforce existing inequalities – or alter the economic opportunities of different groups and trigger conflict over natural resources and the distribution of power – this could have knock-on effects for the quality of institutions and ultimately conflict. Existing inequalities have also been found to lead to differentiated impacts of climate shocks on conflict; for example, Hidalgo et al. (2010) find that in Brazil, climate shocks (leading to negative income shocks) cause twice as many land invasions in highly unequal municipalities compared to municipalities with average land inequality.

2.3.2.2 Incentives
It has been suggested that geography (including climate) matters in the choice of economic policy itself (Gallup et al., 1999). The logic is that the political economy of policy formation depends on the incentives faced by policy-makers. Where growth prospects are weak, the incentive to pursue pro-growth, inclusive economic policies may be weaker than the incentive to pursue 'extractive' type policies that produce short-term benefits for those in power. Alternatively, the decline of aggregate output can diminish government revenues, making the state invest less in state capacity and security. Many developing countries also still display worryingly low levels of access to basic services, including water, electricity and improved sanitation facilities, and this situation tends to be associated with bad governance and the incentives faced to provide broad public goods (Keefer and Khemani, 2005).

Contest models of conflict (for example, Garfinkel, 1990; Skaperdas, 1992) also highlight the association between poverty and conflict through individuals' incentives to maintain order, and therefore predict higher likelihood of conflict in poorer countries or regions. Non-material incentives, including grievances and vengeance, are among the proximate explanations of conflict (Roemer, 1985). Climate change might also play a role here if grievances over resources (for example, water, access to land, grazing rights and so on) are generated by changing environmental conditions.

In any case, climatic conditions, by modifying the growth prospects of poorer nations, might also lead to endogenously worse economic policies. This reasoning is similar in spirit to some of the *resource curse* literature. Natural resource revenues represent a bigger (and more easily appropriable) prize in case of success and also a source of finance for fighting activities (see, for example, Fearon and Laitin, 2003; Besley and Persson, 2008). Natural resources can also make the government less accountable to the population, if resource revenues rather than taxation are relied on to fund the state. This suggests a further political-economy risk associated with climate change; that is, that climate finance flows to developing countries could make their governments less politically accountable.

2.3.2.3 Migration and human capital

There are complex links between climate shocks, migration and conflict. Climate shocks may contribute to conflict, which may in turn trigger migration. But climate shocks may also increase the likelihood of conflict by inducing migration, potentially leading to tensions between displaced people and their putative hosts (see Waldinger, Chapter 11, this volume). Either way, the potential rise in mass migration is one of the main security challenges often associated with climate change (see, for example, Myers and Kent, 1995; although also the criticism of their forecasts by Gemenne, 2011). While the numbers may be speculative at this point, the risks are not so easily dismissed. The security and military communities take these threats seriously, and conduct risk assessments on the basis of considering multiple plausible future scenarios (for example, Campbell et al., 2007).

Another potential risk is the threat to human health posed by large-scale population movements: '[T]he health risks posed by climate-related population movements are likely to become a major source of human suffering, disability, and loss of life – an outcome that, currently, appears more likely than the much-debated possibility of increased violent conflict or state failure' (McMichael et al., 2012, pp. 646–7). But these are not distinct (separate) threats. On the contrary, migration, disease patterns and violent conflict interact in complicated ways, and potentially reinforce each other (see, for example, Miller, 1982 for a discussion of the effects of climate-induced scarcity on migration, disease and migration-induced conflict).

Finally, the opportunities for institutional development depend on levels of human capital (Djankov et al., 2003; Glaeser et al., 2004). Thus, another mechanism through which climate change can deter institutional development is by hindering human capital accumulation – for example, as a result of extreme weather events that cause injuries, illness and death, or disrupt schooling through the (temporary) displacement of people and the destruction of infrastructure (see, for example, Anttila-Hughes and Hsiang, 2013 for evidence on the human capital impacts of environmental disasters).

Ultimately, the sources of conflict are many and complex. However, the discussion in this section has highlighted a number of mechanisms through which climate (change) might be expected to influence both the frequency and severity of conflict. We have also seen the dependence of conflict on institutional quality – and in turn the damaging consequences of conflict for governance. There would thus appear to be a potentially important set of dynamic interactions (and feedback loops) between institutions, climate (impacts and vulnerability) and conflict, which to date have been under-studied. This represents an important research gap in understanding the potential (indirect) implications of climate change for sustaining economic development over the long term.

2.4 CONCLUSIONS

In this chapter we review the role of (past) climatic changes in the process of long-term economic development and poverty reduction. Climate factors affect these processes in a number of important ways. Climate change modifies natural (geographical) conditions relevant in the process of economic development. The literature has already identified significant effects of climate change on economic growth working through multiple channels. Given unequal anticipated effects across rich and poor countries, climate change potentially reinforces both spatial inequalities and poverty trap dynamics. But climate change also has potentially important effects on economic development through its indirect effects on the socio-political environment within which poverty reduction and development take place. First, climate change can alter the context within which institutional development takes place. Second, given its significant role in the likelihood and intensity of conflict, changing climatic conditions can also affect the socio-political stability of countries.

The evidence reviewed confirms distinct effects of climate shocks across rich and poor countries; the macro impacts of a changing climate will be felt more strongly in poorer, and especially in fragile, states. At the same time, it is in these same countries where the indirect effects of climate change become most relevant, potentially reinforcing institutional fragility and in turn vulnerability to climate shocks.

NOTES

1. Except to the extent that mitigation efforts and global climate negotiations might influence domestic politics. However, this is a distinct type of effect – likely operating on the political or ideological make-up of government, as opposed to affecting the fundamental quality of institutions and governance arrangements.
2. Indeed, previous evidence supports the idea of decreased output and rural productivity lowering the opportunity cost of engaging in conflict and increasing the returns to violence. In a study of the Colombian civil conflict, Dube and Vargas (2013) present evidence that steep declines in coffee prices and increases in oil prices reduced workers' wages and increased their propensity to join armed groups.
3. Blattman and Miguel (2010) provide a comprehensive review of war's (economic) causes and consequences, identifying several distinct approaches to modelling the origins of conflict.

REFERENCES

Acemoglu, D. and Robinson, J., 2001. 'A theory of political transitions', *American Economic Review*, **91**(4), 938–63.

Acemoglu, D. and Robinson, J., 2009. *Economic Origins of Dictatorship and Democracy*. Cambridge: Cambridge University Press.

Acemoglu, D. and Robinson, J., 2012. *Why Nations Fail: The Origins of Power, Prosperity, and Poverty*. New York: Crown Publishing Group.

Acemoglu, D., Johnson, S. and Robinson, J., 2001. 'The colonial origins of comparative development: an empirical investigation', *American Economic Review*, **91**(5), 1369–401.

Acemoglu, D., Johnson, S. and Robinson, J., 2002. 'Reversal of fortune: geography and institutions in the making of the modern world income distribution', *Quarterly Journal of Economics*, **117**(4), 1231–94.

Advaryu, A., Kala, N. and Nyshadman, A., 2014. 'The light and the heat: productivity co-benefits of energy-saving technology', Unpublished manuscript, University of Michigan.

Anttila-Hughes, J.K. and Hsiang, S.M., 2013. 'Destruction, disinvestment, and death: economic and human losses following environmental disaster', available at SSRN, http://ssrn.com/abstract=2220501 (accessed February 2016).

Bansal, R. and Ochoa, M., 2009. 'Temperature, growth and asset prices', Duke University Working Paper, Duke University, Durham, NC.

Barr, R., Fankhauser, S. and Hamilton, K., 2010. 'Adaptation investment: a resource allocation framework', *Mitigation and Adaptation Strategies for Global Change*, **15**(8), 843–58.

Barrios, S., Bertinelli, L. and Strobl, E., 2006. 'Climate change and rural-urban migration: the case of Sub-Saharan Africa', *Journal of Urban Economics*, **60**, 357–71.

Barrios, S., Bertinelli, L. and Strobl, E., 2010. 'Trends in rainfall and economic growth in Africa: a neglected cause of the African growth tragedy', *Review of Economics and Statistics*, **92**(2), 350–66.

Barro, R., 1991. 'Economic growth in a cross section of countries', *Quarterly Journal of Economics*, **116**(2), 407–43.

Besley, T. and Persson, T., 2008. 'Wars and state capacity', *Journal of the European Economic Association*, **6**(2–3), 522–30.

Besley, T. and Persson, T., 2011. *Pillars of Prosperity: The Political Economics of Development Clusters*. Princeton, NJ: Princeton University Press.

Blattman, C. and Miguel, E., 2010. 'Civil war', *Journal of Economic Literature*, **48**(1), 3–57.

Boyanowsky, E., 1999. 'Violence and aggression in the heat of passion and in cold blood: the Ecs-TC syndrome', *International Journal of Law and Psychiatry*, **22**(3), 257–71.

Brooks, N., Adger, W.N. and Kelly, P.M., 2005. 'The determinants of vulnerability and adaptive capacity at the national level and the implications for adaptation', *Global Environmental Change*, **15**, 151–63.

Brown, C. and Lall, U., 2006. 'Water and economic development: the role of variability and a framework for resilience', *Natural Resources Forum*, **30**, 306–17.

Brown, C., Meeks, R., Ghile, Y. and Hunu, K., 2013. 'Is water security necessary? An empirical analysis of the effects of climate hazards on national-level economic growth', *Philosophical Transactions of the Royal Society A*, **371**, 20120–416.

Brückner, M. and Ciccone, A., 2011. 'Rain and the democratic window of opportunity', *Econometrica*, **79**(3), 923–47.

Burke, M., Miguel, E., Shanker, S., Dykema, J. and Lobell, D., 2009. 'Warming increase the risk of civil war in Africa', *Proceedings of the National Academy of Sciences*, **106**(49), 20670–74.

Burke, M., Hsiang, S. and Miguel, E., 2015. 'Global non-linear effect of temperature on economic production', *Nature*, doi:10.1038/nature15725

Burke, P. and Leigh, A., 2010. 'Do output contractions trigger democratic change?', *American Economic Journal: Macroeconomics*, **2**(4), 124–57.

Campbell, K.M., Gulledge, J., McNeill, J.R. et al., 2007. *The Age of Consequences: The Foreign Policy and National Security Implications of Global Climate Change*. Washington, DC: Center for Strategic and International Studies and Center for a New American Security.

Chassang, S. and Padro-i-Miquel, G., 2008. 'Conflict and deterrence under strategic risk', NBER Working Paper No. 13964, National Bureau of Economic Research, Cambridge, MA.

Collier, P. and Hoeffler, A., 1998. 'On the economic causes of civil war', *Oxford Economic Papers*, **50**, 563–73.

Collier, P. and Hoeffler, A., 2004. 'Greed and grievance in civil war', *Oxford Economic Papers*, **56**, 563–95.

Collier, P., Conway, G. and Venables, T., 2008. 'Climate change and Africa', *Oxford Review of Economic Policy*, **24**(2), 337–53.

Collier, P., Hoeffler, A. and Rohner, D., 2009. 'Beyond greed and grievance: feasibility and civil war', *Oxford Economic Papers*, **61**, 1–27.

Couttenier, M. and Soubeyran, R., 2013. 'Drought and civil war in sub-Saharan Africa', *The Economic Journal*, **124**(575), 201–44.

Dell, M., Jones, B. and Olken, B., 2012. 'Temperature shocks and economic growth: evidence from the last half a century', *American Economic Journal: Macroeconomics*, **4**(3), 66–95.

Dell, M., Jones, B. and Olken, B., 2014. 'What do we learn from the weather? The new climate-economy literature', *Journal of Economic Literature*, **52**(3), 740–98.

Dercon, S., 2012. 'Is green growth good for the poor?', World Bank Policy Research Working Paper No. 6231, World Bank Group, Washington, DC.

Deryugina, T. and Hsiang, S., 2014. 'Does the environment still matter? Daily temperature and income in the United States', NBER Working Paper No. 20750, National Bureau of Economic Research, Cambridge, MA.

Deschenes, O. and Greenstone, M., 2007. 'The economic impacts of climate change: evidence from agricultural output and random fluctuations in weather', *American Economic Review*, **97**(1), 354–81.

Deschenes, O. and Greenstone, M., 2011. 'Climate change, mortality, and adaptation: evidence from annual fluctuations in weather in the U.S', *American Economic Journal: Applied Economics*, **3**(4), 152–85.

Diamond, J., 1997. *Guns, Germs, and Steel: The Fates of Human Societies.* New York: W.W. Norton.

Diamond, J., 2005. *Collapse: How Societies Choose to Fail or Succeed.* New York: Viking.

Djankov, S., Glaeser, E. L., La Porta, R., Lopez-de-Silane, F. and Shleifer, A., 2003. 'The new comparative economics', *Journal of Comparative Economics*, **31**(4), 595–619.

Dube, O. and Vargas, J.F., 2013. 'Commodity price shock and civil conflict: evidence from Colombia', *Review of Economic Studies*, **81**(2), 1384–421.

Easterly, W. and Levine, R., 1997. 'Africa's growth tragedy: policies and ethnic divisions', *Quarterly Journal of Economics*, **112**(4), 1203–50.

Engerman, S. and Sokoloff, K., 1997. 'Factor endowments, institutions, and differential paths of growth among new world economics', in S. Haber (ed.), *How Latin America Fell Behind.* Stanford, CA: Stanford University Press, pp. 260–304.

Engerman, S. and Sokoloff, K., 2000. 'History lessons: institutions, factor endowments, and paths of development in the new world', *Journal of Economic Perspectives*, **14**(3), 217–32.

Escaleras, M. and Register, C.A., 2011. 'Natural disasters and foreign direct investment', *Land Economics*, **87**(2), 346–63.

Fankhauser, S. and McDermott, T.K.J., 2014. 'Understanding the adaptation deficit: why are poor countries more vulnerable to climate events than rich countries?', *Global Environmental Change*, **27**, 9–18.

Fearon, J. and Laitin, D., 2003. 'Ethnicity, insurgency and civil war', *American Political Science Review*, **97**(1), 75–90.

Findlay, R. and O'Rourke, K.H., 2007. *Power and Plenty: Trade, War and the World Economy in the Second Millennium.* Cambridge: Cambridge University Press.

Gallup, J., Sachs, J. and Mellinger, D., 1999. 'Geography and economic development', *International Regional Science Review*, **22**(2), 179–232.

Garfinkel, M., 1990. 'Arming as a strategic investment in a cooperative equilibrium', *American Economic Review*, **80**(1), 50–68.

Garfinkel, M. and Skarpedas, S., 2000. 'Conflict without misperceptions or incomplete information: how the future matters', *Journal of Conflict Resolution*, **44**(6), 793–807.

Gemenne, F., 2011. 'Why the numbers don't add up: a review of predictions and forecasts for environmentally-induced migration', *Global Environmental Change*, **21**, 41–9.

Glaeser, E., La Porta, R., Lopez-De-Silanes, F. and Shleifer, A., 2004. 'Do institutions cause growth?', *Journal of Economic Growth*, **9**, 271–303.

Grindle, M., 2004. 'Good enough governance: poverty reduction and reform in developing countries', *Governance*, **17**(4), 525–48.

Hallegatte, S., 2014. 'Economic resilience: definition and measurement', World Bank Development Research Group Policy Research Working Paper No. 6852, World Bank Group, Washington, DC.

Heal, G. and Park, J. 2013. 'Feeling the heat: temperature, physiology & the wealth of nations', NBER Working Paper No. 19725, National Bureau of Economic Research, Cambridge, MA.

Heltberg, R., Siegel, P. and Jorgenson, S.L., 2008. 'Addressing human vulnerability to climate change: towards a no regrets approach', *Global Environmental Change*, **19**(1), 89–99.

Henderson, J.V., Shalizi, Z. and Venables, A., 2001. 'Geography and development', *Journal of Economic Geography*, **1**, 81–105.

Henderson, J.V., Storeygard, A. and Deichmann, U., 2014. '50 years of urbanization in Africa', World Bank Policy Research Working Paper No. 6925, World Bank Group, Washington, DC.

Hidalgo, D., Naidu, S., Nichter, S. and Richardson, N., 2010. 'Economic determinants of land invasions', *Review of Economics and Statistics*, **92**(3), 505–23.

Hochrainer, S., 2009. 'Assessing the macroeconomic impacts of natural disasters – are there any?', World Bank Policy Research Working Paper No. 4968, World Bank Group, Washington, DC.

Hsiang, S.M., 2010. 'Temperatures and cyclones strongly associated with economic production in the Caribbean and Central America', *Proceedings of the National Academy of Sciences*, **107**(35), 15367–72.

Hsiang, S.M. and Jina, A., 2014. 'The causal effects of environmental catastrophe on economic growth', NBER Working Paper No. 20352, National Bureau of Economic Research, Cambridge, MA.

Hsiang, S.M. and Narita, D., 2012. 'Adaptation to cyclone risk: evidence from the global cross-section', *Climate Change Economics*, **3**(2).

Hsiang, S.M., Meng, K.C. and Cane, M.A., 2011. 'Civil conflicts are associated with the global climate', *Nature*, **476**, 438–41, 1250011.

IPCC, 2014. *Climate Change 2014: Impacts, Adaptation, and Vulnerability. Contribution of Working Group II to the Fifth Assessment Report of the Intergovernmental Panel on Climate Change.* Cambridge and New York: Cambridge University Press.

Jones, B. and Olken, B., 2010. 'Climate shock and exports', *American Economic Review*, **100**(2), 454–9.

Keefer, P. and Khemani, S., 2005. 'Democracy, public expenditures, and the poor: understanding political incentives for providing public services', *The World Bank Research Observer*, **20**(1), 1–27.

Knack, S. and Keefer, P., 1995. 'Institutions and economic performance: cross-country tests using alternative measures', *Economics and Politics*, **7**(3), 207–27.

Loayza, N., Olaberria, J. and Christiaensen, L., 2012. 'Natural disasters and growth: going beyond the averages', *World Development*, **40**(7), 1317–36.

Martin, R., Muuls, M. and Ward, A., 2011. 'The sensitivity of UK manufacturing firms to extreme weather events. Supporting research for: CCC, 2011', in *Adapting to Climate Change in the UK – Measuring Progress*. London: Climate Change Committee.

Masters, W.A. and McMillan, M.S., 2001. 'Climate and scale in economic growth', *Journal of Economic Growth*, **6**, 167–86.

Maystadt, J. and Ecker, O., 2014. 'Extreme weather and civil war: does drought fuel conflict in Somalia through livestock price shocks?', *American Journal of Agricultural Economics*, **96**(4), 1157–82.

McDermott, T.K.J., Barry, F. and Tol, R.S.J., 2014. 'Disasters and development: natural disasters, credit constraints and economic growth', *Oxford Economic Papers*, **66**(3), 750–73.

McMichael, C., Barnett, J. and McMichael, A.J., 2012. 'An ill wind? Climate change, migration, and health', *Environmental Health Perspectives*, **120**(5), 646–54.

Michaels, G. and Rauch, F., 2013. 'Resetting the urban network: 117-2012', University of Oxford Department of Economics Discussion Paper No. 684, Oxford.

Miguel, E., Satyanath, S. and Sergenti, E., 2004. 'Economic shocks and civil conflict: an instrumental variables approach', *Journal of Political Economy*, **112**(4), 725–53.

Miller, J.C., 1982. 'The significance of drought, disease and famine in the agriculturally marginal zones of West-Central Africa', *Journal of African History*, **23**(1), 17–61.

Myers, N. and Kent, J., 1995. *Environmental Exodus: An Emergent Crisis in the Global Arena*. Washington, DC: Climate Institute.

North, D., 1990. *Institutions, Institutional Change, and Economic Performance*. Cambridge: Cambridge University Press.

Ray, D., 2009. 'Remarks on the initiation of costly conflict', Paper presented at the Yale University Workshop on Rationality and Conflict, New Haven, CT.

Rodrik, D., 1999. 'Where did all the growth go? External shocks, social conflict, and growth collapses', *Journal of Economic Growth*, **4**(4), 385–412.

Rodrik, D., 2008. 'Second-best institutions', *American Economic Review: Papers and Proceedings*, **98**(2), 100–4.

Rodrik, D., Subramanian, A. and Trebbi, F., 2004. 'Institutions rule: the primacy of institutions over geography and integration in economic development', *Journal of Economic Growth*, **9**(2), 131–65.

Roemer, J., 1985. 'Rationalizing revolutionary ideology', *Econometrica*, **53**(1), 85–108.

Sala-i-Martin, X., Doppelhofer, G. and Miller, R., 2004. 'Determinants of long-run growth: a Bayesian averaging of classical estimates (BACE) approach', *American Economic Review*, **94**(4), 813–35.

Schlenker, W. and Lobell, D., 2010. 'Robust negative impacts of climate change on African agriculture', *Environmental Research Letters*, **5**(1), 014010.

Seppanen, O., Fisk, W. and Lei, Q., 2006. *Effect of Temperature on Task Performance in Office Environment*. Berkeley, CA: Lawrence Berkeley National Laboratory.

Skaperdas, S., 1992. 'Cooperation, conflict, and power in the absence of property rights', *American Economic Review*, **82**(4), 720–39.

Smith, A., 1776. *An Inquiry into the Nature and Cause of the Wealth of Nations.* London: Methuen & Co.

Strulik, H., 2008. 'Geography, health, and the pace of demo-economic development', *Journal of Development Economics*, **86**(1), 61–75.

Sudarshan, A. and Tewari, M., 2014. 'The economic impacts of temperature on industrial productivity: evidence from Indian manufacturing', ICRIER Working Paper No. 278, Indian Council for Research on International Economic Relations, New Delhi.

Torres, M. and Anderson, M., 2004. 'Fragile states: defining difficult environments for poverty reduction', PRDE Working Paper No. 1, Department for International Development, London.

UNDP (United Nations Development Programme), 2011. *The Forgotten Billion: MDG Achievement in the Drylands.* New York: United Nations Development Programme.

World Bank, 2010. *World Development Report 2010: Development and Climate Change.* Washington, DC: World Bank Group.

Zartman, W., 1995. 'Introduction: posing the problem of state collapse', in W. Zartman (ed.), *Collapsed State: The Disintegration and Restoration of Legitimate Authority.* Boulder, CO: Lynne Reinner, pp. 1–11.

3. Poverty and climate change

**Stephane Hallegatte, Mook Bangalore,
Laura Bonzanigo, Marianne Fay, Tamaro Kane,
Ulf Narloch, Julie Rozenberg, David Treguer
and Adrien Vogt-Schilb**

3.1 THE IMPACTS OF CLIMATE CHANGE: SHOULD WE FOCUS ON POVERTY INSTEAD OF GROSS DOMESTIC PRODUCT?

Estimates of the economic cost of climate change have always attracted interest and debate from policy-makers and the public. These estimates, however, have mostly been framed in terms of the impact on country-level or global gross domestic product (GDP), which does not capture the full impact of climate change on people's well-being.

One reason is that such estimates do not reflect distribution. The distribution of climate impacts – that is, which countries, regions and people are hit – will determine impacts on well-being. Almost 60 per cent of global income belongs to North America, Europe and East Asia; other regions are economically much smaller, in particular sub-Saharan Africa, which only generates around 3 per cent of global income (World Bank, 2015a). The location of GDP impacts therefore matters.

Equally important, climate change impacts will be highly heterogeneous within countries. If impacts mostly affect low-income people, welfare consequences will be much larger than if the burden is borne by those with a higher income. Poor people have fewer resources to fall back upon and lower adaptive capacity. Moreover, their assets and income represent such a small share of national wealth – and poor people's losses, even if dramatic, are largely invisible in aggregate economic statistics.

Investigating the impact of climate change on poor people and on poverty requires a different approach, focused on people that play a minor role in aggregate economic figures and are often living within the margins of basic subsistence. Such an approach drove a research programme on 'Poverty and climate change' at the World Bank and this chapter is based on some of the programme's results (for a comprehensive presentation of the results, see Hallegatte et al., 2016).

This research starts from the idea that poverty is not static, and poverty reduction is not a monotonic, one-way process. Over time, some people build assets and move out of poverty while others experience shocks and are pulled into poverty. What we call poverty reduction is the net result of these mechanisms. For instance, Krishna (2006) documents poverty dynamics in 36 communities in Andhra Pradesh, India, over 25 years. Every year, on average 14 per cent of households escaped poverty while 12 per cent of non-poor households became poor, so that, overall, poverty was reduced by 2 per cent per year. These numbers show that a relatively small change in the flows in and out of poverty have a significant effect on overall poverty dynamics. For instance, increasing the flow into poverty from 12 to 13 per cent is enough to halve the rate of poverty reduction.

Climate change can affect the flow of people falling into poverty. In the Andhra Pradesh sample, drought is a major factor: a household affected by droughts in the past was 15 times more likely to fall into poverty (Krishna, 2006). Droughts may also result in people falling into poverty traps as a result of asset losses. They often affect human capital, especially for children who may be withdrawn from school or suffer permanent health consequences (Carter et al., 2007). Further, even the risk of a natural disaster keeps people poor by incentivizing low-risk but low-return investment strategies (Elbers et al., 2007). An impact of climate change on the frequency or intensity of natural disasters could therefore worsen poverty reduction with more people falling into and less people escaping poverty.

But natural hazards are not the only climate-sensitive factor to affect the flows in and out of poverty. Agricultural income and food prices matter, as do health shocks. The following sections investigate these major channels through which climate change affects poverty dynamics: agriculture and ecosystems, natural hazards and health. Of course, many other factors play a role, but these three channels already have well-documented impacts on poor people and poverty reduction, and will be affected by future climate change.

3.2   AGRICULTURAL AND ECOSYSTEM IMPACTS

One of the most obvious sectors at the forefront of the climate change and poverty intersection is agriculture. Agriculture is one of the most sensitive activities to climate change because of its direct dependence on weather. And since a large share of poor people globally work in agriculture, any impact of climate change on wages or prices in this sector would affect poverty reduction and the welfare and prospects of poor people. But climate change impacts are not only channelled through the prices and returns determined by markets. Many poor people – especially those residing in rural areas – do not buy or sell consumption goods in markets, but produce them from climate-sensitive ecosystems. This section provides a brief review on how climate change can affect poor people through these two channels – agriculture and ecosystems.

In agriculture, crop yield and harvest quality can be affected directly by changing precipitation and temperature patterns, but also indirectly through water availability for irrigation; and livestock production can also be impacted through pasture yield and quality, heat stress and water availability (Thornton et al., 2009). Climate change will impact agricultural and land productivity, with higher emissions pathways worsening impacts (Porter et al., 2014).

Modelling studies suggest that climate change could result in global crop yield losses as large as 5 per cent in 2030 and 30 per cent in 2080, even accounting for adaptive behaviour such as changed agricultural practices and crops, more irrigation and innovation in higher yield crops (Havlík et al., 2015).

Productivity impacts will also have very uncertain impacts on food prices: the Intergovernmental Panel on Climate Change (IPCC) suggests global food prices may vary anywhere from −30 to +45 per cent by 2050 (Porter et al., 2014). Higher food prices will reduce consumption, but modelling exercises show the final effect will not depend only on the change in climate but also on the socio-economic context, including GDP growth and access to global food markets (Havlík et al., 2015). Food security concerns are lower in a world with fast economic growth and low poverty, compared to a world with slow growth and high poverty.

Any change in food consumption will be particularly severe for poor people, who spend a larger share of their budget on food. Across the developing world, the poorest households spend between 40 per cent and 60 per cent of their income on food items compared to less than 25 per cent for wealthier households (World Bank, 2015b). Poor people in urban areas spend a larger share of income on food than rural people, as the latter may meet some food needs through domestic production.

Losses in the agricultural sector and spikes in food prices can push vulnerable consumers into poverty – take, for example, the 2008 food price spike that caused about 100 million people to fall into poverty, or the 2010–11 episode that increased poverty by 44 million (Ivanic et al., 2012).

But for food producers, an increase in food prices is not necessarily a bad outcome. The final impacts will depend on how changes in prices and productivity balance (an increase in food prices due to reduced productivity does not automatically lead to increased revenues) and on how increased revenues are distributed among farm workers and landowners (Jacoby et al., 2015). Taking a comprehensive view of farm households – both their consumption and production – Hertel et al. (2010) argue they may benefit from climate impacts if the shock is widespread, farm-level demand for their production is inelastic (while supply response is low), there are few sources of off-farm incomes and food represents a relatively small share of expenditures.

More generally, poor people can become more resilient to shocks in agriculture thanks to trade and food reserves that can overcome local shortages in times of need, better access of poor farmers to markets and improved technologies and climate-smart production techniques. Access to functioning markets, however, depends on better infrastructure and better institutions. In Ethiopia, the incidence of poverty decreased by 6.7 per cent following farmers' access to all-weather roads (Dercon et al., 2009). In Burkina Faso, maize price volatility is found to be greatest in remote markets (Ndiaye et al., 2015). Investments in transport infrastructure improve market integration, reduce price uncertainty for farmers and improve food security.

In some areas, however, transformational change for producers will be required. For instance, in Uganda, coffee production is a central activity, employing 2 million people and contributing $400 million to the economy in 2012. But climate change will make coffee growing increasingly difficult in the next decades, making it necessary for the local economy to restructure around a different crop or sector (Jassogne et al., 2013). Such large-scale transformations are highly challenging. In the 1930s, the Dustbowl eroded large sections of the US Great Plains (an area previously renowned for agriculture), with economic impacts enduring for decades (Hornbeck, 2012).

Climate change impacts are not only channelled through the prices and returns determined by markets. Many poor people, especially in rural areas without functioning markets, depend on ecosystems for their livelihood (Barbier, 2010). Ecosystems provide environmental income from the extraction of non-cultivated ecosystem goods (for example, timber, plants, animals and fish), many of which fulfil subsistence needs and are not traded in markets.

Moreover, many poor people are concentrated in less favourable areas, which are most vulnerable to climate risks, such as marginal drylands, degraded forests, fragile mountain ecosystems or low-lying coastal areas. Further, subsistence-based environmental incomes provide an important share of total income for the poorest households. Noack et al. (2015) find that without environmental incomes, an additional 14 per cent of all sampled households (across 58 sites in 24 countries) would fall below the $1.25 poverty line.

Ecosystem resources also serve as a diversification strategy to smooth income volatility. If climate change impacts damage ecosystems and threaten this source of consumption (and safety net), income growth for the poorest will become more volatile, and global poverty could grow significantly. Poor people are affected when climate change affects ecosystems that support their livelihoods. For example, coastal and near-shore habitats such as wetlands, mangroves, coral and oyster reefs and seagrasses support fishing populations and protect coastlines from storm surge, other coastal hazards, pollution and saltwater intrusion (Barbier, 2015).

Importantly, the vulnerability of poor people can be reduced by addressing non-climate stressors to ecosystems. Climate change will only be one of many stressors that needs to be addressed to reduce the livelihood vulnerability of poor people. Climate change will interact with other environmental, social, economic and political stressors, which are mutually reinforcing in determining poverty impacts (Olsson et al., 2014). Conservation and ecosystem-based strategies are critical for making ecosystems more resilient and for protecting the resources on which many poor people in rural areas depend. Healthy ecosystems are generally quite resilient, so protecting them and restoring degraded lands can increase their ability to withstand climate-related disturbances (Bezabih et al., Chapter 9, this volume).

3.3 NATURAL HAZARD IMPACTS

In some regions, natural hazards such as floods, droughts and extreme temperatures will increase in frequency or intensity as a result of climate change (IPCC, 2014). The exposure, vulnerability and lack of adaptive capacity of poor people puts them particularly at risk.

On exposure, it is often the case that poor people live in risky areas. A number of case studies have examined the exposure of poor and non-poor people to past disasters using household surveys. Here we find that poor people are generally more exposed, although there are exceptions – such as Hurricane Mitch in Honduras (Figure 3.1).

The relationship between poverty and exposure to risk is not straightforward. Causality runs in both directions. Poor people sometimes choose to settle in risky areas where land is available or affordable. Living in risky areas can also be a cause of poverty, for example, when hazards destroy assets and livelihoods. Poor people are not always more exposed: for instance, flood-prone coastal or river areas benefit from low transport

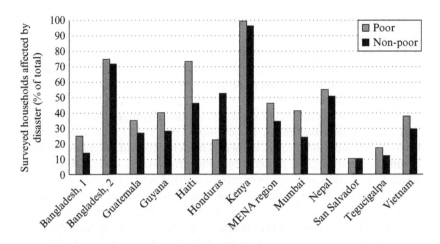

Note: MENA = Middle East and North Africa.

Source: Winsemius et al. (2015).

Figure 3.1   *When disasters hit in the past, poor people were more likely to be affected*

costs that attract firms and opportunities, and wealthier people in a country, potentially leading to greater exposure among rich people.

But in terms of vulnerability, it is clear that poor people are more vulnerable in the sense that they lose a larger fraction of their assets and income when a disaster strikes, for multiple reasons. First, the income and assets of poor people are more vulnerable. Poor people hold a large fraction of assets in material and vulnerable form (rather than as financial savings in a bank), live in lower-quality housing (for example, slums) and depend on lower-quality infrastructure (for example, non-paved roads). For example, Brouwer et al. (2007) examine flood impacts on poor and non-poor households in communities along the Meghna River in southeast Bangladesh. As a share of household income, poor people lost considerably more: 42 per cent of income, as compared to 17 per cent for non-poor people. In Honduras, following Hurricane Mitch in 2000, although poor people were half as exposed to the storm, when affected they lost 31 per cent of their assets compared to 11 per cent for non-poor people (Carter et al., 2007). In the small number of surveys that differentiate asset and income losses by income class, poor people always lose a larger share (Figure 3.2).

In addition to private asset and income losses, natural disasters also result in significant disruptions to infrastructure and services. A survey

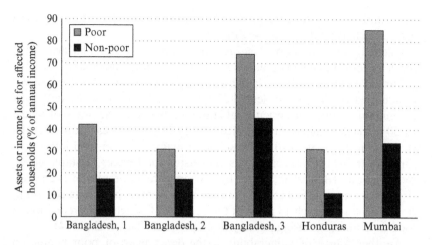

Note: Each study has a different definition of 'poor' and 'non-poor' in their sample. Vulnerability depends on the type of hazard and context in which it occurs; even within the same country (Bangladesh), vulnerability measures vary greatly based on location and severity of flooding. The first three studies use per cent of income loss as a metric, while the Honduras and Mumbai cases use asset loss.

Source: Based on Brouwer et al. (2007) for Bangladesh (1); del Ninno et al. (2001) for Bangladesh (2); Rabbani et al. (2013) for Bangladesh (3); Carter et al. (2007) for Honduras; and Patankar and Patwardhan (2015) for Mumbai.

Figure 3.2 Poor people lose a larger percentage of assets after floods and storms

conducted in Mumbai, India, after the 2005 floods finds that three-quarters of all households report significant disruptions in clean drinking water and electricity, non-availability of transportation and their house becoming flooded with sewage/garbage (Patankar and Patwardhan, 2016). Such impacts are likely to result in significant losses in income generation, due to work closures and the inability to get to work. To make things worse, in many places, factory workers are 'fined' for absenteeism and for even showing up late, as in Ho Chi Minh City, Vietnam, where a study of flood impacts reports factory workers regularly fined for showing up late, including a female migrant worker who arrived 15 minutes late and was fined VND 500,000 (World Bank and Australian AID, 2014).

Second, poor people face multiple vulnerabilities from their consumption patterns and livelihoods. While the above studies examine only direct impacts on assets and income, that is only a subset of the full impact of a disaster on households. What also matter are the indirect impacts, on food prices, on the capital that households depend on to generate their income (for example, productive capital such as farming equipment and natural capital such as land) and on health.

One major indirect impact is through food prices. Natural hazards often result in food price spikes, either by destroying productive assets in agricultural communities or by damaging food infrastructure. The former was evidenced after the unprecedented 2010 floods in Pakistan, which destroyed 2.1 million hectares of agricultural land and increased the prices of wheat by 50 per cent (Cheema et al., 2015). On the latter, Tropical Storm Agatha struck Guatemala in 2010 and resulted in major losses in food infrastructure and transport in urban areas, increasing food prices of staple goods by 17 per cent (Baez et al., 2014). Poor people are hardest hit by such price rises, as discussed in Section 3.2. Indeed, after Agatha, per capita consumption in urban areas fell 13 per cent (40 per cent of which was a reduction in food expenditure), raising poverty by 18 per cent (Baez et al., 2014).

Another source of vulnerability is the dependence of poor people on climate-sensitive income sources such as cropping and forestry, which is higher than for non-poor people (Angelsen et al., 2014). Large-scale events can wreak havoc on natural capital: Cyclone Nargis hit southwest Myanmar in 2008, killing an estimated 140,000 people. In addition to this tremendous human loss, recovery from the cyclone has stumbled off track (World Bank, 2015c). A major reason is the natural capital damage from the cyclone, which resulted in a re-enforcing chain of events. Erosion and destroyed embankments made fields more prone to flooding. The duration of daily and monthly tides became longer after Nargis, making fields more saline and prone to pest infestation. Without funds to repair, affected farming villages became more prone to these external events – flooding, saline intrusion and pest infestation. As a result, yields decreased, as did income. Without outside opportunities, households borrowed money, but many continue to be trapped in a cycle of lower productivity and higher indebtedness.

Poor people – especially children – are vulnerable to indirect impacts through health and education. Following weather shocks in sub-Saharan Africa, asset-poor households provide children with lower-quality nutrition and are less likely to take sick children for medical consultations, with long-term impacts on child development and prospects (Alderman et al., 2006). For instance, after the 1984 drought in Ethiopia, children younger than 36 months at the apex of the famine were less likely to have completed primary school, with long-term income losses of 3 per cent per year (Dercon and Porter, 2014).

In addition, poor people often have more limited access to social protection, a factor that makes them more vulnerable after disasters. A consistent finding across countries is that transfers (from social protection and labour) received are much lower for poor people (ASPIRE, 2015). For example, in Colombia, the poorest 20 per cent receives on average $0.23 per person per day, and the richest 20 per cent, $4.60. Even after a disaster, ad hoc schemes to provide compensation have not targeted poor people, as evidenced after the 2005 Mumbai floods (Patankar, 2015) and the 2011 Bangkok floods (Noy and Patel, 2014). With less income coming from transfers and less savings, poor households are more dependent on their labour income for their consumption, making them more vulnerable to shocks and lost days of work (their inability to smooth consumption can even translate into avoidable health impacts, as discussed in Section 3.4).

It is therefore no surprise that natural disasters have a well-documented impact on poverty (Karim and Noy, 2014). For example, at the municipal level in Mexico, Rodriguez-Oreggia et al. (2013) find that floods and droughts increased poverty between 1.5–3.7 per cent from 2000 to 2005. Local increases in poverty are also documented after specific events, such as floods and hurricanes. In Bolivia, poverty incidence increased 12 per cent in Trinidad City following the 2006 floods (Perez-De-Rada and Paz, 2008).

But looking only at the impact of actual disasters may underestimate the effect of risk on development and poverty. In addition, climate risks affect the behaviour of people, who may reduce investments and asset accumulation because of the possibility of losses and select lower-risk but lower-return activities – a rational strategy to avoid catastrophic outcomes, but one that can keep them in poverty (Cole et al., 2013; Shenoy, 2013). This *ex ante* effect, while much less visible, can dominate *ex post* impacts of disasters (Elbers et al., 2007). While progress has been made in recent years, many poor people remain uninsured and have lower financial inclusion than non-poor people (FINDEX, 2015). This link from natural hazard exposure to poverty may create a feedback loop, in which poor households have no choice but to settle in at-risk zones and as a result face increased challenges to escaping poverty.

While climate change will worsen the frequency and intensity of natural hazards, future impacts depend not only on climate change but also the policies implemented to manage risk. Land-use planning – especially in growing cities – is critical to ensure that new development is resilient and adapted to a changing climate (Hallegatte et al., 2013); early warning systems, hard and ecosystem-based protection against floods, preservation of ground water and improved building quality for poor people are all policies that can save lives and reduce asset losses. Providing options to poor households to save in financial institutions is critical to protect their savings. Social protection that can be scaled up after a disaster and targeting instruments able to identify affected households and deliver aid in a timely fashion to those who need it can help avoid long-term, irreversible consequences and poverty traps (Pelham et al., 2011; Castells-Quintana et al., Chapter 4, this volume).

3.4   HEALTH IMPACTS

Climate change will magnify some threats to health, especially for poor and vulnerable people – such as children. The exact impacts are still highly uncertain in what is still an emerging research field. Past progress on medical treatment offers hope that some of these issues could be solved over the long term thanks to new drugs and better health infrastructure. But short-term impacts could still be significant.

Health shocks are important for poverty dynamics and the impact of climate change for three main reasons. First, the main diseases that affect poor people are diseases that are expected to expand with climate change (such as malaria and diarrhoea). Second, health expenditures are regressive, with poor households largely uninsured against them – such outlays push an estimated 100 million people per year into poverty – and the loss of income for the sick or the caregiver can have a large impact on family prospects (WHO, 2008). Third, children are most vulnerable to these shocks and can suffer from irreversible impacts that affect their lifetime earnings and lead to the intergenerational transmission of poverty.

Malaria: even small temperature increases could significantly affect the transmission of malaria. At the global level, warming of 2°C or 3°C could increase the number of people at risk for malaria by up to 5 per cent, or more than 150 million people. In Africa, malaria could increase by 5–7 per cent among populations at risk in higher altitudes, leading to a potential increase in the number of cases of up to 28 per cent (Small et al., 2003). Further, climate change is projected to intensify malaria along the current edges of its distribution, where malaria control programmes are often non-existent and people have no naturally acquired immunity against the disease.

Diarrhoea: climate impacts could increase the burden of diarrhoea by up to 10 per cent by 2030 in some regions (WHO, 2003). Indeed, higher temperatures favour the development of pathogens, and water scarcity affects water quality and the hygiene habits that can prevent diarrhoea. An estimated 48,000 additional deaths among children under the age of 15 resulting from diarrhoea illness are projected by 2030 (Hales et al., 2014). And climate change could contribute to outbreaks of other waterborne diseases such as cholera and schistosomiasis.

Stunting: in part because of its impacts on agriculture, climate change will increase undernutrition and could sharply increase severe stunting among children. By 2030, an additional 7.5 million children may be stunted (Hales et al., 2014). Climate change could even lead to an absolute increase in the number of stunted children in some parts of Africa, with the negative effect of climate change outweighing the positive effect of economic growth (Lloyd et al., 2011). And recent evidence suggests that the nutritional quality of food (for example, its content in terms of micronutrients such as iron, iodine, vitamin A, folate and zinc) could also be affected by climate change, even though little is known about potential impacts (Myers et al., 2014).

Another concern is that high temperatures will reduce labour productivity of those who are poorer and often work outside or without air conditioning. The impact on outdoor labour productivity could be large and reduce income by several percentage points (Park et al., 2015). Moreover, this effect is not accounted for in any of the studies we reviewed on estimates of agricultural production, although it could magnify food security issues. In addition, new research suggests that extreme temperature stress in either direction – hot or cold – is suboptimal for economic activity, even when considering only non-farm activities. These results imply that the temperature-related loss in performance observed in laboratories and at the individual levels may be observable at the macroeconomic level, and that climate change could hurt overall income through this channel (Heal and Park, 2013; Deryugina and Hsiang, 2014; Park et al., 2015).

We can only begin to measure the global burden of disease from climate change but observed patterns are worrisome. A recent synthesis of five key aspects – undernutrition, malaria, diarrhoea, dengue and heatwaves – estimates that under a base case socio-economic scenario and a medium/high emissions scenario approximately 250,000 additional deaths per year between 2030 and 2050 can be attributed to climate change (Hales et al., 2014).

The future burden of disease will also depend on development. Despite rising temperatures in the twentieth century, malaria rates dropped significantly. This is because socio-economic trends – urbanization, development and improvement of health facilities – matter more for controlling malaria than climate impacts (Gething et al., 2010). An estimated 5.2 billion people will be at risk of malaria when considering climate effects only and an estimated 1.95 billion people will be at risk if GDP growth is factored in – with a peak in 2030 resulting from rapid population growth (Béguin et al., 2011). But even under this optimistic scenario, malaria will remain present in Africa and small parts of Asia. Therefore, in addition to growth, targeted investments in these areas should be made to provide adequate health infrastructure, reach remote and rural areas and develop more effective drugs.

Poor people in low- and lower-middle-income countries have limited access to health care, and face out-of-pocket expenditure exceeding

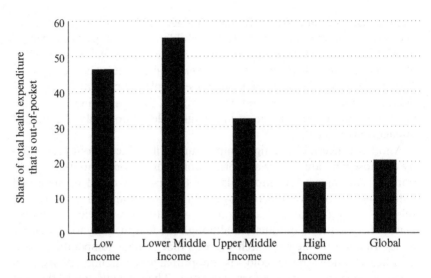

Note: 2011 data. PPP = purchasing power parity.

Source: Based on Watts et al. (2015).

Figure 3.3 A majority of health expenditures in low-income countries come from out-of-pocket

50 per cent of health expenses – much higher than the less than 15 per cent that is common in rich countries (Figure 3.3). Improving health care and working towards universal health coverage in all countries may already be a policy priority, but is made more urgent by climate change. However, benefits from better access to care depend on the quality of care, and in most countries parallel efforts are required to develop and improve health infrastructure. Climate change also makes this need even more important. Countries should have strong monitoring and surveillance systems able to detect new health issues that will periodically arise in response to changing climate conditions. They also need research and development on the diseases that affect poor people and that are expected to increase with climate change.

3.5 HOW TO ACHIEVE CLIMATE-RESILIENT DEVELOPMENT?

While climate change impacts poverty, the previous discussion highlights some of the benefits that development and poverty reduction can bring in terms of reducing climate vulnerability. For instance, better social safety nets, improved access to financial institutions and insurance, and reduced inequality would mitigate the impact of disasters, and especially the irreversible impacts on children through effects on health and education. Improved connection to markets – with better infrastructure and appropriate institutions – would protect consumers against large food supply shocks, and help farmers access the technologies and inputs they need to cope with a different climate. Basic services such as improved drinking water and sanitation and modern energy can also help protect against some of the impacts of climate change – such as waterborne diseases and environmental degradation. Access to health care is already improving with development and growth in most countries, but all countries can strive towards universal health care.

Most importantly, development and climate mitigation are not at odds with each other. Evidence suggests raising basic living standards for the world's poorest will have a negligible impact on global emissions (Rao et al., 2014; Fay et al., 2015). Initiatives such as the United Nations' 'Sustainable Energy for All' can improve access to electricity and be compatible with a warming limit of 2°C (Rogelj et al., 2013). Making mitigation and poverty eradication compatible will require a sequenced approach where richer countries do more, special attention is given to the impacts of land-based mitigation on food production and complementary policies (for example, cash transfers) to protect poor people against negative side-effects of mitigation are implemented (Fay et al., 2015). In many cases, it will also require that richer countries support poorer countries to provide technologies and financing instruments.

Climate change impacts will increase over time. There is thus a window of opportunity to reduce poverty now and thereby reduce vulnerability to future impacts.

But not all development pathways reduce climate risks in the same way. Low-carbon development mitigates climate change and reduces risks over the long term, benefiting everybody, particularly the poorest. In addition, resilient development would go further in reducing climate change impacts. What does it entail? From our analysis, a few recommendations emerge:

- Planning for a different (and uncertain) climate. Many investment and policy decisions have long-term consequences. The effect of transport infrastructure on urban form and economic activity can be observed over long time frames, sometimes even after the infrastructure has become obsolete (Bleakley and Lin, 2010). Policies such as urbanization plans, risk management strategies and building codes can influence development on equally long time scales. Therefore, to ensure development is adapted not only to present but also future conditions, plans must consider the performance of investments and decisions in the short and long term.

But doing so is challenged by deep uncertainty; we cannot predict future climate conditions precisely, we do not know which technologies will appear and we are unsure about socio-economic conditions and future preferences. There is a risk of locking in dangerous development pathways, for instance, by urbanizing impossible-to-protect flood plains or by specializing in agricultural production at risk of climate change. To avoid this, planning needs to investigate a large range of possible futures, and to make sure it does not create unacceptable risks when climate change and other trends are accounted for, especially if these changes differ from what is considered most likely today (Kalra et al., 2014). Such a robust approach leads to strategies that include safety buffers (for example, adding safety margins around what is considered flood prone today), promoting flexibility (for example, select solutions that can be adjusted over time as more information becomes available) and increasing diversification (for example, develop economic sectors less exposed to risk).

- Improving access to health care. Helping households manage health risks is already a priority, considering the role of these shocks in keeping people in poverty. Climate change only makes this task more urgent and more important. Skilled health staff, with equipment and drugs, need to be available in all areas. But even if health care is available, the ability to afford health care is also essential. Increasing health care coverage and decreasing out-of-pocket expenses is a smart investment for development and poverty reduction, and would be an efficient tool to reduce climate change vulnerability. Doing so is possible at all income levels. For instance, Rwanda invested in a universal health coverage system after 1994, with premature mortality rates falling precipitously, and life expectancy doubling (Binagwaho et al., 2014). Climate change does not change dramatically the challenge for the health sector, but emerging issues and diseases increase the importance of monitoring systems that can identify and respond quickly to new – and sometimes unexpected – emergencies.

- Provision of well-targeted, scalable safety nets. Safety nets can help manage weather shocks. During the 1999 drought in Ethiopia, the poorest 40 per cent of the population lost almost three-quarters of their assets (Little et al., 2004). Today, Ethiopia's Productive Safety Net Program supports 7.6 million food-insecure people and builds community assets to counteract the effects of droughts.

The programme has improved food security, access to social services, water supply, productivity, market access and ecosystems (Hoddinott et al., 2013). Safety nets can also play a critical role to avoid irreversible losses from undernutrition, but only if scaled-up and deployed quickly after shocks and targeted to the poorest and most vulnerable (Clarke and Hill, 2013). In addition, an increasing impact of natural disasters makes it essential for safety nets to be able to identify quickly those in need, and to scale-up and retarget support after a shock or disaster (Pelham et al., 2011). One example of a programme with mechanisms for rapid scale-up in response to a shock is the Philippines' Pantawid Pamilyang Pilipino Program (4Ps). After Typhoon Yolanda, the Philippines was able to use the 4Ps' existing conditional cash transfer system to quickly release the equivalent of about $12.5 million between November 2013 and February 2014 in emergency funding (Bowen, 2015).

Further, trends in climate conditions and risks mean that some places will become increasingly less suitable for development. As a result, temporary and permanent migration is an important risk management tool, and can be an adaptation option (see also Waldinger, Chapter 11, this volume on migration). Independently of climate change, migration plays a key role in the ability of poor households to escape poverty by capturing opportunities for better jobs, higher pay and improved access to services and education. Climate change may trigger more migration, for instance, if opportunities disappear because of climate impacts, but may also impair migration, for example, through increased conflict and exclusion (for an extended review, see Adger et al., 2014). Given the importance of mobility as an instrument for poverty reduction, it is critical that social protection does not lock people in places or occupations that will become less able to take them out of poverty. Portability of social protection (geographically and in terms of occupation) is therefore made even more important by a changing climate.

For agricultural and ecosystem impacts, natural hazards and health shocks, climate change only makes existing priorities more urgent for many countries. If done right, this urgency can turn into an opportunity to reduce current poverty and future climate vulnerability simultaneously. Of particular importance is the high economic and health impacts climate change will pose for children. Without action to move towards low-carbon and resilient development now, we may lock ourselves into a future of increased transmission of intergenerational poverty.

REFERENCES

Adger, W.N., Pulhin, J.M., Barnett, J. et al., 2014. 'Human security', in C.B. Field, V.R. Barros, D.J. Dokken et al. (eds), *Climate Change 2014: Impacts, Adaptation, and Vulnerability. Part A: Global and Sectoral Aspects. Contribution of Working Group II to the Fifth Assessment Report of the Intergovernmental Panel on Climate Change.* Cambridge and New York: Cambridge University Press, pp. 755–91.

Alderman, H., Hoddinott, J. and Kinsey, B., 2006. 'Long term consequences of early childhood malnutrition', *Oxford Economic Papers*, **58**, 450–74.

Angelsen, A., Jagger, P., Babigumira, R. et al., 2014. 'Environmental income and rural livelihoods: a global-comparative analysis', *World Development, Forests, Livelihoods, and Conservation*, **64**, Suppl.1, S12–S28.

ASPIRE, 2015. ASPIRE Database, World Bank, Washington, DC.

Baez, J., Lucchetti, L., Salazar, M. and Genoni, M., 2014. *Gone with the Storm: Rainfall Shocks and Household Wellbeing in Guatemala.* Washington, DC: World Bank.

Barbier, E.B., 2010. 'Poverty, development, and environment', *Environment and Development Economics*, **15**, 635–60.

Barbier, E.B., 2015. 'Climate change impacts on rural poverty in low-elevation coastal zones', World Bank Policy Research Working Paper No. 7475, background paper prepared for the report *Shock Waves: Managing the Impacts of Climate Change on Poverty*, Washington, DC, World Bank.

Béguin, A., Hales, S., Rocklöv, J., Åström, C., Louis, V.R. and Sauerborn, R., 2011. 'The opposing effects of climate change and socio-economic development on the global distribution of malaria', *Global Environmental Change*, **21**, 1209–14.

Binagwaho, A., Farmer, P.E., Nsanzimana, S. et al., 2014. 'Rwanda 20 years on: investing in life', *The Lancet*, **384**, 371–5.

Bleakley, H. and Lin, J., 2010. 'Portage: path dependence and increasing returns in US history', Working Paper No. 16314, National Bureau of Economic Research, Cambridge, MA.

Bowen, T., 2015. 'Social protection and disaster risk management in the Philippines', World Bank Policy Research Working Paper No. 7482, background paper prepared for the report *Shock Waves: Managing the Impacts of Climate Change on Poverty*, Washington, DC, World Bank.

Brouwer, R., Akter, S., Brander, L. and Haque, E., 2007. 'Socioeconomic vulnerability and adaptation to environmental risk: a case study of climate change and flooding in Bangladesh', *Risk Analysis*, **27**, 313–26.

Carter, M.R., Little, P.D., Mogues, T. and Negatu, W., 2007. 'Poverty traps and natural disasters in Ethiopia and Honduras', *World Development*, **35**, 835–56.

Cheema, I., Hunt, S., Jakobsen, M., Marzi, M., O'Leary, S. and Pellerano, L., 2015. *Citizen's Damage Compensation Programme: Impact Evaluation Report.* Oxford: Oxford Policy Management.

Clarke, D.J. and Hill, R.V., 2013. 'Cost-benefit analysis of the African Risk Capacity Facility', SSRN Scholarly Paper No. 2343159, Social Science Research Network, Rochester, NY.

Cole, S., Gine, X., Tobacman, J., Topalova, P., Townsend, R. and Vickery, J., 2013. 'Barriers to household risk management: evidence from India', *American Economic Journal of Applied Economics*, **5**, 104–35.

del Ninno, C., Dorosh, P.A., Smith, L.C. and Roy, D.K., 2001. *The 1998 Floods* in *Bangladesh Disaster Impacts, Household Coping Strategies, and Response,* Research Report No. 122. Washington, DC: International Food Policy Research Institute.

Dercon, S. and Porter, C., 2014. 'Live Aid revisited: long-term impacts of the 1984 Ethiopian famine on children', *Journal of the European Economic Association,* **12**, 927–48.

Dercon, S., Gilligan, D.O., Hoddinott, J. and Woldehanna, T., 2009. 'The impact of agricultural extension and roads on poverty and consumption growth in fifteen Ethiopian Villages', *American Journal of Agricultural Economics,* **91**, 1007–21.

Deryugina, T. and Hsiang, S.M. 2014. 'Does the environment still matter? Daily temperature and income in the United States', Working Paper No. 20750, National Bureau of Economic Research, Cambridge, MA.

Elbers, C., Gunning, J.W. and Kinsey, B., 2007. 'Growth and risk: methodology and micro evidence', *World Bank Economic Review,* **21**, 1–20.

Fay, M., Hallegatte, S., Vogt-Schilb, A., Rozenberg, J., Narloch, U. and Kerr, T., 2015. *Decarbonizing Development.* Washington, DC: World Bank.

FINDEX, 2015. Global Financial Inclusion Database, World Bank, Washington, DC.

Gething, P.W., Smith, D.L., Patil, A.P., Tatem, A.J., Snow, R.W. and Hay, S.I., 2010. 'Climate change and the global malaria recession', *Nature,* **465**, 342–5.

Hales, S., Kovats, S., Lloyd, S. and Campbell-Lendrum, D., 2014. *Quantitative Risk Assessment of the Effects of Climate Change on Selected Causes of Death, 2030s and 2050s,* World Health Organization. Available at http://www.who.int/global-change/publications/quantitative-risk-assessment/en/ (accessed February 2016).

Hallegatte, S., Green, C., Nicholls, R.J. and Corfee-Morlot, J., 2013. 'Future flood losses in major coastal cities', *Nature Climate Change,* **3**, 802–6.

Hallegatte, S., Bangalore, M., Bonzanigo, L. et al., 2016. *Shock Waves: Managing the Impacts of Climate Change on Poverty,* Climate Change and Development Series. Washington, DC: World Bank.

Havlík, P., Valin, H., Gusti, M. et al., 2015. 'Climate change impacts and mitigation in the developing world: integrated assessment of agriculture and forestry sectors', World Bank Policy Research Working Paper No. 7477, background paper prepared for the report *Shock Waves: Managing the Impacts of Climate Change on Poverty,* World Bank, Washington, DC.

Heal, G. and Park, J., 2013. 'Feeling the heat: temperature, physiology & the wealth of nations', Working Paper No. 19725, National Bureau of Economic Research, Cambridge, MA.

Hertel, T.W., Burke, M.B. and Lobell, D.B., 2010. 'The poverty implications of climate-induced crop yield changes by 2030', *Global Environmental Change,* **20**, 577–85.

Hoddinott, J., Lind, J., Berhane, G. et al., 2013. *Impact Evaluation of the PSNP and HABP 2012.* London: Institute for Development Studies.

Hornbeck, R., 2012. 'The enduring impact of the American Dust Bowl: short- and long-run adjustments to environmental catastrophe', *American Economic Review,* **102**, 1477–507.

IPCC, 2014. 'Summary for policymakers', in C.B. Field, V.R. Barros, D.J. Dokken et al. (eds), *Climate Change 2014: Impacts, Adaptation, and Vulnerability. Part A: Global and Sectoral Aspects. Contribution of Working Group II to the Fifth Assessment Report of the Intergovernmental Panel on Climate Change.* Cambridge and New York: Cambridge University Press, pp. 1–32.

Ivanic, M., Martin, W. and Zaman, H., 2012. 'Estimating the short-run poverty impacts of the 2010–11 surge in food prices', *World Development*, **40**, 2302–17.
Jacoby, H.G., Rabassa, M. and Skoufias, E., 2015. 'Distributional implications of climate change in rural India: a general equilibrium approach', *American Journal of Agricultural Economics*, **97**, 1135–56.
Jassogne, L., Lderach, P. and van Asten, P., 2013. 'The impact of climate change on coffee in Uganda: lessons from a case study in the Rwenzori Mountains', *Oxfam Policy Practice Climate Change Resilience*, **9**, 51–66.
Kalra, N., Hallegatte, S., Lempert, R. et al., 2014. 'Agreeing on robust decisions: new processes for decision making under deep uncertainty', Policy Research Working Papers, World Bank, Washington, DC.
Karim, A. and Noy, I., 2014. 'Poverty and natural disasters: a meta-analysis', SEF Working Paper Series 04/2014, School of Economics and Finance, Victoria University of Wellington.
Krishna, A., 2006. 'Pathways out of and into poverty in 36 villages of Andhra Pradesh, India', *World Development*, Special Issue, Corruption and Development: Analysis and Measurement, **34**, 271–88.
Little, P., Stone, P., Mogues, T., Castro, P. and Negatu, W., 2004. 'Churning on the margins: how the poor respond to drought in South Wollo, Ethiopia', BASIS No. 21.
Lloyd, S.J., Kovats, R.S. and Chalabi, Z., 2011. 'Climate change, crop yields, and undernutrition: development of a model to quantify the impact of climate scenarios on child undernutrition', *Environmental Health Perspectives*, **119**, 1817–23.
Myers, S.S., Zanobetti, A., Kloog, I., et al. 2014. 'Increasing CO2 threatens human nutrition', *Nature*, **510**(7503), 139–42.
Ndiaye, M., d'Hôtel, E.M. and Tristan, L.C., 2015. 'Maize price volatility: does market remoteness matter?', World Bank Policy Research Working Paper No. 7202, World Bank, Washington, DC.
Noack, F., Wunder, S., Angelsen, A. and Börner, J., 2015. 'Responses to weather and climate: a cross-section analysis of rural incomes', World Bank Policy Research Working Paper No. 7478, background paper prepared for the report *Shock Waves: Managing the Impacts of Climate Change on Poverty*, World Bank, Washington, DC.
Noy, I. and Patel, P., 2014. 'Floods and spillovers: households after the 2011 great flood in Thailand', Working Paper Series No. 3609, School of Economics and Finance, Victoria University of Wellington.
Olsson, L., Opondo, M., Tschakert, P. et al., 2014. 'Livelihoods and poverty', in C.B. Field, V.R. Barros, D.J. Dokken et al. (eds), *Climate Change 2014: Impacts, Adaptation, and Vulnerability. Part A: Global and Sectoral Aspects. Contribution of Working Group II to the Fifth Assessment Report of the Intergovernmental Panel on Climate Change.* Cambridge and New York: Cambridge University Press, pp. 793–832.
Park, J., Hallegatte, S., Bangalore, M. and Sandhoefner, E., 2015. 'The deck is stacked (and hot)? Climate change, labor productivity, and developing countries', World Bank Policy Research Working Paper No. 7479, background paper prepared for the report *Shock Waves: Managing the Impacts of Climate Change on Poverty*, World Bank, Washington, DC.
Patankar, A., 2015. 'The exposure, vulnerability and adaptive capacity of households to floods in Mumbai', World Bank Policy Research Working Paper

No. 7481, background paper prepared for the report *Shock Waves: Managing the Impacts of Climate Change on Poverty*, World Bank, Washington, DC.

Patankar, A. and Patwardhan, A., 2016. 'Estimating the uninsured losses due to extreme weather events and implications for informal sector vulnerability: a case study of Mumbai, India', *Natural Hazards*, **80**(1), 285–310.

Pelham, L., Clay, E. and Braunholz, T., 2011. *Natural Disasters: What is the Role for Social Safety Nets?* London: Overseas Development Institute.

Perez-De-Rada, E. and Paz, D., 2008. *Análisis de la relación entre amenazas naturales y condiciones de vida: El Caso de Bolivia*. Research Report, New York: United Nations Development Programme.

Porter, J.R., Xie, L., Challinor, A.J. et al., 2014. 'Food security and food production systems', in C.B. Field, V.R. Barros, D.J. Dokken et al. (eds), *Climate Change 2014: Impacts, Adaptation, and Vulnerability. Part A: Global and Sectoral Aspects. Contribution of Working Group II to the Fifth Assessment Report of the Intergovernmental Panel on Climate Change*. Cambridge and New York: Cambridge University Press, pp. 485–533.

Rabbani, G., Rahman, S.H. and Faulkner, L., 2013. 'Impacts of climatic hazards on the small wetland ecosystems (ponds): evidence from some selected areas of coastal Bangladesh', *Sustainability*, **5**, 1510–21.

Rao, N.D., Riahi, K. and Grubler, A., 2014. 'Climate impacts of poverty eradication', *Nature Climate Change*, **4**, 749–51.

Rodriguez-Oreggia, E., De La Fuente, A., De La Torre, R. and Moreno, H.A., 2013. 'Natural disasters, human development and poverty at the municipal level in Mexico', *Journal of Development Studies*, **49**, 442–55.

Rogelj, J., McCollum, D.L. and Riahi, K., 2013. 'The UN's "Sustainable Energy for All" initiative is compatible with a warming limit of 2 °C', *Nature Climate Change*, **3**, 545–51.

Shenoy, A., 2013. 'Risk and economic under-specialization: why the pin-maker grows cassava on the side', SSRN Scholarly Research Paper. Available at http://www-personal.umich.edu/~shenoy/files/draft20130605_figin.pdf (accessed February 2016).

Small, J., Goetz, S.J. and Hay, S.I., 2003. 'Climatic suitability for malaria transmission in Africa, 1911–1995', *Proceedings of the National Academy of Sciences*, **100**, 15341–5.

Thornton, P., Van de Steeg, J., Notenbaert, A. and Herrero, M., 2009. 'The impacts of climate change on livestock and livestock systems in developing countries: a review of what we know and what we need to know', *Agricultural Systems*, **101**, 113–27.

Watts, N., Adger, W.N., Agnolucci, P., et al. 2015. 'Health and climate change: policy responses to protect public health', *The Lancet*, **386**(10006), 1861–914.

WHO, 2003. *Summary Booklet: Climate Change and Human Health – Risks and Responses*. Geneva: World Health Organization.

WHO, 2008. *The World Health Report 2008 – Primary Health Care (Now More Than Ever)*. Geneva: World Health Organization.

Winsemius, H., Jongman, B., Veldkamp, T., Hallegatte, S., Bangalore, M. and Ward, P.J., 2015. 'Disaster risk, climate change, and poverty: assessing the global exposure of poor people to floods and droughts', World Bank Policy Research Working Paper No. 7480, background paper prepared for the report *Shock Waves: Managing the Impacts of Climate Change on Poverty*, World Bank, Washington, DC.

World Bank, 2015a. *World Development Indicators*. Washington, DC: World Bank.
World Bank, 2015b. Global Consumption Database, World Bank, Washington, DC.
World Bank, 2015c. *Another Nargis Strikes Everyday: Post-Nargis Social Impacts Monitoring Five Years On*. Washington, DC: World Bank.
World Bank and Australian AID, 2014. *'WHERE ARE WE DURING FLOODING?' A Qualitative Assessment of Poverty and Social Impacts of Flooding in Selected Neighborhoods of HCMC*. Washington, DC: World Bank.

4. Coping with climate risk: the options

David Castells-Quintana,
Maria del Pilar Lopez-Uribe and
Thomas K.J. McDermott

4.1 INTRODUCTION

In this chapter we set out some key considerations for policy makers wishing to design development strategies with climate risk in mind. While much of the economics literature still treats adaptation as a set of self-standing activities to be assessed on a case-by-case basis, we argue instead for a view of adaptation in developing countries as climate-resilient development. In practice, this means embedding climate risk fully into wider development strategies, but also taking account of how adaptation and development will interact dynamically over time – something that has been relatively neglected to date in the adaptation literature. The rapid development in terms of economic growth, capital accumulation and demographics ongoing in many developing countries is fundamentally changing their vulnerability to climate change, for good or ill.

We focus on adaptation as an autonomous response to changing climatic conditions. We explore the barriers to private adaptation of businesses, households and other vulnerable groups to climate risk and the policies that can be used to foster successful long-term adaptation strategies. While most attention in the literature on adaptation has focused on policies undertaken by governments (Fankhauser and Soare, 2013), private agents – households, communities and firms – also undertake important initiatives that help to mitigate or adapt to climate change. Forward-looking private actors should be able to respond appropriately to (slowly evolving) change, without government intervention, provided they have 'adequate information, appropriate incentives, and an economic environment conducive to investing in the required changes' (Collier et al., 2008, p. 346). Ensuring these conditions are met is the primary role for government. As we shall argue, in many cases this begins with removing impediments to efficient adaptation. But there is also an appropriate active role for government, for example, in responding to market failures, providing public goods (for example, information, basic infrastructure and so on) and ensuring that development plans take account of (long-term) climate risk.

The type of initiatives most commonly associated with adaptation to climate change (for example, irrigation schemes and new crop varieties in agriculture) tend to focus on making existing locations, livelihoods and forms of production less vulnerable (or more resilient) to climate change. We might refer to such efforts as *in situ* adaptation. An alternative, in some cases complementary, approach is to reduce vulnerability (or increase resilience) through the movement of people and economic activity across sectors and across space; what we might term *transformational* adaptation. If the productivity of some locations or activities suffers as a result of climate change, then an obvious response is to relocate capital and labour to relatively more productive or less risky locations and sectors. This is also part of the broader development agenda – the standard path of economic development involves structural transformation of the economy, with an accompanying shift from rural to urban locations (see, for example, Lewis, 1954; Harris and Todaro, 1970; Dercon, 2012). While the two forms of adaptation may appear distinct, they are also related, and indeed should be thought of as two dimensions on which a continuum of adaptation strategies might be mapped, rather than discrete or alternative policy options. Some *in situ* adaptation may be required in order to facilitate transformational change, and there are many intermediate cases, such as seasonal migration as a means of coping with risk.

The chapter proceeds as follows. In Section 4.2 we outline a number of important challenges to building climate-resilient development. We begin with the role of poverty as a key determinant of vulnerability and the additional difficulties faced by the poor in coping with risk. We also consider marginalization along various dimensions – including gender, political and geographic – as a further contributor to climate vulnerability. The section concludes with a reflection on the major development trends, such as urbanization, which will influence any climate-resilient development strategy. Section 4.3 sets out a list of responses to the challenges identified, as listed in Table 4.1, with a focus on the appropriate role for government. We divide these according to three broad categories of policy options: building adaptive coping capacity; creating an environment for adaptation; and spatial and industrial policy.

Table 4.1   Adaptation challenges and responses

Challenges		Responses
1. Poverty and vulnerability to risk	➔	1. Building adaptive coping capacity
2. Marginalization	➔	2. Creating an environment for adaptation
3. Development trends	➔	3. Spatial and industrial policy

4.2   CHALLENGES

Climate vulnerability is strongly associated with poverty. One reason the poor are vulnerable to climate risk is their reliance on climate-sensitive economic activities, especially agriculture. Poorer households in urban areas may also be more vulnerable to climate risk as a result of settling in riskier locations (the poor are often priced out of safe areas), with little or no infrastructure and poorly constructed housing. Development and industrialization mean that people in rich countries depend little on weather-contingent production activities and can also use more resources to protect themselves against the direct effects of adverse weather conditions (Fankhauser and McDermott, 2014). Poorer households, on the other hand, tend to be financially constrained. Not only do they lack own resources (by definition), they are also often shut out of credit markets since they lack the collateral required to obtain a loan. This financial insecurity leads to problems coping with risk and constrains long-term investments in productive assets and activities.

The climatic vulnerability of the poor is further compounded by marginalization along various dimensions, including gender, ethnic, political and geographic discrimination (and isolation). As a result, the poor and other marginalized groups face additional difficulties in accessing markets and services, including financial services, and often live in conditions where they lack essential basic infrastructure, including safe shelter, drinking water, sanitation, electricity, transport and telecommunications. These challenges further constrain the adaptive capacity of the poor.

4.2.1   Poverty and Vulnerability to Climate Risk

Since climate vulnerability is strongly associated with poverty, one straight-forward adaptation strategy is the pursuit of (inclusive) economic growth. Indeed, it has been argued that efforts towards adaptation (for example, foreign aid directed towards climate adaptation projects) would be more effectively spent on pursuing basic development goals, such as education and healthcare (Schelling, 1992, 1997). However, development (in the sense of poverty reduction, improvements in livelihoods and the welfare of vulnerable or marginal groups) and adaptation do not derive automatically from aggregate economic growth.

Distinguishing forms of growth (development paths) that are both pro-poor and climate resilient is an important task for policy makers. It is equally important that policy makers do not pursue reduced vulnerability at the expense of longer-term development opportunities. Some development trends (for example, urbanization – which involves the accumulation of assets in high-productivity, but vulnerable locations – and most forms of innovation and entrepreneurial activity) necessarily involve risk taking. Climate-resilient development strategies should therefore emphasize managing that risk, and enhancing adaptive (or risk-coping) capacity, rather than purely focusing on risk reduction.

Two caveats to the adaptation-as-growth perspective are important to note; one is the effect of growth on poverty, which is ambiguous. While growth has been strongly associated with poverty reduction (see, for example, Dollar and Kraay, 2002),[1] translating aggregate growth into poverty reduction is not automatic. Aside from the labour intensity and skill bias of growth, any effect on poverty reduction is also contingent on the mobility of the poor, both across sectors and across space, and their resulting capacity to avail of the opportunities generated by aggregate growth (Dercon, 2012).

The second caveat is the possibility that some forms of growth increase climate risk (Bowen et al., 2012). For example, development initiatives based on climate-sensitive activity (for example, water-intensive crops) or located in high-risk areas (for example, the development of flood plains) risk 'locking in' longer-term vulnerability (Vivid, 2010). In the extreme, any form of *in situ* adaptation in locations that are already economically or agriculturally marginal, and where conditions are expected to deteriorate, might represent maladaptation. More generally, the allure of possible 'quick-wins'[2] needs to be tempered in development strategies by an acute awareness that spurts of short-run growth are rather easily achieved, while sustained long-term growth is considerably more difficult (Easterly et al., 1993; Rodrik, 1999; Easterly, 2006; Broadberry and Gardner, 2013).[3] The former should not be pursued at the expense of the latter.

Climate change will increase the uncertainty and risk faced by vulnerable groups such as poorer households. In spite of this, adaptation to climate change should not be viewed as an entirely defensive project. In fact, Collier et al. (2008) argue that 'defensive flexibility', that is, the ability to cope with, or at least survive, short-run shocks – as in the common informal reciprocal community schemes for coping with individual risks, such as episodes of ill health – tends to be relatively well developed in many traditional, poorer communities. However, the nature of climate risk is that it affects many members of a community simultaneously. This might render these informal neighbourhood schemes inadequate for coping with climate shocks.

The longer-term capacity for sustained adaptation to new circumstances (or the adoption of new technologies), by contrast, is often limited in those same settings, in part because poorer households have less capital-intensive technologies; because their economic activities – whether farming or other – tend to operate at relatively small scales (with implications for management practices and the capacity to experiment with new technologies); due to an aversion to experimentation, deriving from precarious livelihoods; and also because they often lack access to credit and other financial services. Financially constrained households cope with risk in non-efficient ways, both *ex ante* – for example, by holding low-return liquid assets (Rosenzweig and Binswanger, 1993) – and *ex post* – for example, by selling productive assets (Deaton, 1992); sending children to work rather than to school (Jacoby and Skoufias, 1997); or engaging in expensive informal borrowing (Banerjee and Duflo, 2011).[4]

An important constraint on adaptation may be aversion to experimentation, which is prominent especially amongst poor households (Bryan et al., 2014). An inherent obstacle for the poor in escaping poverty – especially for those living close to subsistence – is that any failed experiment can have devastating consequences for household finances and welfare. Aversion to experimentation amongst the poor presents a key challenge for climate change adaptation. For example, in the case of agriculture, efficient adaptation may require the adoption of new technologies (for example, drought-resistant seed varieties, investment in irrigation or changes in production methods) and learning about new weather or growing conditions. Similarly, economic diversification requires entrepreneurial experimentation, while migration strategies often involve experimentation with seasonal migration or sending a household member to look for work in another location.

4.2.2 Marginalization

The climatic vulnerability of the poor is further compounded by marginalization along various dimensions, including gender, ethnic, political and geographic discrimination. For example, the literature on climate impacts appears to show that opportunities for women and the wellbeing of women, including access to education and health, are more severely affected by climate shocks than those of men (see, for example, Maccini and Yang, 2009; Henderson et al., 2014) indicating the potential for climate shocks to exacerbate existing gender inequalities.[5] A lack of access to basic infrastructure (for example, energy and sanitation) might represent an important barrier to the adaptation options available to the poor, especially women and girls, since the burden of domestic activities tends to fall disproportionately on them (UNDP, 2011).

Political and geographic marginalization can also play important roles in reducing or exacerbating the effects of climate stress. Globally, poverty is geographically concentrated in locations that are already marginal from a climate and agricultural productivity perspective. For example, a high proportion of Africa's rural poor live in pastoral and agro-pastoral drylands, with poverty in these regions attributed to climate variability and vulnerability to drought (FAO, 2008). Various measures of human wellbeing have also been found to decline with aridity; for example, infant mortality, child malnutrition, maternal care, adult literacy and access to education – again, particularly amongst women and girls (UNDP, 2011). Political and geographic isolation is also likely to affect the provision of basic infrastructure, access to markets (transport), financial services and the underprovision (by both public and private sectors) of basic services including health and education (Anbarci et al., 2005).

The resilience literature emphasizes that while climate threats are essentially exogenous stressors, the economic and social impacts will depend on a combination of vulnerability, exposure and adaptive capacity (see, for example, Fankhauser and McDermott, 2014). Where adaptive capacity is weak, it is likely that both adverse impacts of climate change will be realized and opportunities missed (Collier et al., 2008; Mendelsohn, 2012). Many of the most pernicious effects of climate shocks tend to occur where basic services and infrastructure are lacking – often in marginal or isolated locations. For example, Burgess et al. (2011) find that weather and mortality remain closely related in post-independence India, but this relationship only exists in rural areas where agricultural yields, wages and prices are adversely affected by hot and dry weather. Similarly, Burgess and Donaldson (2010) show that rainfall shortages affect productivity and led to famine in colonial India, but this rainfall–famine relationship was considerably attenuated after the arrival of railroads in a district. Jayachandran (2006) also shows that wages of rural workers are more responsive (that is, vulnerable) to rainfall shocks in districts with fewer banks or higher migration costs. These studies emphasize geographic isolation as a constraint on adaptive capacity, and the consequent role of transport infrastructure in increasing the flexibility of the local economy, for example, by improving trade and migration opportunities.

The evidence in Jayachandran (2006) also highlights the role of access to finance in risk coping.

4.2.3 Development Trends

The rapid development in terms of economic growth, capital accumulation and demographics occurring in many developing countries is fundamentally changing their vulnerability to climate change, for good or ill. The design of efficient adaptation strategies needs to take account of how adaptation and development will interact dynamically over time – something that appears to have been relatively neglected to date in the adaptation literature. In this subsection we briefly discuss some of the key exogenous trends that will affect adaptation and development paths.

4.2.3.1 (Increasing) location-based inequality

The dramatic differences in the productivity of labour that have been observed across space (for example, in rich versus poor countries) have been shown to derive from location-based characteristics, as opposed to differences in the productivity of workers (Clark, 1987; Hall and Jones, 1999). This finding is supported by empirical work on the earnings of migrants, which tends to find that migrants achieve gains from migration that are roughly equivalent to the wage gap between origin and destination labour markets, while accounting for selection effects (Clemens, 2011). Although it may be that human mobility (especially internal migration) has contributed to productivity differences across locations through the matching of skills or talent with opportunities (as argued by Young, 2013). Spatial externalities – for example, increasing returns to scale linked to location and agglomeration effects – imply that existing inequalities between locations will continue to diverge, regardless of the effects of climate change (Dercon, 2012). This divergence creates the possibility of spatial traps, with persistent poverty in poorer locations (Ravallion and Jalan, 1997; Gallup et al., 1999).

Climate change is likely to increase the challenges faced in lower-productivity locations – that is, those that are already hot, dry, landlocked, suffering from disease burdens, with relatively low agricultural productivity and highly variable rainfall (see, for example, Samson et al., 2011). Thus, climate change can be expected to reinforce existing location-based inequalities, and as a consequence give further momentum to the dynamics and incentives that drive economic migrants towards urban and coastal locations (see, for example, Henderson et al., 2014). An important policy question is whether governments should attempt to counteract these trends or simply manage their inevitable progression. Is an appropriate policy objective to attempt to equalize incomes (or opportunities) across space or across people?

In the extreme – where existing conditions are sufficiently bad, or climate change impacts prove to be especially negative – some marginal areas may no longer be capable of sustaining dense populations and associated economic activity. That means, for some locations, any form of *in situ* adaptation may represent maladaptation. Such cases present a clear policy implication, where efforts to support marginal locations or activities risk both maladaptation and constraining development. However, for intermediate cases, ethical or ideological judgements might support either policy direction.

4.2.3.2   Urbanization: increasing concentration of vulnerability

Demographic trends are one of the key determinants of vulnerability and exposure to future climate change. This is likely to be particularly relevant where existing climatic conditions create challenging environments for sustaining rural livelihoods, where resources per capita (including water, energy, food and finance or capital) are relatively scarce and where rapid population growth is anticipated over the coming decades. The rapid population growth forecast for developing regions will be further concentrated due to continuing rapid urbanization, a trend that is being accelerated by climate stress in rural areas (Barrios et al., 2006; Henderson et al., 2014). While urbanization can offer improved opportunities – by reducing economic dependence on the weather; through agglomeration economies; and by providing better access to trade and financial services (see, for example, UNDP, 2011) – it also carries risks.

The mass movement of (still relatively poor) people into urban areas will involve essentially shifting risk from one location (and type) to another. Urban areas are particularly susceptible to flooding and heat stress, for example, as well as the more rapid spreading of diseases such as cholera – especially where water and waste infrastructure is underprovided (World Bank, 2011). Where urban expansion is occurring most rapidly – in less developed countries – housing and infrastructure are often provided in haste, inadequately or not at all, leaving inhabitants at the mercy of the elements (Anbarci et al., 2005). An estimated one billion people live in slums worldwide, a number that is still growing (UN Habitat, cited in Marx et al., 2013). In some developing countries, the majority of urban residents lives in slums, often lacking access to basic services such as clean water, sanitation facilities and electricity (Castells-Quintana, 2015). When urbanization is dominated by precarious living standards, urban residents become more sensitive and less able to cope with shocks associated with these risks. In developing countries then a major challenge is how to accommodate safely the additional millions who wish to live in economically vibrant urban locations.

4.3   RESPONSES

In this section we set out a set of responses to the challenges identified above, with a focus on the appropriate role for government. We divide these according to three broad categories of policy options: building adaptive capacity; creating an environment for adaptation; and spatial and industrial policy.

4.3.1   Building Adaptive Capacity

The strong association between poverty and vulnerability, and the additional challenges faced by the poor in coping with risk, as discussed in Section 4.1, suggest that building the adaptive capacity of the poor might represent an important response to climate risk, and one that will also support wider development objectives. Adaptive capacity has many dimensions.

4.3.1.1   Access to credit

Relaxing credit or financial constraints on the poor could help them not only to cope better with exogenous risk but also take on riskier (and, theoretically, more efficient) investments (see, for example, Mobarak and Rosenzweig, 2013). Improved access to finance – as a means of coping with greater risk and escaping poverty – could therefore represent an important instrument for adapting to climate change (Hecht, 2008; Ward et al., 2008; Agrawala and Carraro, 2010). However, expanding access to finance for poor or vulnerable households is not easy (Agrawala and Carraro, 2010; World Bank, 2013). The poor often lack collateral. Many vulnerable groups such as pastoralists also tend to live in geographically isolated locations, making market access problematic and provision of services relatively unattractive to the private sector. Microfinance can be a possible remedy. By definition, microfinance schemes rely on small-scale transactions but potentially for many customers. There is therefore a need for service providers to find cost-effective means of reaching a broad customer base. Communications technology is one way to facilitate such a process (see, for example, King, 2012).

From the user's perspective, there are also question marks over the usefulness of microfinance, since it may predominantly benefit those with an a priori propensity to become entrepreneurs (Banerjee et al., 2015). A second issue relates to the design of microfinance schemes; the commonly used joint liability schemes might have the benefit of delivering high repayment rates, but this could also discourage risk taking, making investment in high-return activities less likely (Fisher, 2013). There are also limitations to the effectiveness of financial instruments in coping with risks. In particular, when shocks recur with relative frequency, repeated borrowing could simply result in greater indebtedness.[6]

4.3.1.2 Insurance

One instrument for dealing with income shocks resulting from climate is insurance. In the absence of transaction costs, insurance offers an efficient response to climate risk (Collier et al., 2008), particularly where combined with risk mitigation. An important question is: does insurance lead to more or less risk taking? Perhaps more important again is the normative question: *should* insurance lead to more or less risk taking? If paying actuarially fair premiums, then insurance is 'efficient' in the sense of providing a risk-coping mechanism, while still ensuring that agents internalize risks (and their costs). Subsidized insurance schemes, on the other hand, could lead to inefficient risk-taking behaviour and sub-optimal levels of adaptation.

Providing access to insurance is more complex and difficult than providing other financial services, such as credit. Aside from the standard insurance problems of moral hazard and adverse selection, insuring against weather risk also faces the additional challenge of coping with regional as opposed to individual shocks. For traditional *indemnity insurance*, in which the claim payment depends on the policyholder's loss, the familiar moral hazard problem might be particularly strong where insurance is aimed at poorer households. Observing the effort of many small policyholders can become very expensive, if not impossible – for example, where policyholders are geographically dispersed or isolated (in a rural context) or in the case of the informal economy where business is often not conducted at a fixed location (in an urban setting). An appealing alternative might therefore be *indexed insurance* products (Clarke and Grenham, 2013), where claim payments are triggered by, for example, rainfall dropping below some predefined threshold, reducing the cost of monitoring. However, indexed insurance does not necessarily foster adaptation, while its practical implementation requires good historical data on climate (and its impacts on output). It also requires that these data are a good guide to the future distribution of climatic variables and associated losses (Collier et al., 2008) – which is a challenge in the best of circumstances, but particularly so under uncertain climate change and using the spotty climate data available in many developing countries. One solution might be to combine indemnity and indexed insurance, whereby local community indemnity-based mutual insurance groups would provide protection from individual shocks (with community monitoring), while indexed insurance provides protection to the mutual against aggregate shocks (like climate-related shocks) by transferring the risk to reinsurers (Clarke and Grenham, 2013).

To date, successful (micro)insurance schemes have mostly relied on government funding. Subsidized insurance might promote excessive risk taking (moral hazard). Governments could offer other forms of support, for example, by providing information to customers about the benefits of insurance and improved climate data to providers (public goods). Governments might also partner with insurers to establish maximum thresholds of acceptable risk, and actions to remain below those thresholds (Ward et al., 2008). While insurance has the potential to help society adapt to the impacts of climate change – for example, by promoting the effective management of risks through the provision of better information on risk and vulnerability reduction and through (financial) incentives, such as discounts or making insurance conditional on risk mitigation efforts (Wilbanks and Romero Lankao, 2007; Hecht, 2008) – in practice, the effect of insurance on risk-taking behaviour is unclear. One study of 27 flood insurance schemes in developing countries found that less than half had either a direct or indirect association with risk reduction beyond risk transfer (Surminski and Oramas-Dorta, 2013).

4.3.1.3 Social safety nets
While greater access to financial services (both credit facilities and insurance products) can potentially help the poor to cope with climate risk, practical constraints on both the supply and demand sides, as discussed above, are likely to lead to the underprovision or underutilization of such services. Social safety net schemes offer an alternative, publicly funded form of insurance against climate risk – one that helps among other things to redistribute income to the poorest and most vulnerable, to enable households to make better investments and to manage risk, particularly when faced with unexpected shocks (Grosh et al., 2008; World Bank, 2010). Such schemes can be divided broadly into two categories according to the delivery method, that is, in cash or in kind. For emergencies, the most common type of transfer is the in kind programme, involving, for example, the direct provision of food or shelter. While in kind programmes might be considered less susceptible to corruption or misallocation, there is evidence that in cash programmes have been distributed safely and with positive impacts during emergencies, and even during periods of conflict (Majid, 2007; Pelham et al., 2011).

The advantages of cash transfers include their potential to stimulate local markets, their flexibility and perhaps most significantly their empowering effect, since decision-making power is transferred directly to households. This benefit can be magnified when disadvantaged groups, such as women or the elderly, receive the cash directly. This has been the case in Swaziland, where women have benefited directly from cash transfers (Pelham et al., 2011). However, it is common to observe that households decide to meet other urgent needs (for example, paying debts), with the result that programme objectives, such as health and education, are not met (Bailey, 2008).

This issue might be resolved through the use of conditional cash transfer programmes, which have been successful in promoting both risk coping and other development objectives (for example, in Central and South America – see de Janvry et al., 2006). A possible constraint on the effectiveness of cash payments during a period of crisis – for example, following a natural disaster – is that markets may be (temporarily) disrupted so that providing cash is not sufficient to ensure that affected people are able to access food and other essential supplies. One important caveat to the use of social safety net schemes as public insurance against climate risk is that their availability might reduce incentives to adapt or reduce vulnerability. This concern reinforces the importance of the careful design of such schemes, so that they support efficient risk taking – that is, risks and investments that are productivity enhancing.

4.3.2 Creating an Environment for Adaptation

Alongside building the adaptive capacity of the poor, efficient adaptation will require that private actors have adequate information and appropriate incentives to make decisions that support climate-resilient forms of development.

4.3.2.1 Information
Most adaptation – and certainly the autonomous adaptation of private individuals and firms – will depend on informed decisions by individuals. Actors will respond appropriately to changing conditions when they have adequate information, appropriate incentives and an environment conducive to investing in required changes. However, acquiring information may be costly for individuals. On efficiency grounds, governments should intervene only when markets do not work properly.[7] Lack of information is an important market failure, particularly in smallholder agriculture where incentives to free-ride are strong, resulting in underprovision of information by the private market. This explains why governments usually

provide agricultural extension services. The information deficit problem is intensified when there is a need for adaptation (Collier et al., 2008), and particularly in the context of climate change, where projections of future weather conditions are both complex and highly uncertain (see, for example, Stainforth et al., 2007a, 2007b).

Information on existing climate variability, future climate change and available adaptation strategies are particularly relevant for adaptation in agriculture – for example, to support the adoption of more suitable crops, alternative planting techniques or irrigation methods – but also in an urban context, where resilient development would be fostered through the public provision of information on urban flooding risk (Yohe, 1991; Collier et al., 2008). The quality of available information becomes particularly crucial for *ex ante* adaptation decisions – that is, those made in advance of the actual climate event – especially those involving a degree of irreversibility or vulnerability lock-in (McDermott, 2016). Empirical work in development economics confirms that farmers who are better informed about farming practices and climate change are more likely to adapt (successfully) and experience, on average, higher productivity and output (Di Falco et al., 2011). Relevant information for adaptation decisions might also go beyond making existing modes of production more resilient, to include information that facilitates *transformative* adaptation; for example, information on job opportunities for migrants and on local opportunities for diversification and entrepreneurial activities for those who wish to remain. The provision of information might also improve access to credit for small borrowers, since imperfect information may prevent small borrowers from obtaining credit to finance adaptive investments (Fankhauser et al., 1999).

4.3.2.2 Incentives and property rights

In addition to providing information, a key role for governments in creating an enabling environment for adaptation is to ensure that private sector actors have the incentive to adapt. In many cases, this means that governments commit *not* to act, in order to avoid creating moral hazard, for example, by trying to insulate households and firms from risk. Another crucial component in creating the right incentives for adaptation is the allocation and enforcement of property rights. The evolution of property rights and their effect on, for example, productivity, investment and access to credit, is an important issue in the development economics field and has been seen as a key precondition for economic growth. There are two important channels through which property rights affect efficiency of resource allocation: limiting expropriation and facilitating market transactions (Besley, 1995).

Improved property rights – for example, land tenure – are strongly associated with investment (for example, Besley, 1995). Farmers in Ghana, for example, who lack political influence – and are less confident of their rights as a result – tend to leave their land fallow for shorter periods compared to those who hold political power (Goldstein and Udry, 2008). Improvements in property rights can also increase labour supply of urban slum dwellers via reduced need for guard labour (Field, 2007) and lead to increased housing investment, reduced household size and investment in children's education (Galiani and Schargrodsky, 2010). Improved property rights can also affect access to finance (for example, Wang, 2008; Besley et al., 2012). This literature suggests that improving property rights could have important benefits for poorer households, affecting both their vulnerability to climate risk and their ability to adapt to it.

4.3.2.3 Community-based cooperative resource management

In the case of environmental capital and natural resources – for example, water resources, fisheries, grazing lands and forests – property rights are often poorly defined, or operate under a mixture of private and communal property rights, leading to collective action problems, including the classic 'tragedy of the commons' result of overexploitation (Hardin, 1968). In theory, this further reinforces the case for assigning (private) property rights over natural resources, in order to avoid unsustainable use. However, this may not be feasible where privatization would conflict with traditional rights and practices; for example, those of pastoralist communities. A recent paper on cooperative resource management suggests that the tragedy of the commons can be avoided if cooperative arrangements follow some key design principles. For example, clearly defining the identity of the group and boundaries of the resource; proportional rewards to effort of group members; collective agreement over rules of the group; monitoring, graduated sanctions and simple and fair conflict resolution mechanisms (Wilson et al., 2013). The literature even suggests that 'social norms' enforced by the community can be more effective and have greater staying power than externally imposed systems of monitoring and sanction, in fostering sustainable resource use (see, for example, Ostrom, 2000). Standard agricultural extension services provided by governments might be extended to include training communities in the design of efficient community-based cooperative resource management schemes as an effective adaptive response to climate risk.

4.3.3 Spatial and Industrial Policy

If the productivity of some locations or activities suffers as a result of climate change, then an obvious response is to relocate capital and labour to relatively more productive or less risky locations and sectors (Collier et al., 2008). This is also part of the broader development agenda – the standard path of economic development involves structural transformation of the economy, with an accompanying shift from rural to urban locations (see, for example, Lewis, 1954; Harris and Todaro, 1970; Dercon, 2012).[8]

Facilitating the mobility of the poor and other marginalized groups can therefore contribute both to adaptation and development objectives, by enabling people to escape from vulnerable or low productivity locations or sectors and to avail of the opportunities generated by trends such as globalization, aggregate (national or regional) economic growth and changing climatic conditions (Dercon, 2012). The ability of poorer households to transition out of agriculture into other sectors will depend inter alia on labour market flexibility and the absorptive capacity of the non-farm economy, as well as on measures that facilitate physical movement or relocation across space.

Existing development trends, and the likely effects of future climate change, are driving an increasing concentration of people and economic assets in urban locations, many of which are vulnerable to climate risks, flooding (for example, from sea-level rise) in particular. Reducing the number of casualties from urban disasters needs to be a high priority for governments and international donors, and quick wins in this area might be achieved through improved early warning and emergency response systems. In the longer term, investments in improved (resilient) infrastructure, taking account of disaster risk, will also be required. Long-term development planning should also consider urban disaster risk and how exposure (particularly to flooding) might be minimized, without constraining development opportunities. This might involve development of secondary cities (with lower climate risk), although such strategies will depend on the degree of agglomeration economies already accumulated in existing (risky) urban locations – in other words, the degree of path dependence or historical lock-in already committed to.

4.3.3.1 Infrastructure

The provision of basic infrastructure (transport, energy and sanitation) represents a fundamental role for government, and an important aspect of creating an 'enabling environment' for autonomous adaptation. Such initiatives might have especially strong effects on the adaptive capacity of marginalized groups – for example, by reducing the burden of domestic activities for women or by improving access to markets and other essential services for those living in geographically isolated locations.

Much of this basic infrastructure (for example, electricity, sanitation and transport infrastructure) will be required regardless of climate change and if designed right will likely contribute to building resilience under a range of plausible climate scenarios. However, an important caveat to this view is that any infrastructure provision represents a form of commitment to a specific location. There is also a role for government in ensuring that capital-intensive, long-term investments take account of anticipated future climate trends. To this end, it is important that government policies do not distort information in the form of market signals. For example, government subsidies on scarce resources (including water) might deter vulnerable households from making timely and efficient adaptation decisions. Governments might also choose to support capital-intensive investments (for example, in irrigation), which may not strictly be public goods, but where investment is constrained by lack of resources.

However, public investment in infrastructure projects raises the thorny issue of decision making under (deeply) uncertain climate change (see, for example, Stainforth et al., 2007a, 2007b). This creates an important challenge for policy makers. In general, the thrust of our argument in this chapter is that the role of government in fostering climate-resilient development is to provide an enabling environment for autonomous (private) adaptation. In this sense, policy makers do not have to attempt to predict for every community, location and economic activity when the threshold beyond which *in situ* adaptation becomes maladaptation might be reached. However, as we have already noted, geographic isolation can act as a constraint on the adaptive capacity of poorer households, for example, as a result of a lack of basic infrastructure, and difficulties accessing markets and financial services. In certain circumstances then – particularly in setting priorities for investment in such public infrastructure projects – policy makers will need to take account of the risk of maladaptation in the form of locking in unsustainable development paths. These risks represent an additional motivation to prioritize building adaptive capacity, in particular economic flexibility of vulnerable groups, above defensive infrastructure investments (for example, flood defences), which are much more subject to concerns about uncertainty (see, for example, Watkiss et al., 2014; McDermott, 2016).

4.3.3.2 Mobility across space: migration

The economic benefits and welfare gains from migration derive primarily from the relocation of labour from less to more productive locations (Clemens, 2011; Dercon, 2012) and from the use of temporary or seasonal migration as a mechanism for coping with uncertain income flows, resulting from adverse weather conditions and other external shocks (see, for example, literature cited in Gray and Mueller, 2012a, 2012b and Henderson et al., 2014). However, migration involves substantial up-front costs and there are numerous barriers to migration, especially for poorer households. It is often not the most vulnerable, or those directly affected by climate shocks, that are most likely to move (Ó Gráda and O'Rourke, 1997; Gray and Mueller, 2012a). The element of risk or uncertainty associated with migration is compounded for those already living close to subsistence, for whom failure could be catastrophic (Bryan et al., 2014). The inability to migrate thus represents an important, and relatively neglected, policy concern.

In the context of climate change, migration also carries risks. For example, there is the risk of disorderly or reactive migration in response to climate shocks, potentially leading to disruptions of economic activity and in some cases conflict. A further risk is that internal migration – particularly the rapid urbanization currently occurring in many developing countries – whether driven by economic or environmental forces, will place additional strain on scarce resources (for example, infrastructure and housing) in receiving locations, potentially increasing the vulnerability of migrants to climate risk. These issues are discussed in further detail in Waldinger (Chapter 11, this volume).

4.3.3.3 Mobility across sectors: structural transformation

In creating policies to support adaptation and development under climate change, an important consideration is the potential shift in comparative advantage. For example, yields for various crops may be threatened by shifts in temperature and rainfall patterns resulting from climate change. Similarly, working conditions may be affected by changes in temperature distributions, with stronger effects on some sectors (for example, labour-intensive manufacturing) than others. One obvious adaptive response is to reduce the weather dependence of existing economic activities – for example, through irrigation schemes (in agriculture) or air conditioning (for manufacturing). However, as we have argued previously, for some areas and activities worsening climatic conditions could make any support a form of maladaptation. Instead, policies to identify opportunities and enable diversification should be sought.

Policy support may be required to increase the opportunities available in non-farm employment, whether locally or via migration (as discussed above), to ease movement of workers between sectors (and across space), and to address the barriers to non-farm employment, for rural women in particular, for example, by improving access to basic energy and sanitation services. As Collier et al. (2008, p. 344) have argued, 'a policy priority in responding to climate change should be to raise the factor absorption capacity of the non-agricultural sectors'. But how best can this be achieved? There appears to be renewed interest among some authors in industrial policy as a means of fostering structural change (for example,

Rodrik, 2004; Hausmann and Rodrik, 2006, as cited in Vivid, 2010). However, the standard concerns about such policies – question marks over the ability of governments to successfully 'pick winners' and, perhaps more importantly, 'let the losers fail' (Rodrik, 2014) – are likely exacerbated in developing countries where the business and regulatory environment is less than ideal. These challenges are further complicated by uncertainty over future climate change and its likely effects on comparative advantage – making interventionist policies, particularly those that give support to one industry or sector over others, all the more risky.

If the conditions for establishing competitive industries are lacking, then protectionist policies are likely to prove wasteful at best, and self-defeating at worst, resulting in uncompetitive protected industries draining government resources, forcing higher prices on consumers and ultimately failing to achieve any long-term, sustainable structural change. With that danger in mind, protectionist industrial policies should not be considered without accompanying efforts to improve the conditions required for the development of competitive manufacturing (and other) industries. Priority areas (for government policy) should focus on getting the basics right in providing an enabling environment for the growth of industry, including the provision of infrastructure and reducing the regulatory barriers to the free movement of labour, hiring of employees and the establishment of new enterprises.

4.4   CONCLUSIONS

In this chapter, we began by outlining a number of important challenges to building climate-resilient development. In particular, poverty represents a key determinant of vulnerability, and we emphasize the additional difficulties faced by the poor in coping with risk of various kinds – especially climate risk. In addition to poverty, marginalization along various dimensions – including gender, political and geographic – can act as a further contributor to climate vulnerability and a barrier to climate-resilient development.

We then turned our attention to possible responses to these challenges. Economic development generally involves the accumulation of certain types of risk, whether through movement towards high productivity, vulnerable locations such as coastal areas or through the adoption of new technologies and entrepreneurial activity more generally. We therefore highlight building adaptive capacity amongst the poor and other vulnerable groups – for example, through better access to credit, insurance and social safety nets – as an important response to climate change. Such strategies have the dual benefits of fostering adaptation while also support-ing efficient (that is, productivity-enhancing) risk-taking behaviour, and ultimately economic development. This is the aim of a climate-resilient development perspective.

Private actors also require the right incentives and information in order to undertake efficient adaptation to climate change. The primary role of government is in providing an enabling environment for autonomous private adaptation by, for example, providing necessary information (for example, on existing climate variability, anticipated climate change and associated coping mechanisms), defining property rights or supporting communal resource management arrangements, and also providing basic essential infrastructure.

Successful adaptation strategies should include elements of both *in situ* and *transformational* adaptation. For example, in locations that are already marginal from an economic or environmental perspective, *in situ* adaptation strategies might lock in unsustainable practices. There is also a general risk that adaptation tends to be reactive in nature, for example, in response to extreme weather events. While the 'defensive flexibility' to cope with shocks might be relatively well developed amongst vulnerable groups, more efficient adaptation – that is, that would build longer-term resilience and sustained prosperity – needs to take account of broader development or socio-economic trends, such as population growth and urbanization as well as gradual and in some cases permanent changes in climate.

NOTES

1. This is not universally the case. Periods of rapid growth can of course lead to a widen-ing of (domestic) income inequality and thus an increase in relative poverty. It may also be that aggregate growth is not sufficient to reduce the most extreme (chronic) forms of poverty. However, at a global level, economic growth has been associated with large reductions in absolute poverty (for example, in China). This debate over the links between aggregate growth and poverty has spawned an entire literature, which is some-what beyond the scope of the current chapter. The interested reader should refer to, for example, Ravallion (2012).
2. For example, high-yield crops that depend on unsustainable water use or that are highly vulnerable to variations in growing conditions. In turn, more resilient crop varieties – or diversification of crops – might be adopted at the expense of reduced yields or market value of output. Such trade-offs need to be made explicit so that costs and benefits can be weighed. More generally, the balance between 'quick wins' and longer-term development priorities should also be reflected in setting the appropriate balance between *in situ* and transformational adaptation strategies.
3. For many of the most vulnerable populations, a sustained period of real income growth would be required to overcome the poverty dynamics highlighted in the literature cited here.

4. See Skoufias et al. (2011) for a review of the literature on the poverty impacts of climate change and the role of finance in coping with these impacts.
5. Existing patterns of discrimination against women can also be exacerbated by climatic stress, via income shocks (as noted in Dell et al., 2014). For example, the murder of 'witches' – typically elderly women – in Tanzania has been found to increase in response to extreme rainfall events (Miguel, 2005); the frequency of witch trials also increased in response to cold weather in sixteenth- to eighteenth-century Europe; and dowry killings were found to be higher during recent periods of low rainfall in India (Sekhri and Storeygard, 2011).
6. Frequent shocks that affect large numbers of households, depressing the local economy, could also result in microfinance initiatives themselves becoming indebted or even bankrupt, particularly where these schemes are not well diversified geographically. See Mechler et al. (2014) and Hallegatte et al. (2010) for a discussion of the 'risk-layering' approach to dealing with different categories of risk severity and frequency.
7. Government intervention might also be motivated by equity concerns, as in redistributive taxation systems or initiatives aimed specifically at vulnerable or marginalized groups.
8. Dercon (2012) points to the example of China, where 'in the last two decades, poverty reduction was accompanied by large migration ... with well over 170 million people moving into cities from rural areas since 1990'.

REFERENCES

Agrawala, S. and Carraro, M., 2010. 'Assessing the role of microfinance in fostering adaptation to climate change', OECD Environmental Working Paper No. 15, Organisation for Economic Co-operation and Development, Paris.

Anbarci, N., Escaleras, M. and Register, C.A., 2005. 'Earthquake fatalities: the interaction of nature and political economy', *Journal of Public Economics*, **89**(9–10), 1907–33.

Bailey, S., 2008. *Cash Transfer for Disaster Risk Reduction in Niger: A Feasibility Study*. London: Overseas Development Institute.

Banerjee, A. and Duflo, E., 2011. *Poor Economics: A Radical Rethinking of the Way to Fight Global Poverty*. London: Penguin.

Banerjee, A., Duflo, E., Glennerster, R. and Kinnan, C., 2015. 'The miracle of microfinance? Evidence from a randomized evaluation', *American Economic Journal: Applied Economics*, **7**(1), 22–53.

Barrios, S., Bertinelli, L. and Strobl, E., 2006. 'Climate change and rural-urban migration: the case of Sub-Saharan Africa', *Journal of Urban Economics*, **60**(3), 357–71.

Besley, T., 1995. 'Property rights and investment incentives: theory and evidence from Ghana', *Journal of Political Economy*, **103**(5), 903–37.

Besley, T., Burchardi, K. and Ghatak, M., 2012. 'Incentives and de Soto effect', *Quarterly Journal of Economics*, **127**, 237–82.

Bowen, A., Cochrane, S. and Fankhauser, S., 2012. 'Climate change, adaptation and economic growth', *Climate Change*, **113**, 95–106.

Broadberry, S. and Gardner, L., 2013. *Africa's Growth Prospects in a European Mirror: A Historical Perspective*. London: Chatham House.

Bryan, G., Chowdhury, S. and Mobarak, A., 2014. 'Under-investment in a profitable technology: the case of seasonal migration in Bangladesh', *Econometrica*, **82**(5), 1671–748.

Burgess, R. and Donaldson, D., 2010. 'Can openness mitigate the effects of weather shocks? Evidence from India's famine era', *American Economic Review*, **100**(2), 449–53.

Burgess, R., Deschenes, O., Donaldson, D. and Greenstone, M., 2011. 'Weather and death in India', Tilburg University Working Paper, Tilburg.

Castells-Quintana, D., 2015. 'Malthus living in a slum: urban concentration, infrastructures and economic growth', AQR-IREA Working Papers No. 2015/06, Regional Quantitative Analysis Group, Barcelona.

Clark, G., 1987. 'Why isn't the whole world developed? Lessons from the cotton mills', *Journal of Economic History*, **47**(1), 141–73.

Clarke, D. and Grenham, D., 2013. 'Microinsurance and natural disasters: challenges and options', *Environmental Science and Policy*, **27**(Suppl. 1), S89–S98.

Clemens, M.A., 2011. 'Economics and emigration: trillion-dollar bills on the sidewalk?', *Journal of Economic Perspectives*, **25**(3), 83–106.

Collier, P., Conway, G. and Venables, T., 2008. 'Climate change and Africa', *Oxford Review of Economic Policy*, **24**(2), 337–53.

De Janvry, A., Sadoulet, E., Solomon, P. and Vakis, R., 2006. 'Uninsured risk and asset protection: can conditional cash transfer programs serve as safety nets?', World Bank Social Protection Discussion Paper No. 0604, World Bank Group, Washington, DC.

Deaton, A., 1992. *Understanding Consumption*. Oxford: Oxford University Press.

Dell, M., Jones, B. and Olken, B., 2014. 'What do we learn from the weather? The new climate-economy literature', *Journal of Economic Literature*, **52**(3), 740–98.

Dercon, S., 2012. 'Is green growth good for the poor?', World Bank Policy Research Working Paper No. 6231, World Bank Group, Washington, DC.

Di Falco, S., Veronesi, M. and Yesuf, M., 2011. 'Does adaptation to climate change provide food security? A micro-perspective from Ethiopia', *American Journal of Agricultural Economics*, **93**(3), 829–46.

Dollar, D. and Kraay, A., 2002. 'Growth is good for the poor', *Journal of Economic Growth*, **7**, 195–225.

Easterly, W., 2006. *The White's Man Burden: Why the West's Effort to Aid the Rest have Done So Much Ill and So Little Good.* Oxford: Oxford University Press.

Easterly, W., Kremer, M., Pritchett, L. and Summers, L.H., 1993. 'Good policy or good luck? Country growth performance and temporary shocks', *Journal of Monetary Economics*, **32**(3), 459–83.

Fankhauser, S. and McDermott, T.K.J., 2014. 'Understanding the adaptation deficit: why are poor countries more vulnerable to climate events than rich countries?', *Global Environmental Change*, **27**, 9–18.

Fankhauser, S. and Soare, R., 2013. 'An economic approach to adaptation: illustrations for Europe', *Climate Change*, **118**(2), 367–79.

Fankhauser, S., Smith, J. and Tol, R., 1999. 'Weathering climate change: some simple rules to guide adaptations decisions', *Ecological Economics*, **30**, 67–78.

FAO, 2008. *Water and the Rural Poor: Interventions for Improving Llivelihoods in sub-Saharan Africa.* Rome: Food and Agriculture Organization.

Field, E., 2007. 'Entitled to work: urban property rights and labour supply in Peru', *Quarterly Journal of Economics*, **122**(4), 1561–602.

Fisher, G., 2013. 'Contract structure, risk sharing and investment choice', *Econometrica*, **81**(3), 883–939.

Galiani, S. and Schargrodsky, E., 2010. 'Property rights for the poor: effect of land titling', *Journal of Public Economics*, **94**, 700–29.

Gallup, J., Sachs, J. and Mellinger, A., 1999. 'Geography and economic development', *International Regional Science Review*, **22**(2), 179–232.

Goldstein, M. and Udry, C., 2008. 'The profits of power: land rights and agricultural investment in Ghana', *Journal of Political Economy*, **116**(6), 981–1022.

Gray, C. and Mueller, V., 2012a. 'Drought and population mobility in rural Ethiopia', *World Development*, **40**(1), 134–45.

Gray, C. and Mueller., V., 2012b. 'Natural disasters and population mobility in Bangladesh', *Proceedings of the National Academy of Sciences*, **109**(16), 6000–5.

Grosh, M., Ninno, C. del and Ouerghi, A., 2008. *For Protection and Promotion: The Design and Implementation of Effective Safety Nets*. Washington, DC: World Bank.

Hall, R. and Jones, C., 1999. 'Why do some countries produce so much more output per worker than others?', *Quarterly Journal of Economics*, **114**(1), 83–116.

Hallegatte, S., Henriet, F., Patwardhan, A., et al. 2010. 'Flood risks, climate change impacts and adaptation benefits in Mumbai: an initial assessment of socio-economic consequences of present and climate change induced flood risks and of possible adaptation options', OECD Environment Working Papers No. 27, OECD Publishing, Paris.

Hardin, G., 1968. 'Tragedy of the commons', *Science*, **162**(3859), 1243–8.

Harris, J. and Todaro, M., 1970. 'Migration, unemployment and development: a two-sector analysis', *American Economic Review*, **60**(1), 126–42.

Hausmann, R. and Rodrik, D., 2006. 'Doomed to choose: industrial policy as predicament', Working Paper, Center for International Development at Harvard University, Cambridge, MA.

Hecht, S., 2008. 'Climate change and the transformation of risk: insurance matters', *UCLA Law Review*, **55**(6), 1559.

Henderson, J.V., Storeygard, A. and Deichmann, U., 2014. '50 years of urbanization in Africa – examining the role of climate change', World Bank Policy Research Working Paper No. 6925, World Bank Group, Washington, DC.

Jacoby, H. and Skoufias, E., 1997. 'Risk, financial markets, and human capital in a developing country', *Review of Economic Studies*, **64**, 311–35.

Jayachandran, S., 2006. 'Selling labor low: wage responses to productivity shocks in developing countries', *Journal of Political Economy*, **114**(3), 538–75.

King, M., 2012. 'Is mobile banking breaking the tyranny of distance to bank infrastructure? Evidence from Kenya', IIIS Discussion Paper No. 412, Institute for International Integration Studies, Dublin.

Lewis, W.A., 1954. 'Economic development with unlimited supplies of labour', *The Manchester School*, **22**, 139–91.

Maccini, S. and Yang, D., 2009. 'Under the weather: health, schooling, and economic consequences of early-life rainfall', *American Economic Review*, **99**(3), 1006–26.

Majid, N., 2007. 'Alternative interventions in insecure environments: the case of cash in southern Somalia', Humanitarian Exchange No. 37, Overseas Development Institute, London.

Marx, B., Stoker, T. and Tavneet, S., 2013. 'The economics of slums in the developing world', *Journal of Economic Perspectives*, **27**(4), 187–210.

McDermott, T.K.J., 2016. 'Investing in disaster risk management in an uncertain climate', World Bank Policy Research Working Paper, No WPS7631. World Bank: Washington DC.

Mechler, R., Bouwer, L.M., Linnerooth-Bayer, J. et al., 2014. 'Managing unnatural disaster risk from climate extremes', *Nature Climate Change*, **4**, 235–7.

Mendelsohn, R., 2012. 'The economies of adaptation to climate change in developing countries', *Climate Change Economics*, **3**(2), 1250006.

Miguel, E., 2005. 'Poverty and witch killing', *The Review of Economic Studies*, **72**(4), 1153–72.

Mobarak, A.M. and Rosenzweig, M.R., 2013. 'Informal risk sharing, index insurance, and risk taking in developing countries', *American Economic Review*, **103**(3), 375–80.

Ó Gráda, C. and O'Rourke, K., 1997. 'Migration as disaster relief: lessons from the Great Irish Famine', *European Review of Economic History*, **1**, 3–25.

Ostrom, E., 2000. 'Collective actions and the evolution of social norms', *Journal of Economic Perspectives*, **14**(3), 137–58.

Pelham, L., Clay, E. and Braunholz, T., 2011. 'Natural disasters: what is the role for social safety nets', World Bank Social Protection and Labour Discussion Paper No. 1102, World Bank Group, Washington, DC.

Ravallion, M., 2012. 'Why don't we see poverty convergence?', *American Economic Review*, **102**(1), 504–23.

Ravallion, M. and Jalan, J., 1997. 'Spatial poverty traps?', World Bank Policy Research Paper No. 1862, World Bank Group, Washington, DC.

Rodrik, D., 1999. 'Where did all the growth go? External shocks, social conflict, and growth collapses', *Journal of Economic Growth*, **4**, 385–412.

Rodrik, D., 2004. 'Normalising industrial policy', World Bank Commission on Growth and Development Working Paper No. 3, World Bank Group, Washington, DC.

Rodrik, D., 2014. 'Green industrial policy', *Oxford Review of Economic Policy*, **30**(3), 469–91.

Rosenzweig, M. and Binswanger, H., 1993. 'Wealth, weather risk and the composition and profitability of agricultural investments', *The Economic Journal*, **103**(416), 56–78.

Samson, J., Berteaux, B.J. and Humphries, M.M., 2011. 'Geographic disparities and moral hazards in the predicted impacts of climate change on human populations', *Global Ecology and Biogeography*, **20**(4), 532–44.

Schelling, T., 1992. 'Some economics of global warming', *American Economic Review*, **82**, 1–14.

Schelling, T., 1997. 'The cost of combating global warming: facing the tradeoffs', *Foreign Affairs*, **76**(6), 8–14.

Sekhri, S. and Storeygard, A., 2011. 'The impact of climate variability on crimes against women: dowry deaths in India', Tufts University Working Paper, Tufts University, Medford.

Skoufias, E., Rabassa, M. and Olivieri, S., 2011. 'The poverty impacts of climate change: a review of the evidence', World Bank Policy Research Working Paper No. 5622, World Bank Group, Washington, DC.

Stainforth, D., Allen, M., Tredger, E. and Smith, L., 2007a. 'Confidence, uncertainty and decision-support relevance in climate predictions', *Philosophical Transactions of the Royal Society A: Mathematical, Physical and Engineering Sciences*, **365**(1857), 2145–61.

Stainforth, D., Downing, T.E., Washington, R. and Lopez, A., 2007b. 'Issues in the interpretation of climate model ensembles to inform decisions', *Philosophical Transactions of the Royal Society A: Mathematical, Physical and Engineering Sciences*, **365**, 2163–77.

Surminski, S. and Oramas-Dorta, D., 2013. 'Flood insurance and climate adaptation in developing countries', *International Journal of Disaster Risk Reduction*, **7**, March, 154–64.

UNDP (United Nations Development Programme), 2011. *The Forgotten Billion: MDG Achievement in the Drylands*. New York: United Nations Development Programme.

Vivid, 2010. *Promoting Economic Growth when the Climate is Changing*. London: Vivid Economics and DFID.

Wang, S.Y., 2008. 'Credit constraints, job mobility and entrepreneurship; evidence from a property reform in China', New York University Working Paper, New York.

Ward, R., Herweijer, C., Patmore, N. and Muir-Wood, R., 2008. 'The role of insurers in promoting adaptation to the impacts of climate change', *The Geneva Papers*, **33**, 133–9.

Watkiss, P., Hunt, A. and Savage, M., 2014. 'Early VfM adaptation toolkit: delivering value-for-money adaptation with iterative frameworks & low-regret options'. Available at http://www.evidenceondemand.info/early-vfm-adaptationtoolkit-delivering-value-for-money-adaptation-with-iterative-frameworks-and-low-regret-options (accessed 19 February 2016).

Wilbanks, T. and Romero Lankao, P., 2007. 'Industry, settlement and society', in M.L. Parry, O.F. Canziani, J.P. Paultikof, P.J. van der Linden and C.E. Hanson (eds), *Climate Change 2007: Impacts, Adaptation and Vulnerability. Contribution of Working Group II to the Fourth Assessment Report of the Intergovernmental Panel on Climate Change*. Cambridge: Cambridge University Press, pp. 357–90.

Wilson, D.S., Ostrom, E. and Cox, M.E., 2013. 'Generalizing the core design principles for the efficacy of groups', *Journal of Economic Behavior and Organization*, **90S**, S21–S32.

World Bank, 2010. *World Development Report 2010: Development and Climate Change*. Washington, DC: World Bank Group.

World Bank, 2011. *Building Resilience to Disasters – Delivering Results. Global Facility for Disaster Reduction and Recovery Annual Report 2011*. Washington, DC: World Bank Group.

World Bank, 2013. *World Development Report 2013: Jobs*. Washington, DC: World Bank Group.

Yohe, G., 1991. 'Uncertainty, climate change and the economic value of information: and economic methodology for evaluation of the timing and relative efficacy of alternative response to climate change with application to protecting developed property from greenhouse induced sea level rise', *Policy Sciences*, **24**, 245–61.

Young, A., 2013. 'Inequality, the urban-rural gap and migration', *Quarterly Journal of Economics*, **128**(4), 1727–85.

5. Locking in climate vulnerability: where are the investment hotspots?

Simon Dietz, Charlie Dixon and John Ward

5.1 INTRODUCTION

Hundreds of billions of dollars are invested annually in countries vulnerable to climate variability and change. In 2013, gross investment in the Least Developed Countries totalled about $205 billion, for instance, or about 25 per cent of their gross domestic product (GDP) (World Bank, 2014c). These countries, and others that support them, have a strong interest in ensuring investment is resilient to climate change. The most straightforward concern is that the direct economic, social and environmental returns on investment could be negatively affected by climate change. But, in addition, there is a concern that some investments could indirectly increase climate vulnerability (Klein et al., 2007), for example, road building that attracts development to vulnerable areas.

From the point of view of *ex ante* appraisal, climate-resilient investment is easier in some cases than others. Sometimes the primary purposes of the investment are well aligned with building resilience to climate change, for example, where the investment is intended to reduce vulnerability to current climate variability and this increases resilience to future climatic conditions too, or where the investment is intended to reduce poverty and this reduces climate vulnerability (McGray et al., 2007). In other cases, the project duration is just too short to make future climate a central concern.

But some investments are long-lived and their net present value depends on returns over many years, for instance, various kinds of major infrastructure project. These investments also typically require large sunk costs to be paid, that is, the investment is irreversible or at least costly to reverse. Even if the investment has a short asset life, it may still cast a longer-term, indirect shadow on development patterns. This is often the case with urban planning and development, for instance, and again it is typically costly to reverse such patterns.

As Ranger and Garbett-Shiels (2012) show, this analysis can be used to develop a framework for identifying what kinds of investment decision being made today are likely to require consideration of future climate in their design and implementation. These are decisions that, as well as being large enough to attract attention:

1. affect climate vulnerability (either the performance of the project itself is vulnerable to climate or project outcomes more broadly affect vulnerability to climate)
2. do so in the long run (ten years or more)
3. are quasi-irreversible.

Ranger et al. (2014) went on to analyse 250 development projects from the World Bank and UK Department for International Development (DFID) in three countries and identified the types of project most 'urgent' according to criteria similar to those above. In no particular order they are:[1]

- energy and communications infrastructure
- urban planning, infrastructure and reconstruction
- water supply infrastructure
- transport infrastructure
- major hydropower
- major irrigation infrastructure
- public buildings (schools, hospitals)
- natural resource management.

However, while the conceptual framework is in place, we still lack a quantitative understanding of where these kinds of investment decisions are being made, now and in the coming years. Where are the hotspots that would consequently be deserving of special attention? Much of the agenda here is being driven by organizations engaged in development aid and assistance. Net official development assistance to Least Developed Countries, who are generally the most vulnerable to climate change, totalled about $48 billion in 2013 (World Bank, 2014c).

This chapter seeks to identify potential hotspots for infrastructure investment that affects climate vulnerability and that require consideration of future climate in design and implementation today. The regional focus is on sub-Saharan Africa, though future work could replicate it elsewhere. We use a series of quantitative indicators that are comparable on a national basis across the whole region, obtained from a range of international databases. To help development organizations prioritize across the region, our focus is on aggregate investment flows, rather than flows per capita or shares of GDP. As will become clear, in many cases this paves the way for an important role for the size of countries in terms of GDP and population.

Our analysis is similar in spirit to quantitative analysis of climate vulnerability (for example, Yohe et al., 2006; Barr et al., 2010), but closer inspection reveals that is wholly complementary. Quantitative analysis of climate vulnerability is concerned not with decision-making and investment per se – with the precursors of vulnerability – but with the outcomes for vulnerability. Therefore, the focus in these studies is on measures of exposure/impact such as damage to crop yields, measures of sensitivity such as food import dependency and measures of adaptive capacity such as governance indices (also see IPCC, 2014).

5.2 METHODS

The principal methodological problem confronted in doing a comparative, quantitative analysis of infrastructure investment across a region is that suitable, direct data are in short supply. For some of the above categories of infrastructure, good proxies do exist. For instance, projections can be obtained of population growth in cities in sub-Saharan Africa, which is strongly indicative of likely future urban planning and infrastructure investment. Such data are included here. Yet for the most part this is not the case and reliance must be placed on more indirect proxies. To this end we rely on the notion of infrastructure deficits (Yepes et al., 2008) or *infrastructure intensity gaps*, in order to quantify the potential for future investment (Section 5.3).

The justification for doing so lies in the empirically demonstrated phenomenon of convergence of economies along a growth path (for example, Barro and Sala-i-Martin, 2004). Economies that start further behind gradually catch up with the leaders in terms not only of ultimate living standards but also capital and infrastructure intensity: they grow faster on these dimensions. The implication is that those countries with a large gap relative to a leading, benchmark country in a suitably normalized measure of infrastructure – that is, infrastructure intensity – have the potential to see most investment in the future.

The benchmark country that is chosen for the main analysis is the developing country, anywhere in the world, with the highest infrastructure intensity in a particular category. An alternative would be to benchmark against the leading country in sub-Saharan Africa, but if we can give a cardinal interpretation to the data, then doing so would not convey the potential for further investment even in the leading country in sub-Saharan Africa. Regardless, a potential weakness is that the benchmark country may have unique characteristics, which make it especially infrastructure-intensive. We account for this, wherever it is required, by truncating the benchmark. For example:

- When considering the proportion of the urban population living in slums, countries with an urban population lower than 1 million are excluded.
- When considering the paved road density of total arable land, countries with a total land area of less than 1,000 km² are excluded.

Each of our indicators of intensity is normalized by an underlying absolute variable to ensure comparability across countries. For example:

- The slum population may be normalized by the total urban population. Countries with the largest share of slum-dwellers have the greatest need of urban planning and infrastructure investment to provide adequate conditions for such people, and the greatest potential for future investment according to the convergence story.
- The area of agricultural land that is equipped for irrigation may be normalized by the estimated area of total irrigable land to show where there is potential for investment in further irrigation.

Unless otherwise stated, the results presented in this analysis are the sum of the investment required to first close the current infrastructure intensity gap and second, maintain the benchmark intensity in the future. To calculate what level of investment would be required to close an infrastructure intensity gap relative to the benchmark, the gap is multiplied by the current value of the normalization variable to arrive at an absolute investment potential/requirement. For example, the difference in public spending on education as a percentage of GDP is multiplied by current GDP to arrive at the absolute additional annual spending required to close the gap.

For most of the indicators, the infrastructure intensity benchmark is then multiplied by future forecasts for the normalization variable in order to estimate what investment would be required to maintain infrastructure intensity at the benchmark over time. The latest available forecasts are used for each underlying variable, and the forecasting horizon is 2025. This is not possible for some normalization variables such as irrigable land or potential for hydropower production as they are constant over time or forecasts are unavailable.

Table 5.1 summarizes the indicators we include in our main analysis.

Of course countries do not always neatly follow a process of convergence

Table 5.1   Infrastructure categories and indicators analysed

Category	Indicator	Data sources
National indicators	Produced capital intensity	World Bank (2013, 2014a)
Energy and communications infrastructure	Electricity generation capacity per capita	US Energy Information Administration (EIA) (2014), World Bank (2014a)
	Planned investments in hydropower	The Programme for Infrastructure Development in Africa (2010)
	Hydropower production relative to potential	The Programme for Infrastructure Development in Africa (2010), World Bank (2014a), World Energy Council (2013)
	Fixed broadband internet subscribers per capita	World Bank (2014a, 2014b)
Urban planning and infrastructure	City population growth forecasts	UNDESA (2014)
	Share of urban population living in slums	World Bank (2014b)
Water infrastructure	Share of population with access to improved water	World Bank (2014a)
Transport infrastructure	Paved road density on arable land	World Bank (2014b)
Irrigation infrastructure	Share of irrigable land equipped for irrigation	Food and Agriculture Organization of the United Nations (2014)
Education and health infrastructure	Hospital beds per capita	World Bank (2014a, 2014b)
	Public spending on education as a share of GDP	IMF (2014), World Bank (2014b)
Insurance and social protection	Total spending on social and labour protection measures as a share of GDP	IMF (2014), World Bank (2014b)

(Quah, 1996). The existence of an infrastructure intensity gap does not automatically imply that the gap will be closed; it may exist for a good reason such as weak governance. To account for this, we present two further sets of results.

First, infrastructure intensity gaps can be calculated not with respect to the leading country in each category but what each country might be expected to have achieved given its level of development and other national characteristics. In particular, Yepes et al. (2008) carry out an econometric analysis of the determinants of various kinds of infrastructure intensity in developing countries, showing that they depend, among other things, on national income per capita and population density. We use the statistical estimates from this work to provide a prediction of what degree of infrastructure intensity a country would have given the average effect of national characteristics such as income per capita on infrastructure intensity across all developing countries. If a gap exists, then it is not explained by these characteristics and it might be assumed to be more readily closed. Since we can only follow this alternative approach reliably in a limited number of cases, we present these alternative results as a sensitivity analysis in Section 5.4.

Second, data on infrastructure intensity gaps can be compared with data on governance and the national investment climate. If a large gap exists, yet the investment climate is poor, it can be concluded that it is less likely to be closed (see also Section 5.4).

In Section 5.5 we synthesize the results of Sections 5.3 and 5.4 in a simple way, calculating composite, standardized indicators of investment needs and the enabling environment for investment.

5.3   INFRASTRUCTURE INTENSITY GAPS AND OTHER MEASURES OF INVESTMENT NEEDS

This section presents our main results. Rather than working on an indicator-by-indicator basis through those listed in Table 5.1, for the sake of brevity we focus on the main trends that emerge. Four or five different regional patterns can be observed.

5.3.1   Countries with Large Populations

For many of our indicators, absolute investment needs are largest in the region's most populous countries. Three countries that repeatedly stand out in this category are the Democratic Republic of the Congo (DRC), Ethiopia and above all Nigeria.

Perhaps the best example of this pattern is produced capital intensity. This is the value of the total stock of productive capital per capita, where productive capital includes physical capital such as machinery, buildings and transport infrastructure, as well as urban land. Higher levels of

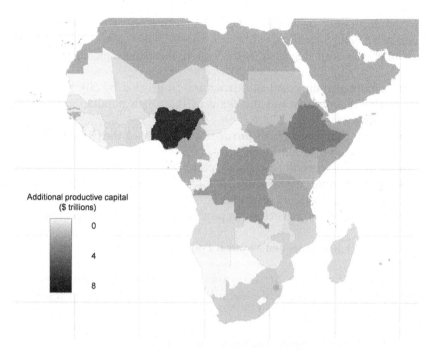

Note: Countries outside sub-Saharan Africa or for which data were unavailable appear as light grey.

Figure 5.1 Potential for investment in produced capital in sub-Saharan Africa

productive capital intensity are associated with increased labour productivity. As countries develop and economic activity shifts away from agriculture towards manufacturing and services, produced capital intensity is likely to increase, which requires investment in a wide range of long-lived assets.

For the purposes of our study, produced capital intensity can be thought of as an overarching indicator, capturing economy-wide potential for investment, rather than focusing on any of the specific categories of infrastructure or spending outlined in the introduction. It sets the scene.

As Figure 5.1 demonstrates, Nigeria has the potential for by far the most future investment in produced capital, $8.4 trillion in all. This is equivalent to over 30 times Nigeria's current stock of produced capital. Ethiopia and the DRC, the second and third highest-placed countries on this measure, require $4.4 trillion and $3.3 trillion investment, respectively. Elsewhere in the north and southeast of the region, a number of countries require between $1 and $3 trillion.

Other indicators that broadly conform to this pattern include:

- Urban planning and infrastructure, as proxied by city population growth forecasts and the share of the urban population living in slums.
- Water infrastructure, as proxied by the share of the population with access to improved water.[2]
- Electricity generation capacity per capita.
- Telecommunications infrastructure, as proxied by fixed broadband internet subscribers per capita.
- Healthcare infrastructure, as proxied by hospital beds per capita.

5.3.2 Water Resources and Physical Potential

We consider two types of infrastructure for which a dominant role is played by countries' physical geography, in particular their water resources and *physical* potential to exploit them.

5.3.2.1 Share of irrigable land equipped for irrigation

Irrigation can dramatically increase crop yields, the productivity of labour and the incomes of agricultural workers. As countries develop, farmers are likely to become richer, gain better access to credit and be more able to invest in the infrastructure required for irrigation, such as irrigation canals and equipment for surface and pressurized irrigation. Thus, the share of land that can be irrigated and that is already equipped with the necessary infrastructure provides an indication of the potential a country has for future investment. Higher shares indicate lower levels of investment are more likely.

Figure 5.2 indicates that the DRC has the largest potential for future investment in irrigation infrastructure, which is mainly attributable to its relatively large area of irrigable land, 7 million hectares, of which only 1.5 per cent is currently equipped for irrigation. Angola, Ethiopia and Mozambique also have large unused potential and require equipment for over 2 million hectares.

5.3.2.2 Planned investments in hydropower

Hydropower production is a particularly capital-intensive form of electricity generation. Moreover, conventional hydroelectric plants typically have large capacities and remain in operation for long periods of time. There are a number of hydroelectric construction projects approved or prioritized

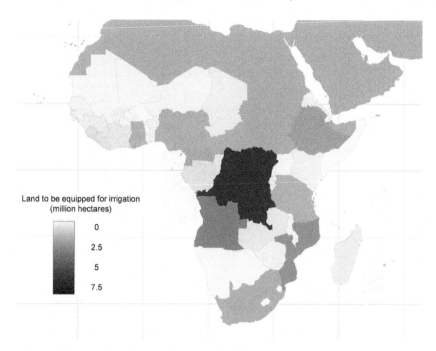

Land to be equipped for irrigation
(million hectares)

0

2.5

5

7.5

Note: Countries outside sub-Saharan Africa or for which data were unavailable appear as
light grey.

Figure 5.2   Irrigation infrastructure intensity gaps in sub-Saharan Africa

for approval in The Programme for Infrastructure Development in Africa's
(2014) *Africa Energy Sector Phase III Report.*
As Figure 5.3 shows, these projects span only 14 countries in sub-Saharan
Africa. The DRC has the largest amount of additional planned capacity
by a considerable margin, 44 GW. Ethiopia has the second largest at 15
GW, while planned construction in all other countries does not exceed 4
GW.
   In addition to planned construction, it can also be insightful to consider
how much of a country's potential for hydropower production is currently
realized. If a country's current production is below its potential, it may be
assumed more likely to invest in hydropower infrastructure in the future to
increase this. Potential production is defined as the level of economically
feasible potential production, that is, the potential for production where the
value of the electricity generated exceeds operational costs. Unfortunately,
there is a paucity of data available to calculate this indicator. What data
are available confirm the pattern in Figure 5.3, insofar as there is strong

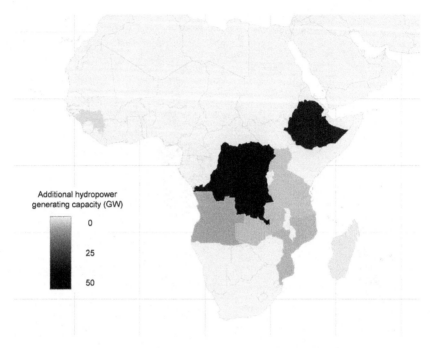

Note: Countries outside sub-Saharan Africa or for which data was unavailable appear light grey.

Figure 5.3   Planned hydropower generation capacity in sub-Saharan Africa

potential in Ethiopia, and modest potential in Angola, Mozambique and Zambia (there were no data for the DRC).

5.3.3   Paved Road Density

As a proxy for investment in transport infrastructure we estimate paved road density on arable land, defined as total kilometres (km) of paved road per square km of arable land. As countries develop, more settlements will become connected to the paved road network and built-up rural settlements will become more densely populated. Paved roads are used as opposed to all roads as both the necessary investment in and asset life of non-paved roads is low. To compare this level of infrastructure across countries, the length of paved road is normalized by the total area of arable land, as opposed to all land, as this excludes large areas of inhospitable land unsuitable for road construction.

In Figure 5.4 we see a more even distribution of likely investment over

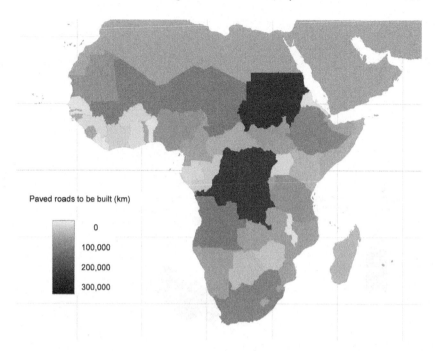

Note: Countries outside sub-Saharan Africa or for which data were unavailable appear as light grey.

Figure 5.4 Paved road infrastructure intensity gaps in sub-Saharan Africa

countries in sub-Saharan Africa, relative to other indicators. While Sudan and the DRC require the most investment to support 324,000 km and 303,000 km of new paved roads, respectively, there is also significant investment potential in Angola, Chad, Ethiopia, Mali, Niger and South Africa. Several countries with a particularly small land area, including Cape Verde, Lesotho and the Seychelles, have been excluded from this analysis. Note that the analysis does not take into account differences in population density, which could affect potential investment in the paved road network. For example, Sudan and the DRC have relatively low population density.

5.3.4 Investment Priorities Driven by National Income

For two of our indicators – public spending on education as a share of GDP, and total spending on social and labour protection measures as a share of GDP – the regional pattern of investment potential that emerges reflects an important role for the scale of the national economy.

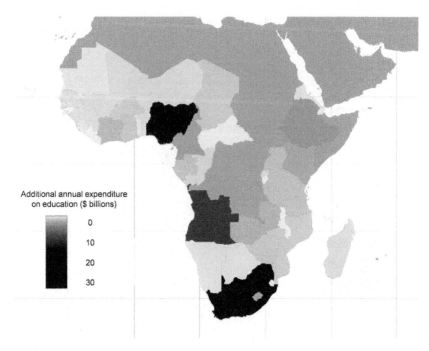

Note: Countries outside sub-Saharan Africa or for which data were unavailable appear as light grey.

Figure 5.5   Education spending gaps in sub-Saharan Africa

Schools are typically built solely from public funds and require several years to plan and construct. As a result, public spending on education is a good leading indicator of when and where investment in school buildings is likely to occur. Examining the level of public spending as a share of GDP provides an approximation of the quality of the education system and hence is a useful metric to compare levels of development. As countries aim to improve the quality of their education system, they are likely to increase public spending on education as a share of GDP and invest in infrastructure for education.

As Figure 5.5 indicates, while Nigeria again has the highest levels of likely investment in educational infrastructure, additional spending of $31 billion per year, South Africa is also likely to invest an additional $23 billion per year. Angola may also invest around an additional $12 billion per year, while most other countries are predicted to experience a relatively small increase in expenditure of below $1 billion per year.

Social and labour protection measures often require several years of planning and substantial amounts of technical infrastructure to implement and monitor. Moreover, as their coverage is often national in size, they can be difficult and costly to adjust in the future. More developed countries are often associated with a more sophisticated, and generous, social safety net and so it is likely, as countries develop, that there will be significant investment in these protection measures.

Expansion of social and labour protection measures has a relatively muted effect on countries other than Nigeria and South Africa, which may increase their annual expenditure by $95 billion and $85 billion, respectively.

5.4   BARRIERS TO CLOSING INFRASTRUCTURE INTENSITY GAPS

As mentioned earlier, it is also possible to calculate infrastructure intensity gaps relative to what we might expect a country's infrastructure intensity to be, given its level of development and other national characteristics. Controlling for national characteristics in this way helps to take into account any intrinsic limitations to investment. This alternative benchmarking method was not used in our main analysis as it is only possible for the subset of indicators that were also considered by Yepes et al. (2008), whose statistical estimates we use.

We would expect the method of benchmarking by the leading developing country to result in higher estimates of investment than this alternative method. The expected intensity method compares a country's actual infrastructure intensity with its expected intensity, given national characteristics that are mostly related to its development level. By contrast, the leading country method compares it with the country's maximum potential intensity, defined as that of the most infrastructure-intense developing country.

The difference that benchmarking makes for our results varies considerably across the indicators for which we can make a comparison, albeit the ranking of countries in terms of investment needs is preserved in most cases. Figures 5.6 and 5.7 contrast the results for, respectively, the share of the population with access to improved water and the number of broadband internet subscribers per capita. These two indicators constitute the extremes of the variation in our results; the two benchmarking methods estimate similar investment needs for access to water, yet very different needs in relation to broadband internet subscribers as a proxy for communications infrastructure.

This difference is likely driven by at least two factors. First, access to improved water is already at relatively high levels in sub-Saharan Africa, so

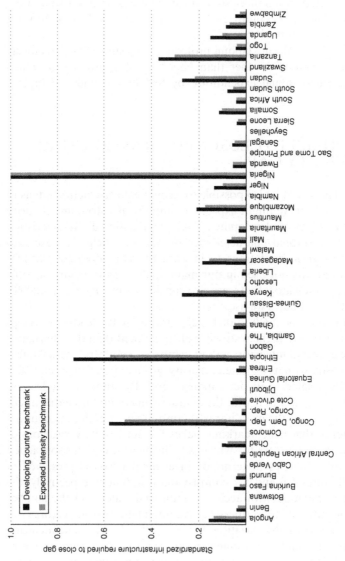

Note: Countries for which data were unavailable appear as zero.

Source: World Bank (2014a), Vivid Economics.

Figure 5.6 Comparing benchmarking methods for access to improved water

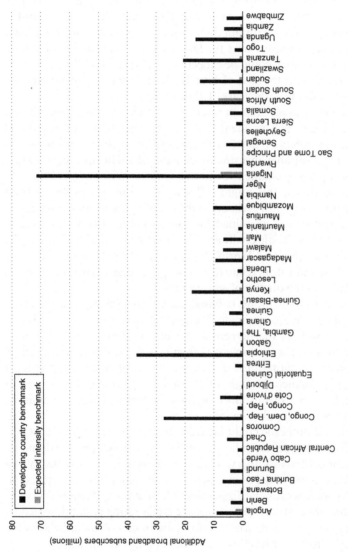

Note: Countries for which data were unavailable appear as zero.

Source: World Bank (2014a, 2014b), Vivid Economics.

Figure 5.7 Comparing benchmarking methods for internet communications infrastructure

that the expected intensity benchmarks range from 85 to 100 per cent, with the vast majority over 90 per cent: not far off the leading country benchmark of 100 per cent. By contrast, the number of broadband internet subscribers per capita is relatively low in the region and has the potential to rise much further in order to catch up with the leading developing country. Second, Yepes et al. (2008) obtain their estimates using data for the period 2001–04. Technical progress over the last ten years may have significantly increased what a country could be expected to achieve, and this seems to be particularly relevant in the case of broadband internet, whose penetration was globally low in the early years of this century.

As well as technical progress in recent years, there is also a concern that statistical problems such as identification and correlation of regressors may prevent the effects of barriers to investment, such as poor access to finance, an unfavourable investment climate or ineffective governance, from being properly accounted for in the work of Yepes et al. (2008). To better understand how this might influence the conclusions drawn from the analysis, three indicators related to the enabling environment for infrastructure investment are examined for each country: a composite credit rating; the level of domestic credit provided by the financial sector; and the average score from the 2014 World Governance Index (WGI) update. The first two of these indicators relate to a country's access to finance, whereas the latter relates to the quality of governance.

The composite credit rating is based on an assessment of a country's rating with all three major rating institutions – Standard and Poor, Moody and Fitch – as well as the perceived stability of those ratings (Trading Economics, 2014). This assessment is then translated into a score out of 100. The composite rating provides an indication of how easy it is for a country to raise finance through international capital markets, as well as the likely costs of borrowing. Both of these factors will play a prominent role in many countries' public investment plans.

The amount of domestic credit provided by the financial sector as a percentage of GDP provides an indication of how well developed the domestic financial sector is. Similarly, this will have direct impacts on the quantity and cost of credit available in the economy both to the public and private sector.

Figure 5.8 compares standardized values of these two indicators for countries in sub-Saharan Africa. The composite credit rating is standardized by the maximum possible score, whereas domestic credit is standardized by the highest value across all (developed and developing) countries. Most sub-Saharan African countries struggle to score more than 40 per cent on either indicator. Some of the countries that were repeatedly identified as having the highest investment requirements – Nigeria and the DRC – have some of the lowest scores, broadly 25 per cent for the composite credit rating and

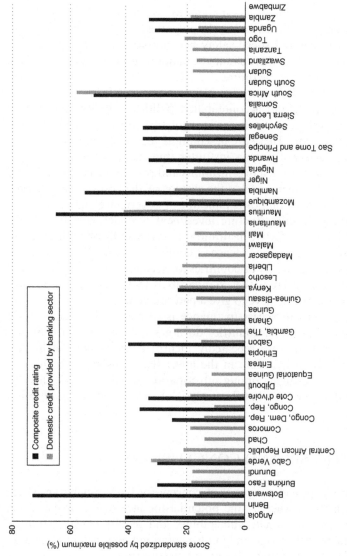

Note: The maximum possible value for domestic credit was taken as the maximum value globally.

Source: Trading Economics (2014), World Bank (2014d), Vivid Economics.

Figure 5.8   Access to finance across sub-Saharan Africa

15 per cent for domestic credit. This suggests that while much investment may be required, if these countries are to meet the infrastructure intensity benchmark identified, they may have difficulty in securing it.

Botswana, Mauritius and South Africa have among the highest scores on both indicators. While Botswana and Mauritius need little investment in absolute terms, South Africa has the potential for significant investment in both educational and social safety net infrastructure. Taken together this suggests that indeed there should be major investment in both of these areas in South Africa in the future.

The WGI reports indicators for 215 economies covering six key areas of governance: voice and accountability; political stability and absence of violence; government effectiveness; regulatory quality; rule of law; and control of corruption. These are based on 32 individual data sources and produced by a variety of surveys, institutes, think tanks, non-governmental organizations, international organizations and private sector firms (World Bank, 2014d). This analysis takes the average of the best estimate of each indicator to provide a composite indicator of governance quality.

Much large-scale infrastructure investment is undertaken by government, which requires effective institutions to successfully plan, finance and implement such investments. Hence, a country's average WGI score is a good indicator of the ability of countries to meet infrastructure investment needs. This average score is then standardized by the maximum possible score a country could achieve to give a percentage value.

A similar pattern to access to finance is seen with the average WGI score in Figure 5.9. Most countries do not score over 40 per cent and those countries that were repeatedly identified as having the highest investment requirements score in the lower half. This suggests that the distribution of investment among sub-Saharan African countries may, in reality, be different from what the analysis of investment *potential* would indicate.

5.5   SYNTHESIS AND CONCLUSIONS

This chapter has provided a proof-of-concept for the sub-Saharan Africa region of a method whereby the potential for investments to be made, which might lock in climate vulnerability and require consideration of future climate in their design and implementation today, can be compared systematically and quantitatively over many countries.

Figure 5.10 synthesizes the results in a straightforward way. It presents an overall indicator of likely future investment by combining a composite score for total investment needs from the data presented in Section 5.3 with

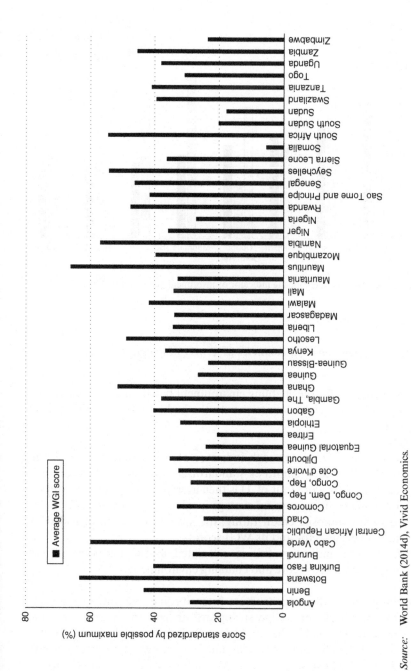

Source: World Bank (2014d), Vivid Economics.

Figure 5.9 Standardized World Governance Index (WGI) scores in sub-Saharan Africa

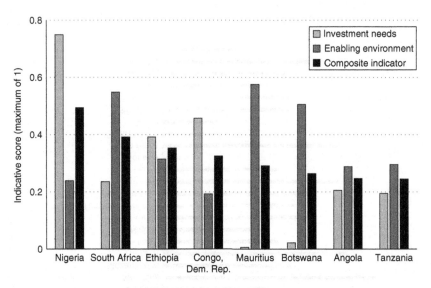

Note: Scores based on a composite indicator of investment needs and enabling environment.

Source: Vivid Economics.

Figure 5.10   The top eight countries in terms of likely future investment

a composite score for the enabling environment based on data presented in Section 5.4, for the eight countries with the highest scores on this overall indicator.

- Investment needs: for each indicator of infrastructure intensity in Section 5.3, each country's standardized investment needs are calculated. This score (out of 1) is then averaged across all indicators.
- Enabling environment: an average is taken of each country's standardized composite credit rating, the amount of credit provided by the financial sector and its WGI score.
- Composite indicator: this is calculated as the midpoint of the investment needs score and enabling environment score.

Looking across the infrastructure intensity gaps for the various categories of infrastructure, Nigeria appears to have the highest absolute investment needs in sub-Saharan Africa – indeed, it has the highest needs for nine of the twelve indicators examined, often by a significant margin. Ethiopia and the DRC also score highly on a wide range of indicators. In all three cases, the key driver of this is the large size of the country, both in terms of population and land area.

However, Nigeria, the DRC and, to an extent, Ethiopia perform poorly when looking at the enabling environment for infrastructure investment. Their composite credit ratings are around the midpoint of sub-Saharan Africa, indicating each country has poor access to finance from international sources. The level of domestic credit available is in the lowest quartile, suggesting resources available domestically are even scarcer. These countries also have a standardized average WGI score between 20 and 30 per cent, which could mean that, even with favourable investment conditions, public institutions may fail to organize and implement such investments.

By contrast, Botswana, Mauritius and South Africa score highly on the enabling environment. This suggests that if there were sufficient demand, investment can be found. Investment needs in Botswana and Mauritius are low due to their small size and their relatively high level of development. However, we estimate that South Africa has relatively high investment needs for both educational and social protection infrastructure due to its relatively high GDP.

NOTES

1. Weather risk insurance and social safety net programmes are mentioned in this paper, though not included in the list.
2. The definition of 'access to improved water' used is consistent with that of the Millennium Development Goals (UN, 2012).

REFERENCES

Barr, R., Fankhauser, S. and Hamilton, K., 2010. 'Adaptation investments: a resource allocation framework', *Mitigation and Adaptation Strategies for Global Change*, **15**(8), 843–58. Available at http://www.springerlink.com/index/10.1007/s11027-010-9242-1 (accessed 14 October 2012).

Barro, R.J. and Sala-i-Martin, X., 2004. *Economic Growth*, 2nd edn. Cambridge, MA: MIT Press.

Food and Agriculture Organization of the United Nations, 2014. *FAO Aqua Statistics*. Available at http://www.fao.org/nr/water/aquastat/data/query/index.html?lang=en (accessed 16 February 2015).

IMF, 2014. World Economic Outlook Database, October.

IPCC (Intergovernmental Panel on Climate Change), 2014. *Climate Change 2014: Impacts, Adaptation and Vulnerability (Fifth Assessment Report of Working Group II of the Intergovernmental Panel on Climate Change)*. Geneva: IPCC.

Klein, R.J.T., Eriksen, S.E.H, Næss, L.O. et al., 2007. 'Portfolio screening to support the mainstreaming of adaptation to climate change into development assistance', *Climatic Change*, **84**, 23–44.

McGray, H., Hamill, A., Bradley, R. et al., 2007. *Weathering the Storm. Options for Framing Adaptation and Development*. Washington, DC: World Resources Institute.

Quah, D., 1996. 'Empirics for economic growth and convergence', *European Economic Review*, **40**(6), 1353–75.

Ranger, N. and Garbett-Shiels, S.-L., 2012. 'Accounting for a changing and uncertain climate in planning and policymaking today: lessons for developing countries', *Climate and Development*, **4**, 288–300.

Ranger, N., Harvey, A. and Garbett-Shiels, S.-L., 2014. 'Safeguarding development aid against climate change: evaluating progress and identifying best practice', *Development in Practice*, **24**(4), 467–86.

The Programme for Infrastructure Development in Africa, 2010. *Africa Energy Sector: Outlook 2040*. NEPAD/African Union/AfDB.

The Programme for Infrastructure Development in Africa, 2014. *Africa Energy Sector Phase III Report*.

Trading Economics, 2014. *Credit Ratings*. Available at http://www.trading economics.com/country-list/rating (accessed 16 February 2015).

UN, 2012. *7.8 Proportion of Population Using an Improved Drinking Water Source*. Available at http://mdgs.un.org/unsd/mi/wiki/7-8-Proportion-of-population-using-an-improved-drinking-water-source.ashx (accessed 14 July 2015).

UNDESA, 2014. *City Population Forecasts*. Available at http://esa.un.org/unpd/wup/Highlights/WUP2014-Highlights.pdf (accessed 16 February 2015).

US Energy Information Administration (EIA), 2014. *International Energy Statistics*. Available at http://www.eia.gov/cfapps/ipdbproject/IEDIndex3.cfm (accessed 16 February 2015).

World Bank, 2013. *Changing Wealth of Nations*. Available at http://data.world-bank.org/data-catalog/wealth-of-nations (accessed 16 February 2015).

World Bank, 2014a. *Health, Nutrition and Population Statistics*. Available at http://databank.worldbank.org/Data/Views/VariableSelection/SelectVariables.aspx?source=Health Nutrition and Population Statistics: Population estimates and projections# (accessed 16 February 2015).

World Bank, 2014b. *The Atlas of Social Protection: Indicators of Resilience and Equity (ASPIRE)*. Available at http://databank.worldbank.org/data/views/variableselection/selectvariables.aspx?source=the-atlas-of-social-protection:-indicators-of-resilience-and-equity-(aspire) (accessed 16 February 2015).

World Bank, 2014c. *World Development Indicators 2014*. Available at http://data.worldbank.org/data-catalog/world-development-indicators (accessed 12 June 2015).

World Bank, 2014d. *Worldwide Governance Indicators*. Available at http://data.worldbank.org/data-catalog/world-development-indicators (accessed 12 June 2015).

World Energy Council, 2013. *World Energy Resources*, p. 468.

Yepes, T. et al., 2008. 'Making sense of Africa's infrastructure endowment: a benchmarking approach', *Africa Infrastructure Country Diagnostic*. Washington, DC: World Bank, pp. 1–42.

Yohe, G. et al., 2006. 'Global distributions of vulnerability to climate change', *The Integrated Assessment Journal*, **6**, 35–44.

6. Assessing climate-resilient development options

Paul Watkiss and Alistair Hunt

6.1 INTRODUCTION

In this chapter we set out some key considerations with respect to assessment methods for climate-resilient development. A key focus has been to capture the changes that have occurred over recent years in three areas: (1) the framing of adaptation; (2) methodological challenges; and (3) considering uncertainty in economic appraisal. In each case, we summarize the current state of knowledge and emerging thinking on assessment methods.

The chapter proceeds as follows. In Section 6.2 we outline a number of important challenges for the assessment of climate-resilient development, highlighting the lack of relevance of older studies, and how these issues are now being addressed. In Section 6.3 we update the state of knowledge on a number of the key methodological challenges for adaptation assessment, highlighting that with mainstreaming, many of these are reduced. In Section 6.4 we investigate the methods that are being adopted for economic appraisal of adaptation, extending existing approaches to address uncertainty. Conclusions are presented in Section 6.5.

6.2 POLICY RELEVANCE AND ADAPTATION ASSESSMENT

Most of the earlier literature on the economics of adaptation used scenario-based 'impact assessment' (see Markandya and Watkiss, 2009). Such studies adopt a logical, scientific and sequential approach, starting with global future socio-economic scenarios and climate model projections, then assessing future impacts and costs from climate change. The analysis of adaptation is then considered as the final step in this chain, with the potential consideration of costs and benefits, and even an analysis of the optimal response. Such an approach has been termed a science-first approach (Ranger et al., 2010; Wilby, 2012).

However, there is a considerable literature (for example, Füssel and Klein, 2006; Ranger et al., 2010; Watkiss and Hunt, 2011) that identifies problems with this classic approach, especially for informing policy makers. This is because:

- The studies have insufficient consideration of immediate and short-term time-scales of relevance for early adaptation.
- They do not consider national to local non-climatic drivers or existing policy – including baseline conditions or programmes of relevance to current and future climate risks.
- They focus on a narrow set of technical (engineering) adaptation responses, excluding the diversity of adaptation options.
- They ignore the factors determining the adaptation process itself, including socio-institutional policy context, actors and governance.

A conclusion is that such studies, on their own, do not provide the necessary information for practical and policy-orientated adaptation, and in particular for early climate-resilient development. This is most important with respect to adaptation in developing countries, where the focus is on short-term planning and where wider non-climatic drivers dominate.

There is also an additional and highly critical challenge for adaptation, which is poorly covered in impact assessment studies; uncertainty. A considerable literature identifies this as the most important challenge for adaptation (for example, Hallegatte, 2009). Climate uncertainty arises in a number of forms. First, at the current time it is not clear what future emission pathway the world is on, that is, whether a future 2°C or a 4°C world. This makes a major difference to the level of adaptation needed. Second, even if this future pathway were known, there is large uncertainty associated with climate models. The range of projected change from alternative models is as large as the scenario uncertainty, and for some parameters such as precipitation, different models can even alter the sign of the change (that is, whether climate change will increase or decrease rainfall, see Christensen et al., 2011).

Impact assessment studies do not take account of this uncertainty, because they are highly stylized and focus on adaptation as a response to a defined future projection. They analyse the idealized response to an individual future projection, even if they subsequently repeat this calculation for a number of alternative simulations (one at a time). This predict-and-optimize approach presents information on how adaptation responses might change across a range of future projections, but it does not inform the policy maker on what to do now, given this future uncertainty exists (and is large). As highlighted by Watkiss et al. (2014), using mean values (or probability weighted expected values) does not address this uncertainty, especially when the direction of change varies across projections, for example, of future rainfall. Optimized responses (to a central scenario) can misallocate resources by over-investing in risks that do not emerge, implementing measures that are insufficient to cope with extreme outcomes or leading to maladaptation by locking in future risks.

As a result of these issues, the framing of adaptation has moved away from impact assessment – at least as the only input to informing adaptation. In this chapter, we identify three key shifts, summarized in turn below.

6.2.1　Policy-orientated Approaches

There has been an observable shift in the literature on adaptation (ECONADAPT, 2015). Many recent studies put more focus on adaptation as the objective, rather than considering it at the end of a classic science-first, impact assessment study. This shift has been termed a 'policy-first' approach (Ranger et al., 2010). Critically, this requires a greater understanding of current drivers, non-climate policy and existing adaptation or resilience measures.

There is also recognition that adaptation needs to address a range of challenges, involving various problems, and thus should not focus only on a single response (that is, a technical solution to a future climate risk). These challenges – and the appropriate responses – are often presented as a set of building blocks or a spectrum of decision types (McGray et al., 2007; Klein and Persson, 2008) and include early activities associated with addressing current vulnerability and building adaptive capacity, longer-term elements associated with mainstreaming climate risks and preparing for and tackling longer-term challenges. More recently, these have been translated into practical frameworks (for example, see Hinkel and Bisaro, 2014), and have been aligned to types of activities and iterative frameworks (for example, Watkiss and Hunt, 2011; Downing, 2012). In these cases, interventions over time are combined to give an overall portfolio of actions, or an 'adaptation pathway'. Importantly, from an economic perspective, each activity (or building block) is a different problem type, requiring different types of information, and varying methods of economic appraisal (Li et al., 2014).

6.2.2　Mainstreaming (Integration)

A second shift, particularly at the national level, is towards mainstreaming adaptation. For example, the National Adaptation Plan (NAP) guidance recommends the mainstreaming of adaptation (LDC Expert Group,

2012). While there is still no formal definition of mainstreaming in the Intergovernmental Panel on Climate Change (IPCC), the term is used interchangeably with 'integration', that is, the integration of adaptation into existing policies and decision making, rather than through implementation of stand-alone adaptation policies, plans or measures. Mainstreaming aligns with the policy-first approach outlined above, in that it centres on existing policy and objectives (for example, underlying agriculture or health sector policy objectives). It also puts greater emphasis on understanding the context for an intervention. Perhaps most importantly in the context of this book, it integrates adaptation as climate-resilient development.

A critical step for mainstreaming is to find relevant entry points (OECD, 2009; UNDP/UNEP, 2011). That is, opportunities in the national, sector or project planning process where climate considerations can best be integrated. Critically, these will differ with each adaptation problem. This makes it essential to understand and integrate adaptation within the existing socio-institutional landscape, especially as adaptation will be one of many policy objectives, and not necessarily the dominant one.

One implication of mainstreaming is that it requires more time and resources when compared to a science-first impact assessment. As it aligns with standard policy practice it considers the reality of multiple drivers and objectives, for example, in relation to the policy background and context, existing objectives and other cost and benefit categories. This can be seen in countries that have applied mainstreaming concepts to adaptation (for example, see HM Government, 2013 in the UK and OECD, 2014 for Ethiopia and Columbia). Mainstreaming also requires a good understanding of the individual organizations, networks and processes for making relevant decisions, recognizing these will differ with sector and application.

6.2.3   Phasing and Timing of Adaptation

A key characteristic of adaptation relates to the profile of costs and benefits over time (DFID, 2014). In many cases, the most important impacts of climate change are likely to arise in the future, in the 2040s and beyond. The benefits of adapting to these changes arise over long time horizons, while the costs may be incurred early on. Using the public discount rates conventionally used in Organisation for Economic Co-operation and Development (OECD) countries, typically being between 3 per cent and 6 per cent, future adaptation benefits from climate change in the medium term (20 years plus) and beyond are relatively small in current terms. For developing countries, where social discount rates (the social opportunity cost of capital) are 10 per cent or higher (as used by international finance institutions (IFIs) or development partners such as the Department for International Development (DFID), see OECD, 2015), the mismatch between future benefits and early costs is critical. Benefits that accrue in 20 years or beyond are very low when expressed in present value terms. Compounding this, the high uncertainty often makes it unclear if these future benefits will actually be realized.

As a response, there has been a shift in thinking to consider the timing and phasing of adaptation, taking account of uncertainty. This has been captured in the literature in terms of the development of conceptual frameworks. Examples include Ranger et al. (2010), Watkiss and Hunt (2011) and Fankhauser et al. (2013). This shift was recognized in the IPCC's *Fifth Assessment Report* through the use of the term 'iterative climate risk management' (IPCC, 2014).

These frameworks follow the concepts of adaptive management and encourage a focus on immediate low-regret actions, combined with an evaluation and learning process to improve future strategies and decisions. An example of such a framework is summarized below (Watkiss, 2014). This frames climate change risks by starting with current climate variability and then looks to future climate change, including uncertainty. The focus is on policy-relevant decisions, that is, those needed and justified (in economic terms) in the next decade, noting that this includes short and long decision lifetimes. Three broad types of adaptation decisions are identified for early adaptation, each with different needs in terms of economic assessment.

First are immediate actions that address the current adaptation deficit and also build resilience for the future. This involves early capacity-building and low- and no-regret actions (for example, IPCC, 2012), as these provide immediate economic benefits: these are usually grounded in current (development) policy and can use existing decision support tools.

Second is the integration of adaptation into immediate decisions or activities with long lifetimes, such as infrastructure or planning (for example, Ranger et al., 2014). This requires different methods to the low-regret actions above because of future climate uncertainty (DFID, 2014), such as a greater focus on risk screening, the risks of lock-in, and for appraisal, a shift away from standard appraisal to methods that consider flexibility or robustness.

Third, there is often an immediate need to start planning for the future impacts of climate change, noting the high uncertainty. This may be due to the long lifetimes of decision choices, or the potential magnitude of future risks. Such problems can be addressed using adaptive management (Tompkins and Adger, 2004; Reeder and Ranger, 2011), and by drawing on lessons from the literature on the value of information and option values and learning (Dixit and Pindyck, 1994).

The three categories can be considered together in an integrated adaptation strategy or adaptation pathway (Downing, 2012). Interestingly, this new framing leads to very different methods and adaptation interventions, with a greater emphasis on early adaptation actions. These are discussed in more detail by Watkiss in Chapter 7 in this volume.

6.3 METHODOLOGICAL ASPECTS OF THE ECONOMICS OF ADAPTATION

Previous studies (EEA, 2007; OECD, 2008; Markandya and Watkiss, 2009; Chambwera et al., 2014) have identified a number of key methodological challenges with the economics of adaptation. These include the choice of discount rate and distributional issues. They also include issues of baselines, analysis of non-technical options, issues of scale and aggregation, and transferability of benefits and costs. These challenges potentially apply at both the policy and programme levels, as well as the project level.

6.3.1 Adaptation Objectives

In any analysis of adaptation, whether at the strategic or project level, the framing and objectives used have a major influence on the costs and benefits of adaptation. Studies with a strong economic perspective will aim to maximize economic efficiency or social welfare by estimating the optimal balance of adaptation costs, benefits and residual impacts. These studies are likely to lead to different outcomes – and costs and benefits – when compared to studies that use predefined objectives, such as the acceptable levels of risk[1] or those with a stronger equity or ethical perspective that aim to reduce damages to pre-climate change (welfare) levels (for example, World Bank, 2010).

Clearly, the choice of objective influences the amount of adaptation and, in turn, the costs of adaptation. Lower costs generally arise when a stronger economic perspective is adopted because a higher level of residual damage is allowed, and adaptation avoids the high cost options towards the upper end of the adaptation marginal cost curve. The problem, however, is that different actors will have alternative views on the most appropriate adaptation objectives to adopt, especially when this relates to the principles of international finance for adaptation in developing countries (and whether one is providing the finance or receiving the finance and bearing the residual impacts).

In practice, however, this may not be such a large problem as initially appears. It is clear that different objectives already exist across various areas and sectors, and for the same sectors in different countries. As an example, the UK uses cost-benefit analysis for appraising flood investment while a number of other European countries use cost-effectiveness analysis around defined levels of acceptable risks. This leads to a different balance of costs, benefits and residual damage. Furthermore, even within the UK, a different approach is used to look at public investment in the health sector (cost-effectiveness) compared to the road transport sector (cost-benefit analysis). Similar issues arise in the developing country context. As there is no standardization of objectives in existing policy, why should this be any different for adaptation? Furthermore, as adaptation becomes mainstreamed, the objectives will be increasingly aligned to the underlying sectoral and policy context, that is, adaptation appraisal will use the existing methods and objectives, rather than introducing 'new' ones.

6.3.2 Baselines and Additionality for Adaptation

In addition to the setting of objectives, there are similar factors involved in defining future baselines (the counterfactual). In theory, different assumptions in the future baseline will lead to large variations in subsequent cost and benefit estimates. There are choices over future socio-economic development levels, the effects on future exposure, changing levels of vulnerability and adaptive capacity, noting these effects can be positive as well as negative. As an example, there are large differences in adaptation costs for future health adaptation in developing countries between studies that consider future development (for example, World Bank, 2010) and those that do not (for example, Ebi, 2008), because of differences in baseline impacts and thus adaptation needs. However, as studies become more policy-orientated, and as they focus more on short-term adaptation, there will be more alignment with existing practice and baseline projections (for example, in the five-year plans and longer-term development planning vision), aligning to future development pathways.

Nonetheless, some important challenges remain. One of these is over the issue of the additionality of finance.[2] A related aspect is the issue of the existing adaptation deficit (the gap between the current (sub-optimal) state of a system and a state that minimizes adverse impacts from existing climate variability). Adaptation to future climate change will be less effective if these have not first been addressed (Burton, 2004) and studies that exclude the gap will have lower adaptation costs, because they assume high levels of existing protection and thus smaller marginal costs.

Some recent studies have started to consider these issues in more pragmatic terms, and this does help in addressing some of these issues. The climate-resilient strategy for Ethiopia (OECD, 2014) is an example. This identified that 63 per cent of the existing agricultural budget was already funding resilience-oriented activities (identifying current baseline activities and the existing measures addressing the current adaptation gap). Indeed, of the adaptation options identified in the strategy, 38 of the 41 priority options were already included in various plans or programmes. The key issue for additionality was therefore to undertake a detailed policy review of existing policies and programmes, to identify the gaps.

6.3.3 Discounting

Any appraisal of strategies that deliver benefits in the future has to identify the appropriate discount rate to use, reflecting the standard practice of discounting costs and benefits in future periods to enable comparison to costs and benefits today. In the mitigation domain, the issue of discount rates has been a major source of contention, notably following *The Stern Review* (2006), which adjusted rates to account for inter-generational wealth transfers.

As highlighted earlier, the discount rate can have a major influence on the justification for adaptation. Nevertheless, discounting for adaptation is not quite as critical as for mitigation for two reasons. First, the focus for adaptation is shorter term. The priority is for low-regret adaptation over the next decade or so, thus benefits are likely to accrue immediately. Even for longer-term interventions, the timeframe will generally be limited to the next few decades, rather than the end of the century, as with mitigation. Second, in many cases (when mainstreaming), there will already be a discount rate in use for the underlying decision context, for example, in the developing country government, IFI appraisal process and so on, and it will usually be appropriate to use these existing rates.

Nonetheless, in developing countries, where appraisal discount rates are high, this still deters longer-term adaptation investment decisions and inhibits adaptation. Therefore, while the use of typical discount rates reflects current preferences, and allows the effective allocation of resources, it reduces the attractiveness of more sustainable options, for example, for sustainable agriculture or green ecosystem-based options that take several years to fully develop (Berger and Chambwera, 2010). It also affects the attractiveness of early action to address longer-term major impacts, even if this uses techniques that address uncertainty (that is, relative to the use of these techniques in the OECD, with lower discount rates).

To address this, investments in adaptation that have long lifetimes could be more appropriately discounted at declining rates (though for consistency, and to ensure adaptation investment are not inappropriately favoured over other development investments, other non-adaptation, public sector investments should be subject to the same profile). While declining schemes are already in place in some OECD countries (HMT, 2007), we have found no examples of their application in developing countries. A key issue – and one that warrants some further research – is what might be the appropriate declining discount scheme for developing countries for adaptation, noting that to have a material impact on future benefits, the scheme would need to start declining rapidly, because of the much higher initial discount rate.

6.3.4   Equity and Distributional Effects

A further issue is the distributional patterns of climate change, which disproportionately impact on poor and vulnerable groups (IPCC, 2014). In economic terms, this is important because a dollar impact to a poor person is not the same as a dollar impact to a rich person (due to the diminishing marginal utility of additional consumption) and similarly an extra dollar spent on adaptation will give more benefit to a person who is poorer (Watkiss, 2011). In the mitigation domain, this is critical when aggregating impacts up over space and time, and is a major source of disagreement and contention as it involves ethical and moral assumptions (see Anthoff and Tol, 2007; Anthoff et al., 2009). While these are important for mitigation and adaptation in global assessments, these aggregation issues are much less important for national to local-scale adaptation.

However, at this level another problem emerges. Cost-benefit analysis does not capture inequality and impacts on the most vulnerable as it focuses on more valuable assets and groups (for example, Cartwright et al., 2013). There is also a question of how costs and benefits can be balanced where one community or stakeholder benefits and another suffers, or the extent to which the costs of adaptation should be borne by the beneficiaries versus shared across a larger population group (Fankhauser and Soare, 2012) – though in the developing country context, where international climate finance is involved, this is less of an issue.

It is possible to take these distributional issues into account in economic appraisal by using equity (distributional) weights or looking at the distributional effects of policies or projects. However, we have found no adaptation studies that have applied such equity weights, and while there is some literature that discusses possible distributional consequences, this remains qualitative. More broadly, this reflects the practice in development economics, especially for more practical-orientated appraisal, where the use of distributional weights is rare. What is clear, however, is that it may be advantageous to consider (and even use) these distributional weights or distributional analysis more frequently than is currently the case, especially when looking to target climate finance to the most vulnerable.

6.3.5   Scale and Transferability

At a practical level, the implementation of adaptation is often at a local scale (for example, flood prevention in a city) but rises up to national and international scales in relation to the overall policy context. Any higher-scale decisions should derive information from the bottom-up perspective and, conversely, lower-level decisions should take account of parameters that are set at regional and national levels. However, in most cases there are no local estimates of the costs of impacts or adaptation, and there are issues with the transferability of aggregated estimates downwards. This leads to a question over the transferability of adaptation costs and benefits over scale and between contexts.

Unlike mitigation costs, adaptation costs and benefits tend to be heavily influenced by local geographic, environmental and economic factors, that is, they are risk, site and location specific. This can be seen in the litera-ture. There are often large differences in the applicability of climate smart agriculture options such as soil and water conservation because of differ-ent climate risks. For example, the International Food Policy Research Institute (IFPRI, 2009) found major differences between high-rainfall and dryland areas. Similarly, the costs of adaptation can vary significantly, even for unit costs: McCarthy et al. (2011) found very large variations for the same climate smart options in different countries. The range of economic benefits can be even larger still. For example, Branca et al. (2011) found very large differences in the benefits between studies for climate smart agri-culture, due to differences in baseline conditions and yield improvements.

What is interesting is that these factors do affect the attractiveness of even low-regret options (DFID, 2014). As an example, while building codes are often cited as a potential low-regret option to address future challenges (IPCC, 2012), the literature reveals a more complex picture. In the USA, very high building codes can be justified because of the high value of property (ECA, 2009). However, in a study of the Caribbean (CCRIF, 2010) and in St Lucia (Hochrainer-Stigler et al., 2010) they were found to have modest to low benefit to cost ratios, with lower values due to a combination of the risk profile and the existing cost and lifetime of the asset. Similarly, findings have emerged for ecosystem-based adaptation (World Bank, 2011), with lower attractiveness in higher income countries due to the large differences in land and labour costs.

All of this means that caution is needed when transferring adaptation costs (and even more so for benefits). This is the case even if these are unit estimates, but especially when transferring overall study results or conclusions as different studies use different methods, objectives, time-scales, climate scenarios and assumptions, and estimates of the costs (and benefits) of adaptation are conditional.

6.4 ANALYSIS OF UNCERTAINTY IN APPRAISAL

This section of the chapter focuses on one particular methodological challenge: the incorporation of uncertainty in appraisal. This is an area that has also developed significantly in recent years, with an increasing focus on the incorporation and treatment in decision support tools.

6.4.1 Decision Making under Uncertainty

Standard public policy and project appraisal generally involves a sys-tematic decision-making process: understanding the problem and setting objectives; identification of options; appraisal of options; planning and implementation; and monitoring and evaluation. This is often formal-ized through guidance on (regulatory) impact assessment or economic appraisal and evaluation.[3] Within this cycle, there are two points where decision support tools are particularly important: (1) for shortlisting options and (2) for prioritizing the shortlisted options.

The process of identifying a shortlist of options (scoping or feasibility) includes, for instance, identifying focus areas for a national plan or strat-egy, options for mainstreaming climate change into a development sector plan or identifying a broad list of options for an individual policy or project. The aim of these processes is to filter options down to a manage-able shortlist, which can then be appraised. There are standard methods for shortlisting options, which include scoping economic analysis, simple attribute analysis and ranking, stakeholder consultation and expert elicitation.

In the climate adaptation context, more recent scoping assessments have started to use iterative climate risk management to help with the phasing and timing of adaptation, as this can actually help the filtering process during initial screening (for example, see FDRE, 2014). This can help identify which types of options to implement first, as well as which options may be warranted to help with future climate change or future decisions. As an illustration, this might identify early enhanced disaster risk management, which addresses the current adaptation deficit and helps to build future resilience, and also highlight opportunities for including 'resilience' in infrastructure development or planning processes, where there are long lifetimes, and advancing research and monitoring to help future longer-term decisions.

The subsequent prioritization of shortlisted options – that is, appraisal – is often assisted with the use of decision support methods and tools, such as cost-benefit analysis and cost-effectiveness analysis. The formal application of such approaches is widespread as part of regulatory impact assessment, but less common in developing countries, where practice is more varied.

There are a number of distinctive factors that are important for decision making for prioritizing adaptation options in appraisal, which makes it particularly challenging (DFID, 2014). Importantly, there are often no common metrics to compare and prioritize different adaptation interventions and these cannot easily be standardized given the highly site- and context-specific nature of adaptation. This is in contrast to mitigation, which targets a common burden (greenhouse gas emissions) and can prioritize options in terms of the cost of abating a tonne of carbon dioxide (CO_2) equivalent, using cost-effectiveness analysis based on simple cost-curves.

The analysis of adaptation options therefore involves additional steps to assess impacts and potential benefits (when compared to mitigation). Furthermore, many impacts are in non-market sectors (for example, health, ecosystems) and adaptation options are often non-technical in nature. While there are techniques for incorporating non-market benefits in cost-benefit analysis, this can be a resource-intensive process.

More unusually, adaptation has to also consider the dynamic and changing nature of climate change over time, including the inter-dependencies in climate risks and, in particular, the issue of future climatic (and socio-economic) uncertainty. As highlighted earlier, this has become central to the appraisal of adaptation in the more recent literature, as it affects both the selection of adaptation options and the decision framework for prioritization.

Due to uncertainty, the most common techniques used in policy appraisal (for example, cost-benefit analysis, cost-effectiveness analysis and multi-criteria analysis) have limitations for adaptation. This point was reinforced by the latest IPCC report, and the chapter on the 'Economics of adaptation', which reported that 'economic thinking on adaptation has evolved from a focus on cost benefit analysis and identification of "best economic" adaptations to the development of multi-metric evaluations' (Chambwera et al., 2014, p. 2).

Therefore, along with a growing evidence-base and examples on the use of traditional decision support approaches for adaptation, there are also new approaches that are being applied that allow for consideration of uncertainty.

6.4.2 Methods for Decision Making under Uncertainty

While there are a potentially large number of possible approaches for considering uncertainty, the adaptation literature focuses on five key methods: real option analysis; robust decision making; portfolio analysis; iterative risk management; and rule-based methods.

A summary of the approaches is shown in Figure 6.1. The methods are categorized into three areas: traditional decision support tools for appraisal; uncertainty framing; and economic decision making under uncertainty. The latter two build on the principles in the first but are

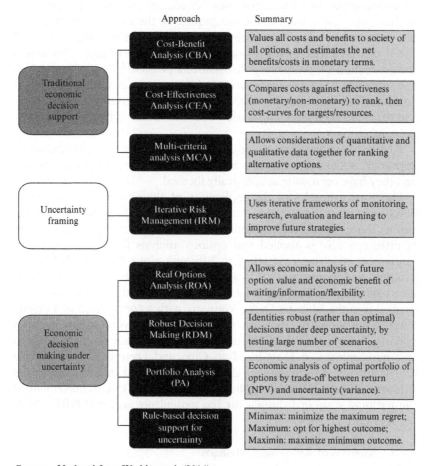

Source: Updated from Watkiss et al. (2014).

Figure 6.1 Decision support tools for adaptation economic appraisal

distinct because they introduce a dynamic component (for example, for iterative risk management and real options analysis), use a different or additional criterion (robust decision making or portfolio analysis) or do not rely on probabilistic data (rule-based methods).

While the traditional methods are often suitable for early low-regret options, the use of uncertainty framing or decision making under uncertainty are needed to tackle longer-term climate change (DFID, 2014). Indeed, these new approaches align to the iterative framework and concepts presented earlier in this chapter.

Interestingly, applications of the new decision-orientated approaches are concentrated in a few sectors, notably coastal and water management, as these lend themselves to the techniques. In the case of coastal zones, this is due to the relative simplicity of the climate change risk, as sea-level rise is characterized by a slow-onset uni-directional change. This makes the generation of probability distributions possible.[4] Coastal protection also often involves large, up-front capital investment favouring real options analysis. For water management, future climate uncertainty is often high, and there has been more application of robust decision making to address deep uncertainty.

To date, these applications have also been used primarily in stand-alone appraisals at the project level, not as part of mainstreaming assessments, and they have been quite academically focused.

There are examples of the application of these methods emerging in developing countries, that is, for climate-resilient development. Several studies have tested real options analysis. For example, Jeuland and Whittington (2013) applied real options analysis for a water resource investment planning case study in Ethiopia along the Blue Nile while Linquiti and Vonortas (2012) analysed investments in coastal protection with case studies in Dhaka and Dar-es-Salaam, and Dobes (2010) applied it in the Mekong Delta, Vietnam, with a comparison of housing alternatives. Similarly, there are a set of applications of robust decision making. Lempert et al. (2013) applied the approach to look at flood risk management in Ho Chi Minh City, and Dyszynski and Takama (2010) applied it to investigate drought index-based micro-insurance in Ethiopia. Finally, there is application of iterative risk management at the national scale in Ethiopia for the agriculture sector (FDRE, 2014; see also OECD, 2014).

6.4.3   Analysis of Assessment Methods

The potential suitability of these new decision support methods for different applications is summarized in Table 6.1, which updates the previous

Table 6.1 Comparing decision support tools

Decision support tool	Strengths	Challenges	Applicability	Potential use
Cost-Benefit Analysis (CBA)	Well-known and widely applied.	Valuation of non-market sectors/non-technical options. Uncertainty limited to probabilistic risks/sensitivity testing.	Most useful when climate risk probabilities are known and sensitivity is small.	To identify low- and no-regret options. As a decision support tool within iterative climate risk management.
Cost-Effective-ness Analysis (CEA)	Analysis of benefits in non-monetary terms.	Single headline metric difficult to identify and less suitable for complex or cross-sectoral risks. Low consideration of uncertainty.	As above, but for non-monetary sectors (e.g. ecosystems) and where social objective (e.g. acceptable risks of flooding).	As above, but for market and non-market sectors where benefits are not monetized.
Multi-Criteria Analysis (MCA)	Analysis of costs and benefits in non-monetary terms.	Relies on expert judgement of stakeholders, and is subjective, including analysis of uncertainty.	When there is a mix of quantitative and qualitative data. Can include uncertainty performance as a criteria.	As above, as well as for scoping options. Can complement other tools and capture qualitative aspects.
Iterative Risk Assessment (IRA)	Iterative analysis, monitoring, evaluation and learning.	Challenging when multiple risks acting together and thresholds are not always easy to identify.	Useful where long-term and uncertain challenges, especially when clear risk thresholds.	For appraisal over medium-longer term. Also applicable as a framework at policy level.
Real Options Analysis (ROA)	Value of flexibility, information.	Requires economic valuation (see CBA), probabilities and clear decision points.	Large irreversible decisions, where information is available on climate risk probabilities.	Economic analysis of major capital investment decisions. Analysis of flexibility within major projects.

Table 6.1   (continued)

Decision support tool	Strengths	Challenges	Applicability	Potential use
Robust Decision Making (RDM)	Robustness rather than optimization.	High computational analysis (formal) and large number of runs.	When uncertainty is large. Can use a mix of quantitative and qualitative information.	Identifying low- and no-regret options and robust decisions for investments with long lifetimes.
Portfolio Analysis (PA)	Analysis of portfolios rather than individual options.	Requires economic data and probabilities. Issues of inter-dependence.	When number of complementary adaptation actions and good information.	Project-based analysis of future combinations. Designing portfolio mixes as part of iterative pathways.

Source: Adapted from Watkiss et al. (2014).

analysis by Watkiss et al. (2014). The assessment suggests that there are no hard or fast rules on when to use each tool and none of them provides a single 'best' method for all adaptation appraisal (they all have strengths and weaknesses). However, certain tools lend themselves more to specific contexts, sectors or problems.

Existing decision support tools, including cost-benefit analysis, can be used for studies that are focused on current climate variability, though adaptation interventions are often in areas that are difficult to value and may involve a lack of quantitative information. In such cases, cost-effectiveness, multi-attribute analysis (or multi-criteria analysis) may be more practical, notwithstanding the limitations of these approaches.

For the analysis of short-term decisions with long lifetimes or longer-term challenges, the use of new decision support tools is warranted. Robust decision making has broad application for current and future time periods. When investments are nearer term (especially with up-front capital investments), and where there is an existing adaptation deficit, real options analysis is a potentially useful tool. For long-term applications in conditions of low current adaptation deficit, iterative risk assessment may be more applicable. Importantly, while the tools are presented individually, they are not mutually exclusive.

While these tools have been developed primarily in the context of project-level appraisal, in principle they can be used to inform the development of policy initiatives at the national and sectoral scales. Iterative risk frameworks and robust decision making have most potential for programme and sector analysis though they are more proven at the project level. However, at this national level, they are principally an organizing framework, with semi-quantitative versions due to data availability.

At the project level, where data are available, all the tools can be applied quantitatively. However, tool selection will be influenced by data availability and the level of uncertainty. Several approaches, such as real options and portfolio theory, require subjective probabilistic inputs and preferably use objective probabilistic inputs. This is a challenge for climate projections, particularly in the developing country context where observed data and future projections are often missing or highly aggregated.

It is worth noting that the differences between the tools are not limited to data and capacity constraints but may have a material impact on the order of prioritization of adaptation. Klijn et al. (2014) demonstrate that applying robust decision making results in a different order from cost-benefit analysis, and cost-benefit analysis produces a different order from cost-effectiveness analysis.

Finally, an analysis of all these new methods – at least when applied formally – is that they are resource-intensive and technically complex. Indeed, this constrains their formal application to large investment decisions or major risks. Therefore, they are more likely to be applied to specific large-scale adaptation projects, rather than contribute to adaptation mainstreaming. They also have limited potential for widespread application to many decision contexts, as might be needed, for example, when implementing a national adaptation plan. These issues are likely to limit future application, especially in developing countries, where data constraints are often a limiting factor in economic appraisal.

A critical question is therefore whether the concepts in these uncertainty approaches can be used in 'light-touch' approaches that capture their conceptual aspects, while maintaining a degree of economic rigour, both at policy and project levels. This would allow a wider application in qualitative or semi-quantitative analysis. This could include the broad use of decision tree structures from real options analysis, the concepts of robustness testing from robust decision making, the shift towards portfolios of options from portfolio analysis and the focus on evaluation and learning from iterative risk assessment for long-term strategies. There has been some progress advancing these types of light-touch applications (Hallegatte et al., 2012; Ranger, 2013). However, more research needs to be undertaken to better understand how and where the trade-offs between quantitative analysis and pragmatic application can be made.

6.5 CONCLUSIONS

In this chapter, we began by outlining a number of important challenges
that are relevant to policy assessment of climate-resilient development,
and assessed how this has led to a change in the framing of adaptation in
recent years – consistent with a more practical and early implementation-
based focus. This has major implications for the economic analysis of
adaptation. A number of key shifts in approach were identified. First,
there has been a move towards a policy-orientated approach, in which the
primary objective of the analysis is framed around adaptation ('adaptation
assessment'). This involves major differences in scope and approach
to the previous literature, which uses a science-first, 'impact assessment' driven method. Second, there is a greater emphasis on integrating
(mainstreaming) adaptation into current policy and development, rather
than implementing as a stand-alone activity, a critical shift with respect to
adaptation as climate-resilient development. Third, there has been a shift
to differentiate the phasing and timing of adaptation, with an increasing recognition of uncertainty. This has led to a framework that starts
with current climate variability and then considers future climate change,
considering early low-regret options and longer-term adaptation interventions, respectively, along with the use of decision making under uncertainty
and iterative adaptive management.

We then turned our attention to underlying methodological challenges
with the economic appraisal of adaptation, analysing the current state-of-
the-art and implementation practice. This includes issues around objectives, baselines, discounting, equity, transferability and additionality. While
the academic theory in many of these areas has advanced, the finding is
that this has not yet transferred into common (appraisal) practice: this is
due to time, resource and capacity constraints, but also because in many
areas there remains no agreed consensus on best practice. What is also
clear is that the assumptions or approaches used to address these issues can
have a large impact on results. However, the increasing use of mainstreaming in adaptation (indirectly) addresses many of these challenges, because
it leads to a greater use of existing development and sector practice, and
the methods, approaches and assumptions already in place for appraisal.

Finally, we focused on one particular methodological challenge: the
incorporation of uncertainty in appraisal. This is an area that has also
developed significantly in recent years. As the most common techniques
used in economic appraisal have limitations in coping with this challenge,
a suite of new decision support tools have emerged that advance decision making under uncertainty. This includes real option analysis, robust
decision making, portfolio analysis, rule-based criteria and iterative risk

management. While the use of these techniques is still at an early stage, there are examples in developing countries. However, none of these approaches provides a single 'best' method for all adaptation. They all have strengths and weaknesses, and their suitability varies with the type of application. It is also highlighted that all of these new methods – at least when applied formally – are complex to use and require high resources. While they have potential application for major development investments, the capacity and resources required represent a barrier to their application in more routine project appraisal. As a result, a key priority is to develop more pragmatic (light-touch) versions of these methods, which can capture their core concepts while maintaining a degree of economic rigour.

NOTES

1. An objective often used in the disaster risk literature, for example, where the objectives might be to provide a 1 in 100-year level of protection against storm-surges or floods, and maintain this under future climate change. For an example in the adaptation context, see Rojas et al. (2013).
2. This term is generally used with respect to international climate negotiation text for developed countries to provide 'new and additional' climate change financing to developing countries. The term 'new' generally refers to the fact that the funds should represent an increase over past and existing climate-related funds.
3. The level of adoption of such appraisal approaches varies in developing countries, though they are often more rigorously introduced when overseas development assistance or finance is involved, as part of project justification, due diligence and safeguards.
4. In practice, even when probabilistic-like projections exist, for example, Murphy et al. (2008), these provide a distribution for individual emission scenarios, rather than a composite probability distribution for all scenario futures and all models together. This is a critical issue, especially for techniques that require probability or expected value (real options analysis and portfolio analysis). This tends to favour robust decision making and iterative risk management tools when climate change uncertainty is large.

REFERENCES

Anthoff, D. and Tol, R.S.J., 2007. *On International Equity Weights and National Decision Making on Climate Change*, FNU-127. Hamburg: Hamburg University and Centre for Marine and Atmospheric Science.

Anthoff, D., Hepburn, C.J. and Tol, R.S.J., 2009. 'Equity weighting and the marginal damage costs of climate change', *Ecological Economics*, **68**(3), 836–49.

Berger, R., and Chambwera, M., 2010. 'Beyond cost-benefit: developing a complete toolkit for adaptation decisions', IIED Briefing Note, London.

Branca, G., McCarthy, N., Lipper, L. and Jolejole, C., 2011. *Climate-Smart Agriculture: A Synthesis of Empirical Evidence of Food Security and Mitigation Benefits from Improved Cropland Management*. Mitigation of Climate Change in Agriculture Series, No. 3. Rome: FAO.

Burton, I., 2004. 'Climate change and the adaptation deficit', in A. French (ed.), *Climate Change: Building the Adaptive Capacity*, Ontario: Meteorological Service of Canada, Environment Canada.

Cartwright, A., Blignaut, J., De Wit, M. et al., 2013. 'Economics of climate change adaptation at the local scale under conditions of uncertainty and resource constraints: the case of Durban, South Africa', *Environment and Urbanization*, **25**, 139. doi: 10.1177/0956247813477814

CCRIF (Caribbean Catastrophe Risk Insurance Facility), 2010. 'Enhancing the climate risk and adaptation fact base for the Caribbean', an informational brochure highlighting the preliminary results of the ECA Study, CCRIF's Economics of Climate Adaptation Initiative, Cayman Islands.

Chambwera, M., Heal, G., Dubeux, S. et al., 2014. 'Economics of adaptation', in *Climate Change 2014: Impacts, Adaptation, and Vulnerability. Part A: Global and Sectoral Aspects. Contribution of Working Group II to the Fifth Assessment Report of the Intergovernmental Panel on Climate Change*. Cambridge and New York: Cambridge University Press, pp. 945–77.

Christensen, O.B., Goodess, C.M., Harris, I. and Watkiss, P., 2011. 'European and global climate change projections: outputs, scenarios and uncertainty', in *The Climate Cost Project, Volume 1: Europe*. Stockholm Environment Institute.

DFID, 2014. *Early Value-for-money Adaptation: Delivering VfM Adaptation Using Iterative Frameworks and Low-regret Options*. London: DFID.

Dixit, A.K. and Pindyck, R.S., 1994. *Investment under Uncertainty*. Princeton, NJ: Princeton University Press.

Dobes, L., 2010. *Notes on Applying Real Options to Climate Change Adaptation Measures, with Examples from Vietnam*. Research Report No. 75, November. Canberra: Crawford School of Economics and Government, Australian National University.

Downing, T.E., 2012. 'Views of the frontiers in climate change adaptation economics', *WIREs Climate Change* 2012. doi: 10.1002/wcc.157

Dyszynski, J. and Takama, T., 2010. 'Robust decision making for sustainable and scalable drought index based micro-insurance in Ethiopia', in E. Morelli, G.A. Onnis, W.J. Ammann and C. Sutter (eds), *Micro-insurance: An Innovative Tool*. Davos: Global Risk Forum, pp. 211–46.

Ebi, K.L., 2008. 'Adaptation costs for climate change-related cases of diarrhoeal disease, malnutrition, and malaria in 2030', *Global Health*, **4**(9). Available at http://dx.doi.org/10.1186/1744-8603-4-9 (accessed February 2016).

ECA, 2009. *Shaping Climate-resilient Development: A Framework for Decision-making*. A report of the Economics of Climate Adaptation Working Group, Economics of Climate Adaptation, ClimateWorks Foundation, Global Environment Facility, European Commission, McKinsey & Company, The Rockefeller Foundation, Standard Chartered Bank and Swiss Re.

ECONADAPT, 2015. *The Costs and Benefits of Adaptation, results from the ECONADAPT Project*. ECONADAPT Consortium. Available at http://econadapt.eu/ (accessed February 2016).

EEA, 2007. *Climate Change: The Cost of Inaction and the Cost of Adaptation*. Technical Report No. 13/2007. Copenhagen: EEA.

Fankhauser, S. and Soare, R., 2012. 'Strategic adaptation to climate change in Europe', EIB Working Papers 2012/01.

Fankhauser, S., Ranger, N., Colmer, J. et al., 2013. 'An independent National

Adaptation Programme for England', Policy Brief, Grantham Research Institute on Climate Change and the Environment, London School of Economics.

FDRE, 2014. *Ethiopia's Climate-resilience Strategy Agriculture.* Federal Democratic Republic of Ethiopia, Environmental Protection Authority, Addis Ababa.

Füssel, H.M. and Klein, R.J.T., 2006. 'Climate change vulnerability assessments: an evolution of conceptual thinking', *Climatic Change*, **75**, 301–29.

Hallegatte, S., 2009. 'Strategies to adapt to an uncertain climate change', *Global Environmental Change*, **19**(2), 240–7.

Hallegatte, S., Shah, A., Lempert, R., Brown, C. and Gill, S. 2012. 'Investment decision making under deep uncertainty: application to climate change', Policy Research Working Paper No. 6193, World Bank, Washington, DC.

Hinkel, J. and Bisaro, A., 2014. 'Methodological choices in solution-oriented adaptation research: a diagnostic framework', *Regional Environmental Change*. doi:10.1007/s10113-014-0682-0

HM Government, 2013. *The National Adaptation Programme Report: Analytical Annex*. London: Economics of the National Adaptation Programme, HM Government.

HMT, 2007. *The Green Book*. London: Her Majesty's Treasury.

Hochrainer-Stigler, S., Kunreuther, H., Linnerooth-Bayer, J. et al., 2010. 'The costs and benefits of reducing risk from natural hazards to residential structures in developing countries', Working Paper No. 2010-12-01, Wharton School, University of Pennsylvania, Philadelphia.

IFPRI, 2009. 'Are soil and water conservation technologies a buffer against production risk in the face of climate change? Insights from Ethiopia's Nile Basin', IFPRI Research Brief.

IPCC, 2012. *Managing the Risks of Extreme Events and Disasters to Advance Climate Change Adaptation, A Special Report of Working Groups I and II of the Intergovernmental Panel on Climate Change*. Cambridge and New York: Cambridge University Press.

IPCC, 2014. *Fifth Assessment Report of the Intergovernmental Panel on Climate Change*. Cambridge and New York: Cambridge University Press.

Jeuland, M. and Whittington, D., 2013. 'Water resources planning under climate change: a "real options" application to investment planning in the Blue Nile', Environment for Development Discussion Paper Series, No. 13-5.

Klein, R J.T. and Persson, Å., 2008. *Financing Adaptation to Climate Change: Issues and Priorities*, European Climate Platform (ECP), Report No. 8. Brussels. Available at https://www.ceps.eu/node/1569 (accessed February 2016).

Klijn, F., Mens, M.J.P. and Asselman, N.E.M., 2014. 'Robustness analysis for flood risk management planning: on risk-based decision making beyond simple economic reasoning, exemplified for the Meuse River (Netherlands)', Paper presented at the 6th International Conference of Flood Management, Sao Paulo, September.

LDC (Least Developed Countries) Expert Group, 2012. *National Adaptation Plans*, Technical Guidelines for the National Adaptation Plan Process, December. Bonn: UNFCCC Secretariat. Available at http://unfccc.int/adaptation/work streams/national_adaptation_programmes_of_action/items/7279.php (accessed February 2016).

Lempert, R., Kalra, N., Peyraud, S., Mao, S. and Tan, S.B., 2013. 'Ensuring robust flood risk management in Ho Chi Minh City', Policy Research Working

Paper No. 6465, May, World Bank, Washington, DC. Available at http://dx.doi.org/10.1596/1813-9450-6465 (accessed February 2016).

Li, J., Mullan, M. and Helgeson, J., 2014. 'Improving the practice of economic analysis of climate change adaptation', *Journal of Benefit Cost Analysis*, **5**(3). doi: 10.1515/jbca-2014-9004

Linquiti, P. and Vonortas, N., 2012. 'The value of flexibility in adapting to climate change: a real options analysis of investments in coastal defense', *Climate Change Economics*, **3**(2). doi: 10.1142/S201000781250008X

Markandya, A. and Watkiss, P., 2009. 'Potential costs and benefits of adaptation options: a review of existing literature', Technical Paper, CDCeCce/mTPb/e2r0 20090/29, UNFCCC.

McCarthy, N., Lipper, L. and Branca, G., 2011. *Climate-smart Agriculture: Smallholder Adoption and Implications for Climate Change Adaptation and Mitigation*, Mitigation of Climate Change in Agriculture Series 4. Rome: Food and Agriculture Organization of the United Nations (FAO).

McGray, H., Hammill, A. and Bradley, R., 2007. *Weathering the Storm: Options for Framing Adaptation and Development*. Washington, DC: World Resources Institute.

Murphy, J.M., Sexton, D.M.H., Jenkins, G.J. et al., 2009. *UK Climate Projections Science Report: Climate Change Projections*. Exeter: Met Office Hadley Centre.

OECD, 2008. *Economic Aspects of Adaptation to Climate Change: Costs, Benefits and Policy Instruments*. Paris: OECD Publishing. Available at http://www.oecd.org/env/cc/economicaspectsofadaptationtoclimatechangecostsbenefitsandpolicyinstruments.htm (accessed February 2016).

OECD, 2009. *Integrating Climate Change Adaptation into Development Co-operation: Policy Guidance*. Paris: OECD Publishing. Available at http://dx.doi.org/10.1787/9789264054950-en (acessed February 2016).

OECD, 2014. *Climate Resilience in Development Planning: Experiences in Colombia and Ethiopia*. Paris: OECD Publishings.

OECD, 2015. *Climate Change Risks and Adaptation: Linking Policy and Economics*. Paris: OECD Publishing.

Ranger, N., 2013. *Topic Guide. Adaptation: Decision Making Under Uncertainty*. Report to DFID, London.

Ranger, N., Millner, A., Dietz, S., Fankhauser, S., Lopez, A. and Ruta, G., 2010. *Adaptation in the UK: A Decision Making Process*. London: Grantham Research Institute on Climate Change and the Environment.

Ranger, N., Harvey, A. and Garbett-Shiels, S-.L., 2014. 'Safeguarding development aid against climate change: evaluating progress and identifying best practice', *Development in Practice*, **24**(4), 467–86.

Reeder, T. and Ranger, N., 2011. *How Do You Adapt in an Uncertain World? Lessons from the Thames Estuary 2100 Project*. Washington, DC: World Resources Report.

Rojas, R., Feyen, L. and Watkiss, P., 2013. 'Climate change and river floods in the European Union: socio-economic consequences and the costs and benefits of adaptation', *Global Environmental Change*, **23**(6). Available at http://dx.doi.org/10.1016/j.gloenvcha.2013.08.006 (accessed February 2016).

Stern, N., 2006. *The Economics of Climate Change: The Stern Review*. Cambridge: Cambridge University Press.

Tompkins, E.L. and Adger, W.N., 2004. 'Does adaptive management of natural resources enhance resilience to climate change?', *Ecology and Society*, **9**,

1. Available at http://www.ecologyandsociety.org/vol9/iss2/art10/ (accessed February 2016).

UNDP/UNEP, 2011. *Mainstreaming Climate Change Adaptation into Development Planning: A Guide for Practitioners.* Nairobi: UNDP-UNEP Poverty-Environment Initiative.

Watkiss, P., 2011. 'Aggregate economic measures of climate change damages: explaining the differences and implications', *Wiley Interdisciplinary Reviews – Climate Change*, **2**(3), 356ff. doi: 10.1002/wcc.111

Watkiss, P., 2014. *Design of Policy-led Analytical Framework for the Economics of Adaptation.* Deliverable 1.2 of the ECONADAPT Project. Available at http://econadapt.eu/ (accessed February 2016).

Watkiss, P. and Hunt, A., 2011. *Method for the UK Adaptation Economic Assessment (Economics of Climate Resilience).* Final Report to Defra, London. Deliverable 2.2.1, May.

Watkiss, P., Hunt, A., Blyth, W. and Dyszynski, J., 2014. 'The use of new economic decision support tools for adaptation assessment: a review of methods and applications, towards guidance on applicability', *Climatic Change*. Available at http://dx.doi.org/10.1007/s10584-014-1250-9 (accessed February 2016).

Wilby, R.L., 2012. *Frameworks for Delivering Regular Assessments of the Risks and Opportunities from Climate Change: An Independent Review of the First UK Climate Change Risk Assessment.* Final Report to the Committee on Climate Change, London, 18 June.

World Bank, 2010. *The Costs to Developing Countries of Adapting to Climate Change: New Methods and Estimates. The Global Report of the Economics of Adaptation to Climate Change Study. Synthesis Report.* Washington, DC: World Bank.

World Bank, 2011. *Natural Hazards, UnNatural Disasters, The Economics of Effective Prevention.* Washington, DC: World Bank.

PART II

Actions

7. Adaptation experience and prioritization

Paul Watkiss

7.1 INTRODUCTION

In this chapter we set out some observations and insights for policy makers on the prioritization of adaptation interventions for climate-resilient development. This draws on current and emerging evidence, applying a practical lens to recent methodological changes in adaptation thinking (see Watkiss and Hunt, Chapter 6, this volume).

The chapter proceeds as follows. In Section 7.2 we outline how the change in assessment methods has altered the nature and mix of adaptation options. In Section 7.3 we review the evidence and state of knowledge on promising early options – both immediate and early actions for longer time-scales. In Section 7.4 we discuss some of the remaining issues that are associated with practical implementation. Finally, conclusions are given in Section 7.5.

7.2 TYPES OF ADAPTATION INTERVENTIONS

The recent shift towards policy-first adaptation and early mainstreaming, set out in Watkiss and Hunt (Chapter 6, this volume), affects the types of adaptation interventions for climate-resilient development. This is particularly relevant for the implementation of adaptation in developing countries, in the context of national, sector and local adaptation plans.

This shift can be seen in recent assessments of adaptation options – especially those that are policy and implementation orientated. These have a greater emphasis on early adaptation interventions; that is, on what to do over the next five years or so. Examples of this can be seen in recent national and sector climate change action plans (reviewed in Watkiss, 2015) as in Bangladesh (MoEF, 2009), Ethiopia (FDRE, 2014), Rwanda (RoR, 2011), Tanzania (URT, 2014) and Zanzibar (RGZ, 2014).

Critically, the options prioritized in these action plans differ significantly from those identified in earlier impact assessment, the latter being focused on technical or engineering options (for example, dikes for flood protection, irrigation for agriculture; see Markandya and Watkiss, 2009). In contrast, recent action plans focus on a broad set of early interventions (non-technical as well as technical options). There is also a focus on 'no- and low-regret' options that address current climate variability as such options offer benefits now and lay the foundation for future resilience (Watkiss and Hunt, 2011; IPCC, 2012; Ranger and Garbett-Shiels, 2011), though the definition of exactly what constitutes 'low-regret' varies.[1] Complementing this, there is an increasing use of approaches and interventions that inform future-orientated climate-smart decisions. These address the risk of lock-in and preserve future option values, as well as encouraging flexibility, robustness, risk diversification and portfolios to address uncertainty (Ranger et al., 2010; Watkiss and Hunt, 2011; Fankhauser et al., 2013; Ranger, 2013; DFID, 2014; Watkiss et al., 2014). These are also forms of 'low-regret' adaptation, but critically they are less focused on delivering immediate benefits or tackling the existing adaptation deficit. They are particularly important, however, in the context of climate-resilient development.

As set out in Watkiss and Hunt (Chapter 6, this volume), these various elements can be combined into a framework for climate-resilient development, which makes sense from an economic perspective and addresses the timing and uncertainty of climate change. This includes three broad groups of adaptation interventions:

- Action to address immediate and short-term risks (current climate variability and extremes, that is, the adaptation deficit).
- Action to improve immediate decisions that have a long lifetime (for example, infrastructure, planning).
- Action to start planning for future long-term risks, taking account of future uncertainty.

For the first of these, the focus is on early options that address immediate risks. Here an important differentiation can be made between interventions that have a strong overlap with current development, which may be more appropriate for implementation through existing country programmes and overseas development assistance, versus interventions that directly address climate variability, which align more strongly with the concept of additionality in climate finance. Nevertheless, both of these are associated with concrete early actions (for example, technical implementation). These options can often be assessed with traditional economic appraisal methods. They typically have high benefit to cost ratios and deliver immediate economic benefits, as well as helping build resilience. Complementing these options, there is a separate category of capacity building, to help deliver effective interventions, focused on the process of adaptation. These include institutional strengthening and awareness raising, but also some specific climate (weather)-orientated information provision, for example, seasonal forecasting, early warning (DFID, 2014).

The second set of options focuses on immediate decisions with a long lifetime (see Fankhauser et al., 2013; Ranger, 2013). These also include technical or outcome-based interventions and capacity building/ information provision. The former can include interventions that build resilience into infrastructure or planning decisions (that is, making them climate-smart) such as low cost over-design, or seeking to reduce lock-in and increase robustness and flexibility. There are also a set of non-technical options, such as information and capacity, processes and assessment that enable or enhance these activities. These involve different methods and approaches for appraisal (compared to the short-term options identified in the previous paragraph), and lead to different types of interventions.

Finally, there is a separate set of longer-term (future-orientated) interventions associated with early planning for addressing future climate challenges. These are areas where early action may be needed to address future long-term risks (Ranger and Reeder, 2011; Watkiss and Hunt, 2011), either because a decision time-scale takes a long time (for example, decades) and thus some early steps are warranted to start planning for the future now, or because there are major (even irreversible) long-term risks – with high uncertainty. Early planning and information gathering can help inform future decisions and also help keep future options open. These interventions are centred on the application of iterative adaptive management, and usually focus on early research, monitoring and learning (the value of information), as well as formal and informal (real) option analysis.

What is critical to note is that these three categories involve different methodological concepts, and require analysis of different types of benefits (over varying time-scales). They also require different information inputs and economic appraisal techniques. As an example, the analysis of capacity building will require different methods and information to a hard flood protection scheme, while future-orientated studies require greater consideration of uncertainty. The distinction in the timing, types and methods are summarized in Table 7.1. More information on these types of adaptation, and the existing evidence base on potential priorities in each of these categories, is given in the following section.

Table 7.1   Differences in timing, types of benefits and analysis methods

Intervention	Timing of benefits	Type of benefits	Analysis
Good development	Now	Increased productivity/ reduced poverty	Classic benefit to cost ratio
Addressing current variability	Now but also resilience for the future	Reduced weather damage costs	As above, but focus on quantification of climate costs and benefits
Early capacity building	Now but also adaptive capacity for the future	Value of information/ increased effectiveness and efficiency	Often qualitative. Multi-criteria analysis, though can quantify value of information
Resilience for the future	Some now, but mostly future	Reduced climate change-induced damage costs	Risk screening, real options, robust decision making etc.
Capacity for the future	Some now, but mostly future	Value of information/ increased effectiveness and efficiency	Qualitative though can quantify value of information
Iterative adaptation and early steps	Future	Value of information Future option value	Iterative pathways, real options analysis

Source: Updated from DFID (2014).

7.3   EVIDENCE ON PROMISING EARLY ADAPTATION OPTIONS

Over the past few years there have been several reviews of the costs and benefits of adaptation (Adger et al., 2007; OECD, 2008; Markandya and Watkiss, 2009; Agrawala et al., 2011; Chambwera et al., 2014). These generally report a low evidence base, and thus they are limited in their application for broader economic prioritization. However, two new evidence lines have started to emerge that have significantly increased the available knowledge, especially for developing countries. First, there have been a large number of national-level initiatives, varying from one or two key sectors through to economy-wide assessments (see UNEP, 2014). Second, there are more studies that focus on early adaptation, considering the application of existing options to new contexts or locations, and for which there is *ex ante* or *ex post* information available. These two factors have led to a substantial increase in the number of studies on the costs and benefits of adaptation. These have been collated as part of the ECONADAPT Project (ECONADAPT, 2015), which identified around 500 studies, a large number of which are in developing countries. This provides a much greater information base on promising early options and thus priorities for adaptation, explored in the next subsection.

7.3.1 Early Low-regret Options

There is a large number of early adaptation options that seek to address the current adaptation deficit.[2] These provide immediate economic benefits, but also provide resilience for the future. They include some general development options, which offer efficiency or generate cost savings (for example, improving irrigation efficiency) or options that address existing problems (for example, reducing post-harvest losses), though many of these are common development options. They also include options that are more targeted to climate-specific risks, and thus more aligned to early climate resilience, such as disaster risk management or soil and water conservation for agriculture. Note, however, that even for these climate-orientated early options, many priorities overlap with existing development activities (see OECD, 2014). There is a good literature emerging on the promising early options for targeting key climate risks. Many of these draw on existing disaster risk management or sustainable practice.

For the risks of coastal flooding, storm surges and sea-level rise, the promising options include climate services and forecasting, early warning systems, disaster risk management and also natural (ecosystem-based) adaptation. There are numerous studies that show high benefit to cost ratios for such options (for example, Mechler, 2012, 2014; DFID, 2014). The benefits of improved forecasting and early warning have been shown in Bangladesh (Paul, 2009) and Southeast Asia (Subbiah et al., 2008). There is also evidence that institutional strengthening, awareness raising, as well as response plans have high benefit to cost ratios (for example, Cartwright et al., 2013 in Durban). Similarly, the use of mangrove conservation, replanting and restoration, as well as shoreline restoration have been found to have high benefit to cost ratios in many studies (for example, ECA, 2009 in Samoa and CCRIF, 2010 in the Caribbean), and there are also risk transfer options including insurance and risk pooling facilities.

Similar options are used to deal with current rainfall variability and flood risks. Mechler et al. (2014) undertook a systematic review of the costs and benefits of flood risk management looking at appraisals (*ex ante*) and evaluations (*ex post*) in 27 studies: he found an average benefit to cost ratio of just under 5 to 1 for flood related risks. This review was further expanded in ECONADAPT (2015). Options with high benefit to cost ratios included enhanced meteorological and climate services and early warning systems (for example, World Bank, 2012), disaster risk management and emergency, contingency and preparation response plans and awareness raising (for example, Hawley et al., 2012), enhanced maintenance regimes for drainage and sewage systems (for example, Moench et al., 2009; Ranger et al., 2011), integrated water resource management (for example, Mechler, 2005), risk transfer including insurance, reserve funds and risk facilities (for example, Jongman et al., 2014) and ecosystem-based adaptation.

A number of these options are also relevant for drought risks. Complementing these, there are more targeted options for this risk that show high benefits, such as early disaster response and resilience (for example, Cabot Venton et al., 2013 in Mozambique, Bangladesh, Niger, Kenya and Ethiopia) and social protection through cash transfer payments (DFID, 2011). There are also high benefit to cost ratios for interventions that reduce waterborne disease through enhanced water and sanitation (see Hunt, 2011 for a review). There are a set of more general options with high benefit to cost ratios for water management that includes knowledge and awareness, integrated watershed management (de Bruin et al., 2009), enhanced hydrological monitoring and information (Flörke et al., 2011), metering (Darch et al., 2011), water allocations (Nkomo and Gomez, 2006), water efficiency measures (ECA, 2009; Flörke et al., 2011; Lunduka et al., 2012), leakage reduction (Darch et al., 2011) or reclaimed water (Máñez and Cerdà, 2014), as well as ecosystem-based adaptation, river restoration and water retention measures (de Bruin et al., 2009; Flörke et al., 2011).

In the agricultural sector, much of the recent focus in developing countries has been on climate-smart agriculture (FAO, 2013). These are forms of sustainable agricultural land management and include agroforestry, soil and water conservation, reduced or zero tillage and use of cover crops (see also Bezabih et al., Chapter 9, this volume). These options improve soil water infiltration and holding capacity, as well as nutrient supply and soil biodiversity. They also reduce risks from rainfall variability (for rain-fed agriculture) and soil erosion, increase soil organic matter, soil fertility and productivity, and reduce greenhouse gas emissions (Branca et al., 2011). The costs of these measures have been assessed by McCarthy et al. (2011). Specific examples of cost-effectiveness assessment and even cost-benefit analysis also exist such as Branca et al. (2012) in Malawi and ECA (2009) in Mali, and these studies generally report that climate-smart agriculture is win-win for food security and climate change adaptation, as well as providing mitigation (reduced greenhouse gas) benefits. Some options also lead to direct co-economic benefits, for example, agroforestry can generate additional income streams from fuel wood, building material and food. Complementing these, there are other options that exist that lead to high benefit to cost ratios, noting these often overlap with existing agricultural development strategies. Such options include climate information, agro-meteorological information, seasonal forecasting and early warning (Ranger and Garbett-Shiels, 2011; ECONADAPT, 2015; see also Clements, 2013); research and development; crop switching/planting (agronomic management); pest and disease management, including post-harvest losses; water management ecosystem-based adaptation and insurance. Some countries have assessed and costed these options in agriculture sector adaptation plans (for example, FDRE, 2014; URT, 2014).

Many of the most promising options for the risks and sectors above are 'behavioural' or soft measures – information and education, preparedness, forecasts and warning systems, emergency responses and so on. Indeed, in many cases, these have been found to be among the priorities (in terms of benefit to cost ratios) from all options considered. These include capacity building,[3] which is an important precursor or complement to successful adaptation, providing the architecture to enable and improve current as well as future decision making, strengthening relevant institutions, enhancing baseline information and so on.

Critically, these soft measures are highly synergistic to technical or engineering-based options, creating the enabling environment or increasing the effectiveness of delivery. There are therefore benefits in introducing complementary packages of options, for example, portfolios rather than single technical solutions (see Di Falco and Veronesi, 2012 for an example in agriculture combining improved seeds, soil and water conservation and better extension services). This highlights that successful adaptation is likely to involve a combination of outcome- and process-based adaptation (technical and socio-institutional interventions). Importantly, this moves away from the sequential and linear approach used for mitigation appraisal (with cost-effectiveness curves).

However, these non-technical and capacity building options have very different characteristics to technical options. They are generally low cost to implement, though not cost-free. They also have benefits that are more difficult to assess quantitatively, though it is possible to assess using the value of information or quasi-option value: information has a value, as it leads to different actions with learning, and allows higher benefits or lower costs as a result. To place an economic value on this, the analysis can calculate the value or cost without information, and then compares this to value or cost if learning takes place and action is taken. The difference between these is the economic value of information. When these benefits are included, it is clear that capacity building leads to high benefit to cost ratios. As an example, a review of the cost-benefit studies of enhanced climate services (for example, seasonal forecasts, information for early warning) was found to produce high benefit to cost ratios (Clements, 2013) and there are similar findings for enhanced hydrological information (World Bank, 2012). Cartwright et al. (2013) report high benefit to cost ratios for disaster risk management plans (contingency, awareness) and institutional strengthening (cross-sectoral disaster forums), and similar benefits are found for flood forecasting and institutional reform and incentives to reduce vulnerability (Wilby and Keenan, 2012) and for improved watershed management (Mechler, 2005; de Bruin et al., 2009).

It is worth highlighting, however, that low-regret options, on their own, may not be sufficient to address more extreme risks from longer-term change (see World Bank, 2011). Furthermore, it is important to ensure that changing climate trends are taken into account in advancing these early options. This often involves doing something slightly different, as implementation takes place in a situation where the historical climate is no longer a good predictor of the future. This may mean that the nature or emphasis of an intervention may need to change. As an illustration of this, Conway and Schipper (2011) identify that under conditions of a changing climate, existing social protection programmes will need to invest in monitoring to learn and may need more flexible programmes.

7.3.2   Early Decisions with a Long Lifetime

The second major group of interventions focuses on early decisions that will be impacted by climate change in the future. They may be associated with climate-sensitive infrastructure (for example, hydro-plants or critical infrastructure) that could be affected by changing trends (for example, river flows) or extremes (for example, floods). It also applies to decisions on land use (urban or rural), due to the long-term multi-decadal nature of the changes that these decisions involve (Ranger et al., 2014). They are therefore highly relevant for climate-resilient development.

There are some additional challenges when looking at the promising or priority options for this category of intervention. There is an important trade-off between early actions – which are likely to incur potential costs – versus future longer-term benefits, due to the importance of discounting (DFID, 2014). In the developing country context, this is a particular issue, due to high discount rates (or the rates of return on investment). This means that the choice of options has to be made carefully, to avoid misallocation of resources in relation to additional up-front investment versus long-term benefits that accrue in the future. This factor is complicated by future climate uncertainty. This makes it very difficult to design optimal interventions with foresight, and indeed the focus has been on the use of decision making under uncertainty to address this.

This includes climate risk screening, to avoid or minimize future risks at the outset, and indeed many organizations are introducing such systems (for example, AfdB, 2011). These can be justified on the basis that it is often more expensive (and sometime impossible) to retrofit later. A number of elements are possible.

First, it is possible to focus on simple siting (avoiding high risk locations). This may be for the individual site (for example, of infrastructure) or the analysis of risks as part of urban or land-use planning decisions, to avoid areas of increased future risk or minimize the risk of lock-in. Some studies report high cost-effectiveness if climate risk screening is included at the design stage, because of the avoided reconstruction costs from floods and storms (for example, ADB, 2005 in the Micronesia and Cook islands). The siting of critical infrastructure such as hospitals and water treatment facilities away from high risk areas is also an early priority option. There have been studies of the use of land-use planning and set-back zones (where development is prohibited) that report high benefit to cost ratios, for example, for wind storm protection under current climate variability and future climate change (ECA, 2009; CCRIF, 2010; Cartwright et al., 2013), although some caution is needed, as these can often involve a high opportunity cost due to land-use exclusion.

Second, it is possible to alter design to take account of changing risks. There are studies that highlight that the upgrading of design standards (Wilby and Keenan, 2012) is a potential option for enhancing the climate resilience of infrastructure. However, this is only likely to make sense where the additional costs are very low or the future benefits are very high (or generate co-benefits), because of discounting (DFID, 2014). The balance between costs and benefits is particularly important in the developing country context, where over-design has the potential to divert key sources of finance away from investments that could give greater short-term economic benefits. As an example, for rural road development projects, it may be better to spend resources to maximize the length of roads built, rather than spend these resources on a small number of highly resilient roads, especially noting the design lifetime is short. In contrast, it may be worth over-designing critical infrastructure (World Bank, 2011), such as bridges or water treatment plants, even if this involves higher costs, because of the importance in post-disaster scenarios in reducing wider indirect and even macro-economic costs.

It is clear that the level of risks (and thus benefits) influences the trade-off here, and that there is the important issue of transferability. A good example can be seen with building codes for future enhanced climate resilience. These are often cited as a potential low-regret option (IPCC, 2012), but the literature shows more variation: while some studies find high benefits, for example, in Florida (ECA, 2009) and Samoa (World Bank, 2010), others report low benefit to cost ratios, for example, in the Caribbean (CCRIF, 2010; Hochrainer-Stigler et al., 2010) due to differences in risk levels, the costs of resilience, existing cost and asset lifetime, and discount rates.

A further option is to provide the opportunity for changes in the future by providing flexibility. In some case this may be low or zero-cost (for example, allowing the space for future upgrade as part of future maintenance and refurbishment cycles). In other cases it may be much more expensive, for example, increasing the foundation size of a hydro-electric dam to allow upgrade against future flood risks as higher flows in the future can increase costs significantly. Importantly, in many cases, this flexibility will have a cost. An alternative can be to introduce soft- or ecosystem-based protection, as these often have lower capital costs and greater flexibility for enhancing protection levels in the future, although higher maintenance costs (though also ecosystem service co-benefits).

Finally, there is a set of interventions that seek to enhance the use of robustness, in this context, defined as designing against many scenarios (or climate futures) rather than optimizing to one. There is a literature on this, often captured through the use of robust decision making (Dessai and Hulme, 2007; Lempert and Groves, 2010). These focus on the application of this approach to water management, primarily in the Organisation for Economic Co-operation and Development (OECD), although developed country examples are emerging.

Importantly, all of these areas of intervention involve a more considered analysis, that is, there are potentially attractive options, from a cost-benefit perspective, but these must be carefully chosen, and may even vary with site or context. Their analysis also requires a set of additional economic techniques to allow the economic valuation to be extended to capture the added component (for example, the flexibility or robustness) when compared to a baseline study where uncertainty is excluded.

7.3.3   Early Action to Address Long-term Risks

The final category relates to early planning for major risks, for example, through early research, monitoring and planning. In terms of low-regret options, this centres on the use of iterative adaptive management. Most examples of this type of activity are from the OECD, notably in countries such as the Netherlands (Delta Programme, 2014; Eijgenraam et al., 2014; Kind, 2014) and the UK (EA, 2011), where iterative adaptive management and dynamic adaptation pathways have been advanced in practical policy settings (for national coastal and flood planning policy and protecting London from sea-level rise, respectively).

While this has a potentially high resonance for future major changes in climate, in developing countries, there are fewer examples to date, though there are some studies in the agricultural sector (including FDRE, 2014 and Matiya et al., 2011). In these cases, there is a strong focus again on the value of information. In the context of climate change adaptation, better information about future climate change risks is likely to prove beneficial in making decisions on resource allocation. For example, information on changes in temperature and sea level, or the severity of future droughts, can help to design and leverage resources as part of future decision cycles. There is also the formal application of these concepts as part of real options analysis (Watkiss and Hunt, Chapter 6, this volume).

7.4   ISSUES WITH PRACTICAL IMPLEMENTATION

The final set of issues relates to the additional aspects in moving from the identification and appraisal of priority options to their practical implementation.

One lesson from recent policy-orientated studies is that adaptation decisions are more complex, and costs are often higher, when working within the current policy environment, as this involves multiple risks and wider non-climatic drivers when compared to more theoretical appraisals (ECONADAPT, 2015). This is an important finding given the trend towards mainstreaming (integration) and leads to a greater need to balance many competing priorities and stakeholder views. Of interest for researchers and policy makers, it is also clear that real-world studies involve greater time and resources to undertake, due to the need to understand the background policy context and to address these issues.

These policy-orientated and practical studies also reveal important opportunity and transaction costs associated with implementation of low-regret options, which will lead to much higher out-turns in practice (that is, *ex post*). This replicates the lessons from the emissions reduction domain, where it was found that negative no-regret cost options were rarely as easy or as cheap to implement as predicted in the technical cost-curve analysis (for example, Ecofys, 2009). Many low-regret adaptation options have opportunity, transaction or policy costs (DFID, 2014), which have not been included in many studies or estimates to date. Examples include the opportunity costs of climate-smart agriculture (McCarthy et al., 2011), the land acquisition opportunity costs of set-back zones or planning controls (Cartwright et al., 2013) or the enforcement costs for ecosystem-based options (Watkiss et al., 2014). These factors need to be included in the appraisal and prioritization of options, and the estimates of costs for programming and implementation.

A final issue relates to the additional challenges of implementing adaptation in developing countries, and especially the least developed countries. This will be more difficult due to the existing capacity, development and governance challenges. As a result, there may be additional technical assistance and programming costs, as well as additional aspects that need to be included to address key barriers to adaptation, to ensure the effective and continued delivery of benefits. This highlights an important issue of the transferability of priorities, and their costs and benefits, to different countries and contexts.

7.5   CONCLUSIONS

In this chapter, we began by outlining how methodological shifts in adaptation assessment have led to a change in the types of adaptation interventions currently being considered, reinforced by the changing needs of policy makers towards short-term adaptation implementation. The result has been a much broader and more comprehensive set of interventions that extend beyond the previous focus on technical (engineering) options. The changes have also led to a much greater focus on the timing and sequencing of adaptation and the prioritization of low-regret options for climate-resilient development.

We then explored the emerging priorities for early adaptation across different time-scales, for immediate climate risks (weather and extremes) and also for future climate change and future decisions under uncertainty. This has drawn on recent literature and evidence on the costs and benefits of interventions. A number of key findings emerge. First, there are a number of promising interventions that form the basis for early action planning, that is, that are initial priorities. These include capacity building and interventions targeting existing climate variability, but also actions that introduce climate into longer-term decisions and start planning (and learning) for the future. Second, and related to this, to capture current and future risks, a complementary portfolio of interventions is needed, noting this involves different problem types and timing, and varying economic concepts and appraisal methods. Third, while promising options can be identified, there is a large variation in costs and benefits, and it is important to consider the transferability, risk and timing for the specific context as part of the prioritization process.

Finally, we turned our attention to a number of key challenges with the practical prioritization and programming of adaptation, especially in the context of real-world decision making and mainstreaming (integration). We identify a number of additional challenges that are important when implementing adaptation, including opportunity and transaction costs, as well as potential economic and socio-institutional barriers, and highlight the need for these to be considered as part of prioritization.

NOTES

1. No-regret adaptation is defined in the Intergovernmental Panel on Climate Change (IPCC) glossary as adaptation policies, plans or options that 'generate net social and/or economic benefits irrespective of whether or not anthropogenic climate change occurs'. There is, however, no agreed definition of low-regret options, and a review of various studies (DFID, 2014) identifies the following: (1) options that are no-regret in nature, but have opportunity, transaction or policy costs; (2) options that have benefits (or co-benefits) that are difficult to monetize; (3) low cost measures that can provide high benefits if future climate change emerges; (4) options that are robust or flexible, and thus help with future uncertainty.
2. The IPCC's *Fifth Assessment Report* (2014) defines the adaptation deficit as 'the gap between the current state of a system and a state that minimizes adverse impacts from existing climate conditions and variability'. However, in this chapter we introduce a caveat with this definition, which recognizes that it is usually not economically efficient (or optimal) to completely minimize the adaptation gap to zero (indeed, even highly developed countries have an adaptation deficit).
3. Capacity building is a broad term (UKCIP, 2009) that involves: gathering and sharing information, that is, undertaking research, collecting and monitoring data and raising awareness through education and training initiatives; creating a supportive institutional framework that might involve changing standards, legislation and best practice guidance, and developing appropriate policies, plans and strategies; and creating supportive social structures, such as changing internal organizational systems, developing personnel, providing the resources to deliver the adaptation actions and working in partnership.

REFERENCES

ADB, 2005. *Climate Proofing: A Risk-based Approach to Adaptation*. Manilla: Asian Development Bank.

Adger, W.N., Agrawala, S., Mirza, M.M.Q. et al., 2007. 'Assessment of adaptation practices, options, constraints and capacity', in M.L. Parry, O.F. Canziani, J.P. Palutikof, P.J. van der Linden and C.E. Hanson (eds), *Climate Change 2007: Impacts, Adaptation and Vulnerability. Contribution of Working Group II to the Fourth Assessment Report of the Intergovernmental Panel on Climate Change*, Cambridge: Cambridge University Press, pp. 717–43.

AfDB (African Development Bank Group), 2011. *Climate Screening and Adaptation Review & Evaluation Procedures*, Tunis: AfDB.

Agrawala, S., Bosello, F., Carraro, C., de Cian, E., and Lanzi, E., 2011. 'Adapting to climate change: costs, benefits, and modelling approaches', *International Review of Environmental and Resource Economics*, 5, 245–84.

Branca, G., McCarthy, N., Lipper, L. and Jolejole, M.C., 2011. *Climate-smart Agriculture: A Synthesis of Empirical Evidence of Food Security and Mitigation Benefits from Improved Cropland Management*, Mitigation of Climate Change in Agriculture Series 3, December. Rome: Food and Agriculture Organization of the United Nations (FAO).

Branca, G., Lipper, L. and Sorrentino, A. 2012. 'Benefit-costs analysis of climate-related agricultural investments in Africa: a case study', Italian Association of Agricultural and Applied Economics Congress Papers 2012, First Congress, 4–5 June, Trento, Italy.

Cabot Venton, C., Coulter, L. and Schmuck, H. 2013. *The Economics of Early Response and Resilience: Summary Report*. Report to DFID, London.

Cartwright, A., Blignaut, J., De Wit, M. et al., 2013. 'Economics of climate change adaptation at the local scale under conditions of uncertainty and resource constraints: the case of Durban, South Africa', *Environment and Urbanization*, 25, 139. doi: 10.1177/0956247813477814

CCRIF (Caribbean Catastrophe Risk Insurance Facility), 2010. 'Enhancing the Climate Risk and Adaptation Fact Base for the Caribbean', an informational brochure highlighting the preliminary results of the ECA Study.

Chambwera, M., Heal, G. and Dubeux, S., 2014. 'Economics of adaptation', in *Climate Change 2014: Impacts, Adaptation, and Vulnerability. Part A: Global and Sectoral Aspects. Contribution of Working Group II to the Fifth Assessment Report of the Intergovernmental Panel on Climate Change*. Cambridge and New York, Cambridge University Press, pp. 945–77.

Clements, 2013. *The Value of Climate Services Across Economic and Public Sectors*. Report to the United States Agency for International Development (USAID) prepared by Engility/International Resources Group (IRG). Available at http://www.climate-services.org/wp-content/uploads/2015/09/CCRD-Climate-Services-Value-Report_FINAL.pdf (accessed February 2016).

Conway, D. and Schipper, L., 2011. 'Adaptation to climate change in Africa: challenges and opportunities identified from Ethiopia', *Global Environmental Change*, 21, 227–37.

Darch, G., Arkell, B. and Tradewell, J., 2011. *Water Resource Planning under Climate Uncertainty in London*. Atkins Report (Reference 5103993/73/DG/035) for the Adaptation Sub-Committee and Thames Water. Epsom: Atkins.

De Bruin, K., Dellink, R.B., Ruijs, A. et al., 2009. 'Adapting to climate change in the Netherlands: an inventory of climate adaptation options and ranking of alternatives', *Climatic Change*, 95, 23–45.

Delta Programme, 2014. *Working on the Delta: Promising Solutions for Tasking and Ambitions*. The Hague: The Delta Programme.

Dessai, S. and Hulme, M., 2007. 'Assessing the robustness of adaptation decisions to climate change uncertainties: a case study on water resources management in the East of England', *Global Environmental Change*, 17, 59–72.

DFID, 2011. *Guidance for DFID Country Offices on Measuring and Maximising Value for Money in Cash Transfer Programmes. Toolkit and Explanatory Text*, edited by A. Hodges, P. White and M. Greenslade. October.

DFID, 2014. *Early Value-for-money Adaptation: Delivering VfM Adaptation Using Iterative Frameworks and Low-regret Options*. London: DFID. Available at http://www.vfmadaptation.com (accessed October 2015).

Di Falco, S. and Veronesi, M., 2012. 'How African agriculture can adapt to climate change? A counterfactual analysis from Ethiopia', Working Paper Series No. 14, Department of Economics, University of Verona.

EA, 2011. *Thames Estuary 2100: Strategic Outline Programme*. Bristol: UK Environment Agency.

ECA, 2009. *Shaping Climate-resilient Development: A Framework for Decision-making*. A Report of the Economics of Climate Adaptation Working Group. Economics of Climate Adaptation. ClimateWorks Foundation, Global Environment Facility, European Commission, McKinsey & Company, The Rockefeller Foundation, Standard Chartered Bank and Swiss Re.

Ecofys, 2009. *The Hidden Costs and Benefits of Domestic Energy Efficiency and Carbon Saving Measures*. For Defra, London, Apri.

ECONADAPT, 2015. *The Costs and Benefits of Adaptation, Results from the ECONADAPT Project*. ECONADAPT Consortium. Available at http://econa-dapt.eu/ (accessed February 2016).

Eijgenraam, C., Kind, J., Bak, C. et al. (2014). 'Economically efficient standards to protect the Netherlands against flooding', *Interfaces*, **44**(1). Available at http://dx.doi.org/10.1287/inte.2013.0721 (accessed February 2016).

Fankhauser, S.N., Ranger, J., Colmer, S. et al., 2013. 'An independent national adaptation programme for England', Policy Brief, Grantham Research Institute on Climate Change and the Environment, London School of Economics.

FAO, 2013. *Climate Smart Agriculture*. Available at http://www.climatesmartagriculture.org (accessed February 2016).

FDRE, 2014. *Ethiopia's Climate-resilient Green Economy: Climate-resilient Strategy for Agriculture*. Federal Democratic Republic of Ethiopia, Environmental Protection Authority.

Flörke, M., Wimmer, F., Laaser, C. et al., 2011. *Climate Adaptation – Modelling Water Scenarios and Sectoral Impacts. Final Report*. Kassel: ClimWatAdapt Project. Available at http://climwatadapt.eu/sites/default/files/ClimWatAdapt_final_report.pdf (accessed February 2016).

Hawley, K., Moench, M. and Sabbag, L., 2012. *Understanding the Economics of Flood Risk Reduction: A Preliminary Analysis*. Boulder, CO: Institute for Social and Environmental Transition-International.

Hochrainer-Stigler, S., Kunreuther, H., Linnerooth-Bayer, J. et al., 2010. 'The costs and benefits of reducing risk from natural hazards to residential structures in developing countries', Working Paper No. 2010-12-01, Wharton School, University of Pennsylvania, Philadelphia.

Hunt, A., 2011. 'Policy interventions to address health impacts associated with air pollution, unsafe water supply and sanitation and hazardous chemicals', Environment Working Paper No. 35, OECD, Paris.

IPCC, 2012. *Managing the Risks of Extreme Events and Disasters to Advance Climate Change Adaptation, A Special Report of Working Groups I and II of the Intergovernmental Panel on Climate Change*. Cambridge and New York: Cambridge University Press.

IPCC, 2014. *Fifth Assessment Report of the Intergovernmental Panel on Climate Change*. Cambridge and New York: Cambridge University Press.

Jongman, B., Hochrainer-Stigler, S., Feyen, L. et al., 2014. 'Increasing stress on disaster-risk finance due to large floods', *Nature Climate Change*, **4**(4), 264–8.

Kind, J.M., 2014. 'Economically efficient flood protection standards for the Netherlands', *Flood Risk Management*, **7**, 103–17.

Lempert, R.J. and Groves, D.G., 2010. 'Identifying and evaluating robust adaptive policy responses to climate change for water management agencies in the American West', *Technological Forecasting & Social Change*, **77**, 960–74.

Lunduka, R.W., Bezabih, M. and Chaudhury, A., 2012. *Stakeholder-focused Cost Benefit Analysis in the Water Sector: A Synthesis Report*. London: International Institute for Environment and Development (IIED).

Máñez, M. and Cerdà, A., 2014. *Prioritisation Method for Adaptation Measures to Climate Change in the Water Sector*, CSC Report 18. Hamburg: Climate Service Center.

Markandya, A. and Watkiss, P., 2009. 'Potential costs and benefits of adaptation options: a review of existing literature', Technical Paper, CDCeCce/mTPb/e2r0 20090/29, UNFCCC.

Matiya, G., Lunduka, R. and Sikwese, M., 2011. *Planning and Costing Agricultural Adaptation to Climate Change in the Small-scale Maize Production System of Malawi*. London: International Institute for Environment and Development (IIED).

McCarthy, N., Lipper, L. and Branca, G., 2011. *Climate-smart Agriculture: Smallholder Adoption and Implications for Climate Change Adaptation and Mitigation*, Mitigation of Climate Change in Agriculture Series 4. Rome: Food and Agriculture Organization of the United Nations (FAO).

Mechler, R., 2005. 'Cost-benefit analysis of natural disaster risk management in developing countries' Deutsche Gesellschaft für Technische Zusammenarbeit (GTZ), Arbeitskonzept, Eschborn, Germany.

Mechler, R., 2012. *Reviewing the Economic Efficiency of Disaster Risk Management*. Review commissioned by Foresight Project: Reducing Risks of Future Disasters. Priorities for Decision Makers. IIASA.

Mechler, R., Czajkowski, J., Kunreuther, H. et al., 2014. 'Making communities more flood resilient: the role of cost benefit analysis and other decision-support tools in disaster risk reduction', White Paper, Zurich Flood Resilience Alliance, opim.wharton.upenn.edu/risk/library/ZAlliance-decisiontools-WP.

MoEF, 2009. *Bangladesh Climate Change Strategy and Action Plan (BCCSAP)*. Ministry of Environment and Forestry, Government of the People's Republic of Bangladesh.

Moench, M., Hochrainer, S., Mechler, R. et al., 2009. 'Rethinking the costs and benefits of disaster risk reduction under changing climate conditions', in M. Moench, E. Fajber, A. Dixit, E. Caspari and A. Pokhrel (eds), *Catalyzing Climate and Disaster Resilience*. Kathmandu, Nepal: ISET-Nepal.

Nkomo, J.C. and Gomez, B., 2006. *Estimating and Comparing Costs and Benefits of Adaptation Projects: Case Studies in South Africa and the Gambia*. Final Report submitted to Assessments of Impacts and Adaptations to Climate Change (AIACC), Project No. AF 47. Washington, DC: International START Secretariat.

OECD, 2008. *Economic Aspects of Adaptation to Climate Change: Costs, Benefits and Policy Instruments*. Paris: OECD Publishing. Available at http://www.oecd.org/env/cc/economicaspectsofadaptationtoclimatechangecostsbenefitsandpolicyinstruments.htm (accessed February 2016).

OECD, 2014. *Climate Resilience in Development Planning: Experiences in Colombia and Ethiopia*. Paris: OECD Publishing.

Paul, B.K., 2009. 'Why relatively fewer people died? The case of Bangladesh's Cyclone Sidr', *Natural Hazards*, **50**, 289–304.

Ranger, N., 2013. *Topic Guide. Adaptation: Decision Making Under Uncertainty*. Report to DFID, London.

Ranger, N. and Garbett-Shiels, S.L., 2011. *How can Decision-makers in Developing Countries Incorporate Uncertainty about Future Climate Risks into Existing Planning and Policy-making Processes?* London: Grantham Research Institute on Climate Change and the Environment in collaboration with the World Resources Report.

Ranger, N., Millner, A., Dietz, S., Fankhauser, S., Lopez, A. and Ruta, G., 2010. *Adaptation in the UK: A Decision Making Process*. London: Grantham Research Institute on Climate Change and the Environment.

Ranger N., Hallegatte, S., Bhattacharya, M. et al., 2011. 'A preliminary assessment of the potential impact of climate change on flood risk in Mumbai', *Climatic Change*, **104**(1), 139–67.

Ranger, N., Harvey, A. and Garbett-Shiels, S.L., 2014. 'Safeguarding development aid against climate change: evaluating progress and identifying best practice', *Development in Practice*, **24**(4), 467–86.

Reeder, T. and Ranger, N., 2011. *How do You Adapt in an Uncertain World? Lessons from the Thames Estuary 2100 Project*. Washington, DC: World Resources Report.

RGZ, 2014. *Zanzibar Climate Change Strategy and Action Plan (2014)*. Revolutionary Government of Zanzibar.

RoR, 2011. *Rwanda Green Growth and Climate Resilience (National Strategy for Climate Change and Low Carbon Development), 2011*. Republic of Rwanda.

Subbiah, A., 2008. 'Assessment of the economics of early warning systems for disaster risk reduction', Background Paper for World Bank-UN Project on the Economics of Disaster Risk Reduction, World Bank, Washington, DC.

UKCIP, 2009. *Identifying Adaptation Options*. Oxford: UK Climate Impacts Programme.

UNEP (United Nations Environment Programme), 2014. *The Adaptation Gap Report 2014*. Available at http://www.unep.org/climatechange/adaptation/gap report2014/ (accessed October.2015).

URT, 2014. *Tanzania Agriculture Climate Resilience Plan*. United Republic of Tanzania.

Watkiss, P., 2015. 'A review of the economics of adaptation and climate-resilient development', Grantham Research Institute on Climate Change and the Environment Working Paper No. 205, London School of Economics.

Watkiss, P. and Hunt, A., 2011. *Method for the UK Adaptation Economic Assessment (Economics of Climate Resilience)*. Final Report to Defra. Deliverable 2.2.1, May.

Watkiss, P. et al., 2014. 'The use of new economic decision support tools for adaptation assessment: a review of methods and applications, towards guidance on applicability', *Climatic Change*. Available at http://dx.doi.org/10.1007/s10584-014-1250-9.

Wilby, R.L and Keenan, R., 2012. 'Adapting to flood risk under climate change', *Progress in Physical Geography*, **36**(3). Available at http://dx.doi.org/10.1177/0309133312438908 (accessed February 2016).

World Bank, 2011. *Natural Hazards, UnNatural Disasters: The Economics of Effective Prevention*. Washington, DC: World Bank.

World Bank, 2013. *Weather, Climate and Water Hazards and Climate Resilience: Effective Preparedness through National Meteorological and Hydrological Services*. Washington, DC: World Bank.

8. Climate-resilient cities

Hélia Costa, Graham Floater and Jared Finnegan

8.1 INTRODUCTION

Cities, and the people living in them, face substantial risks from climate change. Cities are concentrations of people, assets, infrastructure networks and major sectors of national economies. In larger cities, this means that a single climate-related disaster such as a major storm can affect millions of people and damage buildings and infrastructure worth billions of dollars. At the same time, three-quarters of all large cities in the world are located on the coast, with the associated risk of sea flooding (UNEP-UN Habitat, 2005). Furthermore, city infrastructure itself can increase the risk of damages. Extensive use of concrete and asphalt raises the temperature in cities and the sealed surfaces of the urban landscape lead to more intense flooding.

Even without the amplifying effects of climate change, many cities are already highly vulnerable to existing weather-related risks, particularly in the developing world. As a result, developing more climate-resilient cities is becoming a greater priority for governments and businesses. In addition, if governments are to create effective strategies for improving urban climate resilience, adaptation policies will need to be placed in the context of rapid urban growth.

Over half the global population now lives in urban areas. The urban population is expected to grow by 1 billion people in less developed countries and by 70 million people in developed countries by 2030 (UN DESA Population Division 2012, as cited in IPCC, 2014). Urban growth is also a key driver of the global economy. Recent research suggests that over 60 per cent of global economic growth will be concentrated in just 470 large cities, predominantly in Asia, North America and Europe (Floater et al., 2014b).

This growth phenomenon is largely the result of economies of scale and agglomeration effects (Brueckner, 2011). Economies of scale lead to the creation of large business enterprises, with the resulting job creation being a major pull factor for cities. At the same time, agglomeration economies, such as reduced transport costs in more compact urban areas and enhanced innovation through knowledge spill-overs, lead to business clustering, contributing to the formation of large cities. As a consequence, the perception of better opportunities, employment and living conditions attracts an increasing number of migrants to cities every year.

While the potential benefits of urban growth for development, poverty alleviation and quality of life are significant, the scale and pace of today's urbanization brings a range of substantial costs if poorly planned and managed (Floater et al., 2014b). Cities in developing countries face an acute shortage of well-planned infrastructure and services to support the rapid growth of urban populations. As a result, the number of people living in poverty in slums, informal settlements and on the periphery of large cities is rising rapidly (Bhatta, 2010). Other costs of poorly managed urban growth include traffic congestion, air pollution, social exclusion and higher carbon emissions. Consequently, policies for climate resilience need to be integrated into wider urban policy programmes.

In this chapter, we examine the economic risks faced by cities from climate change and discuss the importance of integrated policy programmes that can deliver the co-benefits of well-managed urban growth along with a resilient economy. Section 8.2 discusses the major climate-related hazards faced by cities. Section 8.3 examines the characteristics of cities that are particularly vulnerable to these hazards, including location, infrastructure, economic activity and people. Section 8.4 then discusses a model for integrating climate resilience into urban growth strategies, along with the economic policy instruments required. Section 8.5 concludes.

8.2   CLIMATE-RELATED HAZARDS IN CITIES

8.2.1   Urban Hazards

Cities are vulnerable to climate change hazards in specific ways that differ from non-urban areas (IPCC, 2014). Climate-related hazards affecting cities include extreme weather events, such as sea and tidal flooding, inland flooding (fluvial and pluvial), heat waves, storms, drought, landslides, wild fires and snow storms, as well as slow-onset events, such as sea level rise, mean temperature increase, rising air pollution or the spread of invasive species and diseases.

Each hazard affects different cities in different and often complex ways, and will usually have both direct and indirect costs. Direct costs include the costs of repairing physical damage to buildings and infrastructure following a storm or flood, or the costs associated with hospital admittances due to a heat wave. Indirect costs are also likely to occur in the wider economy and over the longer term. Examples include costs to production due to transport disruptions, interruptions in production due to energy shortages and knock-on effects through the supply chain.

Of all the climate-related hazards affecting cities, the main economic threats worldwide are from heat waves, floods and storms, and droughts. The following sections discuss these major threats in more detail.

8.2.2 Heat

Higher temperatures tend to be more frequent and prolonged in cities than in rural areas. This is known as the urban heat island effect (IPCC, 2007). The relative warmth of cities is due in part to the extensive use of concrete and asphalt, a lack of shade-bearing vegetation and moisture-trapping soils, and the production of excess heat from equipment such as air conditioning. Built surfaces are composed of a high percentage of non-reflective and water-resistant construction materials that absorb sunlight and incident radiation, releasing heat. The urban heat island effect is expected to be exacerbated by climate change. Indeed, the difference in temperature between cities and rural areas could increase by 1°C per decade (Voogt, 2002).

One of the most important consequences of increased urban heat waves is the impact on human health. Higher temperatures result directly in increased mortality rates, and indirectly through famine, exacerbation of non-infectious health problems and the spread of infectious diseases (OECD, 2010). In addition, heat exhaustion and heat stroke can exacerbate a wide range of medical conditions, particularly in vulnerable groups such as the elderly and children.

Recent research suggests that reduced worker productivity due to heat waves could translate by 2100 into annual costs of up to 10 per cent of a city's economic output in northern Europe without associated adaptation measures (Costa et al., 2015). Higher temperatures may also possibly affect health by exacerbating air pollution (Harlan and Ruddell, 2011), though the evidence for this is as yet uncertain.

Heat waves can damage transport infrastructure with associated disruption costs. If temperatures reach between 39 and 43°C, railway tracks can buckle and deform (Dobney et al., 2009). In addition, increased temperatures tend to increase energy demand through the intensified use of air conditioning. Global energy demand for air conditioning is projected to increase rapidly over the 2000–2100 period, while overall winter heat demand may decrease in cities in cooler regions.

8.2.3   Floods and Storms

Urban flooding is a major climate change hazard. Costs of flooding include direct damage to buildings and their contents (both residential and commercial), disruption of transport networks due to flooded rail tracks, roads and underground systems, and associated disruption of business activities (Floater et al., 2014c). Severe flooding may limit access to water and electricity, with important impacts to the urban economy, while human health can be affected as sewage systems overflow and water-borne diseases are spread more extensively.

Sea flooding can lead to substantial economic damages in cities as well as loss of life. Before the building of the St Petersburg flood barrier, the total average annual direct damages from sea flooding in the city were estimated at $94 million at 2002 prices (Hunter, 2012).

Globally, damages from sea flooding are expected to rise substantially over the coming decades, both due to the urban growth of coastal cities and increased threats from climate change. Recent research suggests that damages from sea flooding in the 136 largest coastal cities in the world could exceed $993 billion a year by 2050 (Hallegatte et al., 2013). With city ports being central to international trade, costs in wider regional economies are also likely to increase.

Flooding commonly results from heavy rainfall (pluvial flooding) and river overflows (fluvial). Due to the extensive areas of sealed surfaces in urban areas, flash floods are a major hazard in cities (EM-DAT, 2014). As a result, the costs of flooding can be substantial. For example, the 2011 flash floods in the state of Rio de Janeiro, Brazil, resulted in an estimated $1.68 billion of damages (World Bank, 2012).

Many cities in developing countries are at particular risk from pluvial flooding, due to the development of informal settlements and housing stock constructed from lower quality materials. The flood of 1908 that devastated the city of Hyderabad in India is estimated to have destroyed around 80,000 homes and killed 150,000 people (Apte, 2009). The city is now protected from fluvial flooding by upstream dams.

Storm damage in cities can result from strong winds, as well as from associated heavy rainfall, hail or snow (EEA, 2011). Storm surges are also a common cause of sea flooding in urban areas. For example, the damages from Hurricane Katrina in New Orleans resulted largely from flooding. With high concentrations of buildings and energy systems, cities are particularly susceptible to storm damage. Direct economic costs result from damage to buildings, vehicles, boats, scaffolding, cranes and overhead power networks (Barredo, 2010).

8.2.4 Drought

Drought can lead to a range of impacts in cities, including building subsidence, water shortages, power failures and increased health risks. Drought in the surrounding agricultural region of a city can also result in food shortages, along with increased rural to urban migration.

One of the main impacts of drought in cities is water shortage, particularly in developing countries. Today, around 150 million people are estimated to live in cities with perennial water shortages, and this figure could rise to 1 billion people by 2050, largely due to rapid urbanization in Asia (McDonald et al., 2011; IPCC, 2014). The health impacts associated with droughts also include increased risks of diseases, malnutrition and famine (Logar and van den Bergh, 2011).

Drought can lead to extensive subsidence as the ground under buildings changes in volume due to water loss. Drought can also have less obvious effects on building stock. Despite being located on a canal system, the City of Amsterdam has become increasingly aware that a large proportion of the city's buildings are at risk from periods of reduced rainfall, as the traditional houses are built on wooden piles that dry out and crumble if the water level drops.

8.3 URBAN VULNERABILITY

8.3.1 What is Vulnerability?

Climate vulnerability can be defined as the 'inability to cope with external changes including avoiding harm when exposed to a hazard', which includes 'people's inability to avoid the hazard (exposure), anticipate it, and take measures to avoid or limit its impact; cope with it; and recover from it' (Revi et al., 2014, p. 547).

Compared to rural or small urban areas, cities have large and concentrated populations, a high concentration of buildings, extensive and interdependent infrastructure networks and concentrated economic activity (Satterthwaite et al., 2007; OECD, 2010). These all pose specific risks for cities. The effectiveness of health and emergency services also determines a city's vulnerability where high concentrations of people may be affected by a natural disaster. Furthermore, cities in developing countries are often more vulnerable due to rapid urban population growth, higher levels of poverty, extensive slums, low quality infrastructure and greater future exposure to climate hazards (Hunt and Watkiss, 2011).

Given the large combination of characteristics that affect a city's vulnerability, and the extensive data and information required for its analysis, assessing the vulnerability of any one city is a major task (Hallegatte and Corfee-Morlot, 2011). For example, damages from a hurricane will likely depend on a city's proximity to the coast, the quality of its buildings, the location of populations and key infrastructure within the city, the main economic sectors of the urban economy and the preparedness of people and government services to respond. In this subsection, we attempt to simplify this complexity by examining four broad characteristics that make cities particularly vulnerable to climate-related hazards: location, infrastructure, economic activity and people.

8.3.2 Location

At the regional scale, cities lying in a hurricane belt, on a low-lying river delta or in a high temperature zone will tend to be more vulnerable to climate-related hazards simply due to their geographical location. One of the highest socio-economic risks from climate change is urban coastal flooding, with 65 per cent of large cities located in low elevation coastal zones (McGranahan et al., 2007). Coastal assets exposed to climate risks are an estimated \$3 trillion globally, and this could rise to \$35 trillion or 9 per cent of global gross domestic product (GDP) by 2070. Coastal infrastructure assets in rapidly developing Asian port cities, such as Guangzhou, Shanghai and Kolkata, are particularly vulnerable (Nicholls et al., 2008; OECD, 2010).

The topography of a city and its surrounding environment can also increase its vulnerability to climate hazards. Low-lying districts are more prone to flooding, while neighbourhoods located on or near steep slopes may have higher risks of landslides following storms and flooding. For example, the mountains around Rio de Janeiro have been progressively deforested over time and as a result are now prone to landslides, decomposition and erosion (Sherbinin et al., 2007).

8.3.3 Infrastructure

Cities rely on extensive infrastructure systems to support them, making them more vulnerable to climate impacts than less urbanized areas (OECD, 2010). Well-functioning urban infrastructure is essential for providing public health and safety, supporting economic productivity, reducing social exclusion and promoting the overall well-being of residents (Rode et al., 2014).

Buildings, water distribution networks, sewage systems, energy networks, transport systems and communication grids are all potentially vulnerable to extreme weather events (Revi et al., 2014). Furthermore, a disruption in one system produces cascading effects across others, reducing economic efficiencies and imposing costs on the local and national economy. For example, a disruption to energy infrastructure can impede the delivery of electricity to homes, offices and factories, as well as transportation networks and electronic communication.

The quality and positioning of infrastructure also influences its vulnerability to hazards. For example, transport networks located in low-lying areas and underground are more vulnerable to flooding. Flooding of the underground metro system in London cost more than $12 million in passenger delays between 1999 and 2004 (Arkell and Darch, 2006). At the same time, heat waves in London are now an increasing threat to buckling rail lines that are not manufactured to withstand high temperatures. Similarly, the quality of a city's stormwater drainage and sewage system can determine its vulnerability to pluvial flooding.

Energy and digital networks are key to a city's resilience as many other types of infrastructure and economic sectors rely on energy. For example, in New York City, flooding from Hurricane Sandy disrupted a third of the city's electricity generating capacity and parts of its natural gas distribution system, leaving 2 million city-dwellers without electricity and 80,000 households without gas (City of New York, 2013). The New York Stock Exchange closed for two days, while hospital patients had to be evacuated as emergency power failed.

Flooding and storm damage to poorly adapted buildings is one of the highest risks that cities face from climate change. Elevation, construction materials, number of floors, presence of a basement, shape and age all influence a building's vulnerability to flooding and storms (Acero et al., 2013). Buildings are also often the first line of protection for people. Housing protects people from weather-related injuries, damage and displacement, especially infants, the elderly and those with disabilities or illness (Revi et al., 2014). Consequently, people living in low-quality housing face higher risks. For example, a United Nations study on the slums of Ethiopia's capital, Addis Adaba, found that half of the houses had mud floors, and most had corrugated iron roofs or no ceiling at all (UN Habitat, 2006). These fragile shelters are typical of informal settlements around the world.

8.3.4 Economic Activity

Cities concentrate economic activity (Hallegatte et al., 2011a). As a result, natural disasters can lead to an immediate contraction in economic output, reduce tax revenue, limit investment opportunities, deteriorate fiscal balances and exhaust funds for infrastructure and innovation (OECD, 2010).

Additional costs of climate-related hazards include productivity loss, provision of emergency and post-disaster aid, transport disruption, increased healthcare expenses, relocation and retraining, lost heritage and urban ecosystem damage; all of which can reduce a city's competitiveness.

To understand a city's overall economic vulnerability it is important to account for all components of socio-economic activity and their interdependent relationships (Hallegatte et al., 2011a). Direct costs result from the destruction of physical assets from storms, floods and other extreme events (Krousky, 2013). They can include damages to homes, office buildings, factories, inventories, infrastructure and services.

Additional indirect costs can include the diffusion of costs into the wider economy both in the short term (for example, disruption of basic services) and long term (for example, inflation due to a surge in demand, increased energy costs, bankruptcy, increased public deficit, change in housing prices). Other indirect costs include responses to the economic shock (for example, loss of confidence, change in expectations, increased inequality); financial constraints that slow or prevent reconstruction (for example, limited access to public funding and private capital); and technical constraints that hinder reconstruction (for example, lack of skilled workers or materials) (Hallegatte et al., 2011b).

The composition of a city's economic activity can play a significant role in the vulnerability of an urban economy. For example, a city with a large manufacturing sector may be more vulnerable to disruptions in electricity supply and transportation networks due to pluvial flooding, while a city with a large construction sector may suffer disproportionately from reduced worker productivity due to outdoor heat exhaustion. Cities with a large tourism sector may become less attractive to visitors in peak summer seasons (Revi et al., 2014). Similarly, if vulnerable to climate hazards, cities with large finance or high-tech sectors may become less attractive to international high-skilled workers, who may compare cities on their quality of life.

8.3.5   People

Vulnerable individuals and social groups tend to be less able to avoid a hazard, anticipate it, limit its impact, cope with it or recover from it (Revi et al., 2014). Factors that influence social vulnerability include a lack of access to quality housing; basic infrastructure and services such as water, transportation, energy and sewage; income and technological resources; social networks and connections (Cutter et al., 2003). In addition, age, illness, disability, gender and ethnicity can all increase individual vulnerability.

Poverty increases people's vulnerability. Residents of informal settlements often occupy the cheapest land, which may be prone to flooding such as the Dharavi slums in Mumbai (Ranger et al., 2011) or landslides such as the favelas of Rio de Janeiro. Globally, the numbers of people at risk are substantial. In 2001, 924 million people lived in slums: 32 per cent of the world's population (UN Habitat, 2003). In Mumbai alone, half the population live in slums. As the global population grows rapidly over the next decades (particularly in sub-Saharan Africa and Asia), the concentration of urban poverty, inadequate services and informal settlements is likely to increase substantially (Floater et al., 2014b).

The urban poor typically live in substandard housing made of cheaper materials such as mud, corrugated iron and wood, which increases the likelihood that they will be damaged or collapse from high-intensity storms (OECD, 2010). Even in the richest countries, lower income groups tend to be more at risk. For example, the poorer communities in New Orleans were disproportionately impacted by Hurricane Katrina (Logan, 2006; Masozera et al., 2007). Extreme weather may also increase urban poverty if income levels drop, home enterprises are destroyed or government benefits and services are constrained following a disaster.

Children and the elderly tend to face higher risks of extreme weather due to their physiology. Older people are more prone to heatstroke and are more susceptible to disease. Similarly, children have a higher disease risk as their respiratory and immune systems are not fully developed (Bunyavanich et al., 2003), while they are also less able to care for themselves, communicate effectively and employ coping skills during a disaster (Wisner et al., 1994).

8.4 DEVELOPING RESILIENT CITIES

8.4.1 Market Failure: The Costs of Poorly Managed Urban Growth

The potential benefits of urban growth are substantial. Urbanization has already lifted millions of people out of poverty and continues to contribute significantly to global economic growth. However, evidence suggests that where urbanization is unplanned or poorly managed, the potential economic benefits are reduced while also leading to significant negative impacts on the environment and on the quality of life of urban citizens (Davis et al., 2010; Bourdic and Salat, 2012). These costs are a result of market failure, or the inability of governments to address market failure effectively.

Where markets operate effectively, efficiently and equitably governments should not intervene. However, urban growth that is purely market-based leads to a number of market failures, which in turn can hinder productivity and overall economic growth. Examples of these market failures include urban sprawl, congestion and longer travel times, negative externalities of pollution and carbon emissions, network externalities, reduced agglomeration effects on innovation and skills matching, and imperfect and asymmetric information (for a discussion of these market failures, see Floater et al., 2014a and references therein).

Urban sprawl can be particularly costly. Sprawl can be defined as the uncontrolled expansion of urban development into low density areas, with segregated land use and insufficient infrastructure provision, or leapfrog development (Rode et al., 2014). It increases commuting times, which undermines agglomeration economies based on reduced transport costs. Motorization as a result of urban sprawl also leads to health impacts from increased air pollution, vehicle-related deaths and climate impacts from higher carbon emissions. Urban sprawl also leads to less efficient public provision of goods and services, as costs per capita are higher in dispersed areas. These costs are partly borne by taxpayers, making dispersed development artificially cheap. For example, Litman (2015) has estimated that the external cost of urban sprawl to US taxpayers is over \$400 billion annually.

If cities across the world are to adapt to climate change, governments will need to understand how climate vulnerability interacts with the global phenomenon of rapid urban growth. Let us take the example of urban sprawl once again. In many cities, sprawling suburbs have spread into flood plains or landslide-prone areas, exposing assets and infrastructure to higher risks. The high commuting costs of sprawling urban form become even higher during or following natural disasters, such as storms or floods, when severe transport disruptions take place. Similarly, the cost of replacing public infrastructure after a disaster is higher in these expansive areas than equivalent costs in more densely settled districts. A recent study has also found that urban sprawl is an important factor in influencing the level of emergency public assistance spending, including post-disaster relief efforts, in the United States (Lambert and Catchen, 2013). This demonstrates that while the complexities of developing climate resilience in a rapidly urbanizing world are daunting, there are at the same time potential co-benefits that can be exploited.

8.4.2   The 3C Model: Harnessing the Benefits of Urban Growth

Addressing the market failures associated with poorly managed urban growth requires an alternative model of urban development that locks urban form into a path of greater economic and climate benefits. The Global Commission on the Economy and Climate, in association with the United Nations Secretary General, suggests that an alternative model of well-managed urban growth should be underpinned by three distinct but interconnected pillars: compact urban growth; connected infrastructure; and coordinated governance (Floater et al., 2014b). While this approach, known as the 3C model, requires further testing and refinement, initial empirical evidence suggests that the model can deliver substantial benefits, not only for economic growth but also for social inclusion, health, quality of life and the urban environment.

Improving resilience while simultaneously delivering the 3C model of urban growth requires an integrated approach that combines economic and social development with capacity and climate resilience building. Figure 8.1 summarizes how climate resilience can be integrated into the 3C model to capture the co-benefits of urban growth and resilience policies, while at the same time recognizing some of the tensions between them. The following subsections explore some of the potential opportunities and challenges of this integrated approach for each of the three pillars of the model: compact, connected and coordinated.

8.4.3 Compact Urban Growth

Compact urban growth realizes the benefits of agglomeration economies, through higher densities, contiguous development, functionally and socially mixed neighbourhoods, walkable and human-scale local urban environments, the redevelopment of existing brownfield sites and provision of green space (Floater et al., 2014b). Compact growth represents relatively dense, proximate development, with high levels of accessibility to local employment and services. This type of development is not about urban containment or solely about high density but rather about how urban expansion is managed to develop dense, transit-oriented urban forms.

Compact urban growth can strengthen climate resilience by promoting development in less hazardous zones, affordable housing developments with heat and flood protection and cost-efficient development that frees resources for resilient infrastructure. Compact cities also have more rapid response times to natural disasters and greater efficiency gains in terms of emergency aid spending (Lambert and Catchen, 2013).

Although for the most part compact urban growth and climate adaptation policies have co-benefits – avoiding unnecessary sprawl that both decreases resilience and hampers urban economies – potential policy conflicts will sometimes arise. For example, extreme cases of higher density

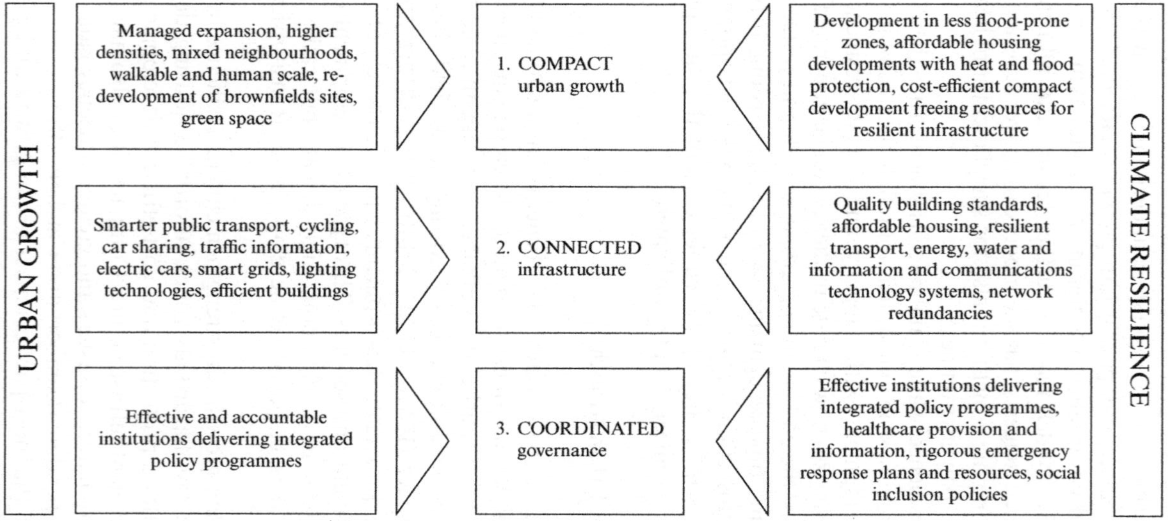

CLIMATE RESILIENCE

Development in less flood-prone zones, affordable housing developments with heat and flood protection, cost-efficient compact development freeing resources for resilient infrastructure	Quality building standards, affordable housing, resilient transport, energy, water and information and communications technology systems, network redundancies	Effective institutions delivering integrated policy programmes, healthcare provision and information, rigorous emergency response plans and resources, social inclusion policies

1. COMPACT urban growth

2. CONNECTED infrastructure

3. COORDINATED governance

Managed expansion, higher densities, mixed neighbourhoods, walkable and human scale, re-development of brownfields sites, green space	Smarter public transport, cycling, car sharing, traffic information, electric cars, smart grids, lighting technologies, efficient buildings	Effective and accountable institutions delivering integrated policy programmes

URBAN GROWTH

Figure 8.1   Compact, Connected, Coordinated: the 3C model of urban growth and climate resilience

living can generate higher temperatures in cities. This implies that compact urban growth policies will need to integrate and be balanced by climate resilience policies, such as zoning for green spaces as part of development planning.

Realizing the benefits of urban agglomeration through the reduction of sprawl, while at the same time strengthening climate resilience, requires strategic spatial planning for transport, land use and urban infrastructure, as well as pricing and information. Urban governments can set the planning and regulatory framework that zone particular areas of the city for particular uses – residential, commercial and industrial – and set building standards. Zoning can prevent high-risk areas such as flood plains from being settled in. At the same time, effective planning can help to provide affordable housing in alternative lower risk zones, a particular priority for low-income groups in developing countries (Satterthwaite et al., 2007).

8.4.4 Connected Infrastructure

Connected infrastructure is cost and energy efficient, climate resilient and socially inclusive, and enables the benefits of urban compact growth (Floater et al., 2014b). It includes innovative urban infrastructure and technology such as efficient transport systems, urban utilities that deliver resource-efficient public services, and energy-efficient buildings.

Connected infrastructure can reduce the impact of climate hazards substantially. Examples include buildings, transport, energy and digital networks, water treatment and sewage systems that are resistant to flooding, buildings that provide heat protection and public transport systems that are reliable and well connected. Connected infrastructure also includes system redundancies that allow networks to continue functioning even when parts of the network are damaged. Infrastructure resilience can be increased with the installation of ventilation systems for cooling buildings, rail tracks with higher heat resistance or construction materials and methods that are more storm resistant.

Delivering infrastructure that is both well connected and climate resilient should draw on a mix of low- and high-tech solutions to take account of future climate risks. For example, New York City has implemented requirements for new hospital buildings to meet construction code standards for flood-resistant construction while at the same time facilitating retrofits for existing hospitals (City of New York, 2013). As part of Copenhagen's climate adaptation plan, the city will be supplementing traditional sewers with a new system of landscaped over-ground water boulevards and large water storage areas in parks and football fields (City of Copenhagen, 2011).

In terms of transport, planning should ensure, for example, that developments near railways have adequate drainage systems or that new rail tracks are raised, since the development of land near railways can increase the risk of flooding.

8.4.5   Coordinated Governance

Cities will need strong leadership, institutions and integrated policies to deliver the 3C model of urban growth and resilience (Floater et al., 2014b). City-level governance is critical for collective action, particularly for the integrated policy intervention needed for infrastructure development and spatial planning. Effective multilevel governance requires horizontal coordination across city-level agencies as well as vertical coordination with regional and national governments (Kern and Alber, 2008). It also requires the facilitation of citizen- and community-led initiatives.

Effective institutions are necessary to deliver climate resilience through integrated policy programmes, including large infrastructure projects, healthcare provision and information, and rigorous emergency response plans. Coordinated governance can strengthen climate resilience by improving the collection and distribution of information on climate and resilience, coordinating adaptation efforts to increase their efficiency and sharing financial resources across departments to fund the most effective measures.

Many adaptation measures can be implemented through the actions of the city government alone. However, in other cases, powers and responsibilities at the municipal level overlap with higher levels of government (Ostrom, 2009). For example, national governments can establish formal mandates for urban resilience that help to mainstream climate adaptation at the city level, insulating it from local-level interests and leadership changes. Similarly, funding from national and regional governments is often required for delivering large urban infrastructure projects.

Coordination is particularly important for an effective emergency response. In the aftermath of a disaster, with hampered communication lines and diverse actors involved, government coordination is key. Rio de Janeiro has created a Centre of Operations, housing representatives from over 30 different departments, with the main purpose of coordinating emergency response. The centre is also used to manage day-to-day city services that can be repurposed during emergencies, thereby increasing efficiency in the use of resources (Resurgent India, 2014). Similarly, Shanghai has developed a multi-hazard early warning system, integrated coordination and cooperation across agencies (Tang et al., 2012).

Health policy is also highly dependent on the coordination of information and funding across different actors to enable individual behavioural changes that successfully increase resilience. For example, workers can decrease the negative impact of heat waves by changing their working hours or clothing if they are aware of the benefits for their health. Hospitals can improve their response to heat-induced health problems if they have access to adequate funding and information.

8.4.6 Policy Tools for Urban Resilience

The effective delivery of climate-resilient cities that are compact, connected and coordinated requires a range of urban policy instruments. These can be divided into four main categories: planning, pricing, finance and information (Table 8.1).

Table 8.1 Policy instruments for developing resilient cities

	City strategies	Examples of policy instruments
Compact urban growth	Development in less flood-prone zones, affordable housing developments with heat and flood protection, cost-efficient compact development freeing resources for resilient infrastructure	Planning and regulation (e.g. Land Value Capture that facilitates compact transport networks) Pricing (e.g. taxation on building in risky areas; pricing to discourage sprawl) Information (e.g. information on risky areas)
Connected infrastructure	Quality building standards, affordable housing, resilient transport, energy, water and information and communications technology systems, network redundancies	Planning and regulation (e.g. building standards) Pricing (e.g. congestion charges) Finance (e.g. public private partnerships, multilateral development banks and international funding) Information (e.g. information on resilient construction materials, future climate change)
Coordinated governance	Effective institutions delivering integrated policy programmes, healthcare provision and information, rigorous emergency response plans and resources, social inclusion policies	Information (e.g. health, information sharing across levels of government) Funding (e.g. cross-departmental public funding)

Urban planners have a critical role to play in increasing the resilience of cities to climate change, especially in developing countries where cities are growing rapidly (Corfee-Morlot et al., 2011). Decisions made today by city planners will have consequences for urban residents for years to come, including their vulnerability to climate change.

The uncertainties surrounding climate outcomes and their impacts require that policy making comprises adequate risk management strategies to avoid harmful lock-in effects that hamper both economic growth and climate resilience. For example, the location and quality of urban infrastructure, such as electricity, transport, communications and water systems, will affect the ability of urban residents and economic activity to withstand and recover from extreme events.

Pricing instruments such as taxes and permit trading can be used to correct for market failures and have been used extensively to reduce carbon emissions and pollution. Taxes and fees can also be used to correct for agents' overly risky behaviour by internalizing existing risk. For example, land use and property taxation could be used to discourage construction in hazardous areas. Licences and tradable permits, similar to those in emissions trading systems, could be used to incentivize the provision of public goods (Bräuninger et al., 2011), such as flood barriers. However, limited evidence exists on the use of pricing instruments to deliver adaptation measures.

A major challenge for cities is the lack of finance for delivering large urban infrastructure projects, particularly in developing countries. In 2013, the World Bank estimated that cities in developing countries required an extra $700 billion a year of investment in public infrastructure simply to keep pace with population growth (World Bank, 2013).

A particularly effective method of funding infrastructure projects is Land Value Capture (LVC). Under LVC, the government captures the increase in the value of land and development that new public infrastructure, such as a new metro line, generates. In Hong Kong the 'Rail plus Property' model of LVC has resulted in compact urban development and delivered multi-million dollar profits for the city's transport corporation (Rode and Floater, 2013). Economically, LVC is well targeted in terms of raising finance specifically from those agents that derive benefits from the investment. Furthermore, LVC not only raises substantial finance but can also focus development around mass transit corridors leading to more compact urban growth (Floater et al., 2014a). In effect, LVC can be seen as a pricing and planning instrument, as well as one of financing.

While traditional sources of funding are necessary, there is an increasing focus on leveraging private finance. For instance, London's Thames Barrier was financed through a public private partnership (PPP)

(Bräuninger et al., 2011). In another example, the World Bank has been developing a City Creditworthiness Initiative to increase access to long-term investment for cities in developing countries through the use of municipal bonds (World Bank, 2015). However, PPP deals need to be well prepared and managed in order to reap the benefits.

International funding will also need to play a key role in financing urban infrastructure projects in developing countries. Multilateral Development Banks (MDBs) and Multilateral Climate Funds both support sustainable and climate-relevant urban activities. However, a limited number of projects currently target urban resilience. Only around 13 per cent of the 186 transport projects funded in 2012 by MDBs were both urban and sustainable. Similarly, only 5 per cent of the $1.83 billion approved for adaptation from 2010 to 2015 by climate funds targeted cities (Floater et al., 2014a; Barnard, 2015).

City governments play a key role in providing information directly or providing funding to independent bodies for research and development activities. Information on future climate can incentivize investments that are resilient and financially sound. Research can help determine the most efficient practices, such as car and cycle sharing, smart grids, information systems, smart utility systems and smart buildings. Allowing for the effective dissemination of information in urban settings can also change individual behaviour and increase the efficacy of emergency responses.

8.5 CONCLUSION

Owing to the concentration of people, assets and economic activity, cities are highly vulnerable to climate-related hazards, and the risks are expected to increase substantially with climate change. As a result, there is growing recognition that adaptation policies that strengthen the resilience of cities need to be integrated into policy making at all levels of government. At the same time, policy makers in many parts of the world will need to develop urban resilience in the context of rapid urban growth. This represents a major challenge not only for many city mayors but also governments responsible for national economic and disaster planning, particularly in the developing world.

This challenge is exacerbated by a lack of available data and measurable indicators at the city level, both in terms of urban growth and urban resilience. Nonetheless, international and national policy makers are beginning to join municipal governments in recognizing not only the scale of the challenge globally but also the role that all levels of government will need to play.

In this chapter, we argue that the first step in developing effective economic policies for resilient cities is understanding the importance of integrating climate adaptation into urban growth strategies. This means recognizing the importance of the 3C model – compact urban growth, connected infrastructure and coordinated governance – for the future growth of cities. It also means a more sophisticated approach to developing resilience in cities.

REFERENCES

Acero, J., Boettle, M., Costa, L. et al., 2013. 'Physical and cost typology for buildings and infrastructure/project database', Deliverable 2.2 of RAMSES Project, European Commission.

Apte, N.Y., 2009. 'Urban floods in context of India', Paper presented at the Economic and Social Commission for Asia and the Pacific Expert Group Meeting on Innovative Strategies towards Flood Resilient Cities in Asia-Pacific, Bangkok, 21–3 July.

Arkell, B.P. and Darch, G.J.C., 2006. 'Impacts of climate change on London's transport systems', *Proceedings of the ICE – Municipal Engineer*, **159**(4), 231–7.

Barnard, S., 2015. 'Climate finance for cities. How can international climate funds best support low-carbon and climate resilient urban development?', ODI Working Paper No. 419.

Barredo, J.I., 2010. 'No upward trend in normalised windstorm losses in Europe: 1970–2008', *Natural Hazards and Earth System Sciences*, **10**, 97–104.

Bhatta, B., 2010. 'Analysis of urban growth and sprawl from remote sensing data', *Advances in Geographic Information Science*, chapter 2. doi: 10.1007/978-3-642-05299-6_2

Bourdic, L. and Salat, S., 2012. 'Building energy models and assessment systems at the district and city scales: a review', *Building Research & Information*, **40**(4), 518–26.

Bräuninger, M., Butzengeiger-Geyer, S., Dlugolecki, A. et al., 2011. *Application of Economic Instruments for Adaptation to Climate Change*, Final Report, CLIMA.C.3./ETU/2010/0011.

Brueckner, J.K., 2011. *Lectures on Urban Economics*, Vol. 1. Cambridge, MA: MIT Press.

Bunyavanich, S., Landrigan, C., McMichael, A. and Epstein, P., 2003. 'The impact of climate change on child health', *Ambulatory Pediatrics*, **3**(1), 44–52.

City of Copenhagen, 2011. *Climate Adaptation Plan*.

City of New York, 2013. *A Stronger, More Resilient New York*. Available at http://www.nyc.gov/html/sirr/html/report/report.shtml (accessed 17 February 2016).

Corfee-Morlot, J., Cochran, I., Hallegatte, S. and Teasdale, P., 2011. 'Multilevel risk governance and urban adaptation policy', *Climatic Change*, **104**, 169–97.

Costa, H., Floater, G., Hooyberghs, H. and de Ridder, K., 2015. 'Climate change, heat stress and labour: a framework for assessing adaptation costs in the city economy', Mimeo, London School of Economics and VITO Urban Climate Service Centre.

Cutter, S., Boruff, B. and Shirley, W.L., 2003. 'Social vulnerability to environmental hazards', *Social Science Quarterly*, **84**(2), 242–61.

Davis, S.J., Caldeira, K. and Matthews, H.D., 2010. 'Future CO^2 emissions and climate change from existing energy infrastructure', *Science*, **329**(5997), 1330–3.

Dobney, K., Baker, C.J., Quinn, A.D. and Chapman, L., 2009. 'Quantifying the effects of high summer temperatures due to climate change on buckling and rail related delays in southeast United Kingdom', *Meteorological Applications*, **16**(2), 245–51.

EEA, 2011. 'Mapping the impacts of natural hazards and technological accidents in Europe. An overview of the last decade', Technical Report No. 13/2010, European Environment Agency.

EM-DAT, 2014. 'Glossary' in EM-DAT, the International Disaster Database. Available at http://www.emdat.be/glossary/ (accessed 15 July 2015).

Floater, G., Rode, P., Friedel, B. and Robert, A., 2014a. 'Steering urban growth: governance, policy and finance', New Climate Economy Cities, Paper 02, LSE Cities, London School of Economics and Political Science.

Floater, G., Rode, P., Robert, A. et al., 2014b. 'Cities and the new climate economy: the transformative role of global urban growth', New Climate Economy Cities, Paper 01, LSE Cities, London School of Economics and Political Science.

Floater, G., Bujak, A., Hamill, G. and Lee, M., 2014c. *Review of Climate Change Losses and Adaptation Costs for Case Studies*. Brussels: RAMSES, European Commission.

Hallegatte, S. and Corfee-Morlot, J., 2011. 'Understanding climate change impacts, vulnerability and adaptation at the city scale: an introduction', *Climatic Change*, **104**, 1–12.

Hallegatte, S., Henriet, F. and Corfee-Morlot, J., 2011a. 'The economics of climate change impacts and policy benefits at city scale: a conceptual framework', *Climatic Change*, **104**, 51–87.

Hallegatte, S., Ranger, N., Mestre, O. et al., 2011b. 'Assessing the climate change impacts, sea level rise and storm surge risk in port cities: a case study on Copenhagen', *Climatic Change*, **104**, 113–37.

Hallegatte, S., Green, C., Nicholls, R. and Corfee-Morlot, J., 2013. 'Future flood losses in major coastal cities', *Nature Climate Change*, **3**, 802–6.

Hardoy, J., and Pandiella, G., 2009. 'Urban poverty and vulnerability to climate change in Latin America', *Environment and Urbanization*, **21**(1), 203–24.

Harlan, S.L. and Ruddell, D.M., 2011. 'Climate change and health in cities: impacts of heat and air pollution and potential co-benefits from mitigation and adaptation', *Current Opinion in Environmental Sustainability*, **3**(3), 126–34.

Hunt, A. and Watkiss, P., 2011. 'Climate change impacts and adaptation in cities: a review of the literature', *Climatic Change*, **104**, 13–49.

Hunter, P., 2012. *The St Petersburg Flood Protection Barrier: Design and Construction*, Paris: CETMEF PIANCs.

IPCC, 2007. *Climate Change 2007: The Physical Science Basis. Contribution of Working Group I to the Fourth Assessment Report of the Intergovernmental Panel on Climate Change*, edited by S. Solomon, D. Qin, M. Manning et al. (eds). Cambridge: Cambridge University Press.

IPCC, 2014. *Climate Change 2014: Impacts, Adaptation, and Vulnerability. Part A: Global and Sectoral Aspects. Contribution of Working Group II to the Fifth Assessment Report of the Intergovernmental Panel on Climate Change*, edited by C.B. Field, V.R. Barros, D.J. Dokken et al. (eds). Cambridge and New York: Cambridge University Press.

Kern, K. and Alber, G., 2008. 'Governing climate change in cities: modes of urban climate governance in multi-level systems', *Competitive Cities and Climate Change*, OECD Conference Proceedings, Milan, Italy, 9–10 October. Paris: Organisation for Economic Co-operation and Development, pp. 171–96.

Krousky, C., 2013. 'Informing climate adaptation: a review of the economic costs of natural disasters, their determinants, and risk reduction options', Resources for the Future Discussion Paper, Resources for the Future, Washington DC.

Lambert, T. and Catchen, J., 2013. 'The impact of urban sprawl on disaster relief spending: an exploratory study', MPRA Paper No. 51887.

Litman, T., 2015. 'Analysis of public policies that unintentionally encourage and subsidize sprawl', New Climate Economy Cities, Paper 04, LSE Cities, London School of Economics and Political Science.

Logan, J., 2006. *The Impact of Katrina: Race and Class in Storm-damaged Neighborhoods*, S4, Spatial Structures in the Social Sciences, Hurricane Katrina Project. Providence, RI: Brown University.

Logar, I. and van den Bergh, J.C.J.M., 2011. *Methods for Assessment of the Costs of Droughts*, CONHAZ WP05_1 Final Report.

Masozera, M., Bailey, M. and Kerchner, C., 2007. 'Distribution of impacts of natural disasters across income groups: a case study of New Orleans', *Ecological Economics*, **63**, 299–306.

McDonald, R.I., Green, P., Balk, D. et al., 2011. 'Urban growth, climate change, and freshwater availability', *Proceedings of the National Academy of Sciences*, **108**(15), 6312–17.

McGranahan, G., Balk, D. and Anderson, B., 2007. 'The rising tide: assessing the risks of climate change and human settlements in low elevation coastal zones', *Environment and urbanization*, **19**(1), 17–3.

Nicholls, R.J., Hanson, S., Herweijer, C. et al., 2008. 'Ranking port cities with high exposure and vulnerability to climate extremes', OECD Environment Working Papers. doi: 10.1787/19970900

OECD, 2010. *Cities and Climate Change*. Paris: OECD Publishing.

Ostrom, E., 2009. 'A polycentric approach for coping with climate change', Background Paper to the 2010 World Development Report, Policy Research Working Paper No. 5095, World Bank, Washington, DC.

Ranger, N., Hallegatte, S., Battacharya, S. et al., 2011. 'An assessment of the potential impact of climate change on flood risk in Mumbai', *Climatic Change*, **104**, 139–67.

Resurgent India, 2014. *Smart Cities*. Available at http://www.credai.org/sites/default/files/Conclave-2014-Report-smart-cities.pdf (accessed 17 February 2016).

Revi, A., Satterthwaite, D.E., Aragón-Durand, F. et al., 2014. 'Urban areas', in *Climate Change 2014: Impacts, Adaptation, and Vulnerability. Part A: Global and Sectoral Aspects. Contribution of Working Group II to the Fifth Assessment Report of the Intergovernmental Panel on Climate Change*, edited by C.B. Field, V.R. Barros, D.J. Dokken et al. (eds.). Cambridge: Cambridge University Press, chapter 8.

Rode, P. and Floater, G., 2013. *Going Green: How Cities are Leading the Next Economy: Final Report*. London: LSE Cities and ICLEI.

Rode, P., Floater, G., Thomopoulos, N. et al., 2014. 'Accessibility in cities: transport and urban form', New Climate Economy Cities, Paper 03, LSE Cities, London School of Economics and Political Science.

Satterthwaite, D., Huq, S., Pelling, M., Reid, H. and Romero Lankao, P., 2007. 'Adapting to climate change in urban areas: the possibilities and constraints in low- and middle-income nations', Human Settlements Discussion Paper Series, Theme: Climate Change and Cities – 1, International Institute for Environment and Development, London.

Sherbinin, A., Schiller, A. and Pulsipher, A., 2007. 'The vulnerability of global cities to climate hazards', *Environment and Urbanization*, **19**(1), 39–64.

Tang, X., Feng, L., Zou, Y. and Mu, H., 2012. 'The Shanghai multi-hazard warning system: addressing the challenge of disaster risk reduction in an urban megalopolis', in M. Golnaraghi (ed.), *Institutional Partnerships in Multi-hazard Early Warning Systems*. Heidelberg: Springer, pp. 159–79.

UN Habitat, 2003. *The Challenge of Slums: Global Report on Human Settlements*. London: Earthscan Publications.

UN Habitat, 2006. *Situation Analysis of Slum Settlements in Addis Ababa*. Nairobi: United Nations Human Settlements Programme (UN-HABITAT).

UNEP-UN Habitat, 2005. *Local Capacities for Global Agendas*, Brochure. Available at http://www.unep.org/urban_environment/PDFs/Coastal_Pollution_Role_of_Cities.pdf (accessed 17 February 2016).

Voogt, J.A., 2002. 'Urban heat island', in I. Douglas (ed.), *Encyclopaedia of Global Environmental Change*. New York: John Wiley and Sons, pp. 660–6.

Wisner, B., Blaikie, P., Cannon, T. and Davis, I., 1994. *At Risk: Natural Hazards, People's Vulnerability and Disasters*, 2nd edn. London: Routledge.

World Bank, 2012. *Avaliação de Perdas e Danos Inundações e eslizamentos na Região Serrana do Rio de Janeiro – Janeiro de 2011*, Brazil: World Bank Group.

World Bank, 2013. *Feature Story. Financing Sustainable Cities: How We're Helping Africa's Cities Raise their Credit Ratings*. Available at http://www.worldbank.org/en/news/feature/2013/10/24/financing-sustainable-cities-africa-creditworthy (accessed 17 February 2016).

World Bank, 2015. *Brief. City Creditworthiness Initiative: A Partnership to Deliver Municipal Finance*. Available at http://www.worldbank.org/en/topic/urbandevelopment/brief/city-creditworthiness-initiative (acessed 17 February 2016).

9. Climate-resilient development in agrarian economies

Mintewab Bezabih, Stefania Lovo, Gregor Singer and Courtney McLaren

9.1 INTRODUCTION

The negative impacts of climate change are arguably most felt by the predominantly agrarian and rain-fed economies of many developing countries (Kurukulasuriya et al., 2006; Dinar et al., 2012). It is such vulnerability that has underscored the importance of mechanisms that enhance the agricultural sector's capacity to cope better with the adverse impacts of climate change (Maddison, 2007; Bryan et al., 2011).

Climate change poses an additional challenge to the mainstay agricultural sector, which is already faced with resource degradation, caused by heavy dependence on natural resources and agricultural stagnation, forming a nexus of deepening poverty and further dependence on ecologically fragile environments (Mellor, 1988; Dasgupta and Mäler, 1994; Berry et al., 2003). The need for substantial increases in food production to meet the demands of a growing population adds further pressure for growth in the agricultural sector (Berry et al., 2003; New Climate Economy, 2014).

Improved climate resilience is required such that adaptive capacity is built in a manner that is compatible with the needs of the agricultural sector to meet increasing demand and to replenish the natural resource base. Indeed, in the case of the more severe states of nature of climate change, modifying existing agricultural practice will be insufficient and instead an integrated approach addressing the aforementioned challenges is emphasized (Howden et al., 2007). Accordingly, climate-resilient development is focused on integrating consideration of climate impacts in development strategies, such that climate adaptation and mitigation activities are compatible with pre-existing development objectives (USAID, 2014).

Despite the challenges, substantial evidence justifies optimism that with adaptation the adverse effects of climate change on agriculture can be significantly reduced. A 2007 study found that alterations made to existing agricultural systems could achieve substantial climate resilience (Howden et al., 2007). Several studies in the African context have identified substantial potential for adaptation to improve the resilience and productivity of agriculture (Benhin, 2006; Mano and Nhemachena, 2007; Kurukulasuriya and Mendelsohn, 2008).

Embarking on a climate-resilient development path, however, is not without its difficulties. The very low level of development of many agrarian economies itself is a testament to the monumental policy challenges. Furthermore, the inherently future-oriented nature of climate adaptation and mitigation objectives may not always align with the urgency and multifaceted features of existing challenges. Therefore, a clearer understanding is required of what climate-resilient development entails in terms of design and implementation. This chapter assesses the opportunities and challenges for climate-resilient development in agrarian economies.

The chapter is structured as follows. Section 9.2 looks at the intervention options available for climate-resilient development. Section 9.3 evaluates the policy and institutional challenges faced in the path of climate-resilient development in the context of wider green growth objectives. Section 9.4 concludes.

9.2 INTERVENTION OPTIONS FOR A CLIMATE-RESILIENT AGRICULTURE

This section primarily explores various practices that support a 'double win', that is, opportunities for growth in productivity and consequently income, as well as resilience to a changing climate. These include the successes already achieved, as well as the potential to support future developmental and environmental gains.

9.2.1 Soil Conservation Investment

The emphasis on soil conservation as a climate change adaptation tool, primarily in the form of contour farming or terracing and building of soil conservation structures on the farm, stems from the strong and significant impact of climate change on soil erosion rates (Boardman and Favis-Mortlock, 1993; O'Neal et al., 2005). Particular to developing countries, soil conservation is considered one of the major strategies farmers employ to adapt to the threat of climate change (Deressa et al., 2009). Based on their study in the Nile Basin of Ethiopia, Di Falco and Bulte (2012) show that the adoption of soil conservation structures and tree planting reduces the impact of climate-related shocks. In addition, Kato et al. (2009) find that in response to perceived long-term changes in temperature and rainfall, more than 30 per cent of farmers adopted soil and water conservation measures.

9.2.2 Afforestation and Agroforestry

Following extensive cultivation, soils in sub-Saharan Africa are far less nutrient rich relative to other regions, with substantial depletion of important nutrients including nitrogen, phosphorus and potassium (Henao and Baanante, 2006). Additionally, African soils have been found to be particularly low in carbon, whose content promotes moisture and nutrient retention, that is so important given the region's heightened exposure and vulnerability to climate change (Winterbottom et al., 2013). While the use of fertilizer has been shown to improve soil fertility, some studies have found fertilizer's cost-effectiveness to be dependent on threshold levels of organic matter contents (Marenya and Barrett, 2009).

Certain varieties of trees and shrubs have been found to retain and redistribute moisture throughout the surrounding soil (Caldwell et al., 1998). The integration of perennial plants – trees or shrubs – on cropland supports increased soil fertility through increased nutrient content (Allison, 1973) and the carbon released by the decomposition of organic matter (Winterbottom et al., 2013). Moreover, in providing a supplementary income source, agroforestry can spread and minimize risk should another crop fail, while also promoting a broader and more resilient ecosystem compared to crop plants alone. Evidence from Niger shows that increasing tree cover between 10- to 20-fold (New Climate Economy, 2014) increased resilience during the 2004–05 floods. Further, the restoration of degraded lands also increased yields to effectively double annual incomes across a million rural households, equivalent to food security for 2.5 million people (Winterbottom et al., 2013; New Climate Economy, 2014). Additionally, agroforestry initiatives across East Africa have obtained yields comparable to those associated with fertilizer use (Akinnifesi et al., 2008).

9.2.3 Conservation Agriculture

Classified as the 'means of reproducing plants and water recurrently and sustainably from landscapes and the soils that cover them', conservation agriculture is a composite of three main agricultural practices: (1) reduction or elimination of tilling; (2) retaining or fostering crop cover; and (3) diversification of crops (Derpsch et al., 2010). By increasing the water retention qualities of the soil, conservation agriculture can increase resilience to climatic volatility. Further, these techniques are compatible with smallholders' minimal financial, capital and labour assets, requiring no specialized tools, irrigation and minimal labour with low or limited tillage (Hobbs, 2007; Derpsch et al., 2010; Kassie et al., 2010). However, the approach requires tailoring to the specific context. It has the highest likelihood of achieving its objectives when those within the community work together to determine and implement the specific techniques most appropriate for their particular conditions and constraints (Dumanski et al., 2006); a challenge not to be understated.

9.2.3.1 Reduced or eliminated tillage

While formerly a mainstay of farming, extensive and long-running tilling has since been recognized as a primary contributor to soil erosion and degradation via weakened water infiltration, nutrient run-off and disturbed microbial activity (Hobbs, 2007). Reducing or eliminating excessive tilling allows degraded soils to be restored and extends the maturity period to facilitate a more robust growing season (Derpsch et al., 2010). As an example, a South Asian study found no tillage methods more cost-effective (Hobbs et al., 2008). Moreover, its reduced labour requirements facilitated labour allocation to other income generating activities (Hobbs, 2007).

Despite a growth in global implementation from 45 to 111 million hectares (ha) between 1999 and 2009, low tillage methods have not yet been widely adopted in Africa; however its potential is being increasingly recognized (Derpsch et al., 2010). Following farmer-focused promotion, Tunisia's use of no tillage increased from 27 ha on ten farms in 1999 to 6,000 ha on 78 farms in 2007 (Derpsch et al., 2010). In southern and eastern Africa, no tillage has been incorporated for rehabilitation purposes across over 100,000 smallholders in highly degraded areas in Zambia, Zimbabwe and Swaziland, and within conservation initiatives in Kenya, Tanzania, Lesotho, Swaziland, Mozambique and Malawi (Derpsch et al., 2010).

9.2.3.2 Ground cover/mulch

Coverage of the ground surface and cover crops has been widely noted to increase biodiversity in the soil, improve water retention and nutrient development (Hobbs, 2007), and prevent compaction (Scopel et al., 2013). Ground cover has been associated with reduced likelihood of weed germination (Hobbs, 2007), while other studies found that increased ground cover and no-tillage methods promote soil fauna and increased microbial activity that aid in pest resilience (Kennedy, 1999).

9.2.3.3 Diversification

Climate change is predicted to impact both the biotic (pests and pathogens) and abiotic (solar radiation, hydrological cycles, temperature) systems, adversely affecting agricultural systems and production (Lin, 2011). Crop diversification supports climate resilience in two key ways. First, agricultural systems are better able to suppress pest transmissions and outbreaks and second, it acts as a shock absorber against increased climatic variability (Di Falco et al., 2010; Lin, 2011). While diversification is primarily an effective strategy against environmental variability, for diversification to render sufficient productivity benefits, the level of environmental variability needs to be sufficiently high (Bezabih and Gaeback, 2010) or risk-prone areas with high rainfall variability need to be targeted (Di Falco and Chavas, 2009).

9.2.4 Adoption of Adaptive New Varieties

While conventional improved varieties are largely associated with yield improvement (for example, Asfaw et al., 2011), research into varietal development is increasingly focused on the development of technologies that have risk reducing features. Examples include the system of rice intensification (SRI) package used in many countries on the Indian subcontinent and increasingly in sub-Saharan Africa (Moser and Barrett, 2003) and the drought resistant and and high yielding package for South Asia, Southeast Asia, and Africa (Kumar et al., 2014).

9.2.5 Water Harvesting

A predominately rain-fed agricultural system also poses challenges regarding the strategic behaviour of smallholder farms in terms of their coping mechanisms and risk minimization in the face of yield variability (Cooper et al., 2008). Adequately improving water harvesting systems requires a paradigm shift where the water governance issues of rain-fed agriculture are conceptualized in terms of supply variability as opposed to an absolute supply issue (Rosegrant et al., 2002). In this regard, the past three decades have seen the development of several water harvesting methods to support resilience to precipitation variability (Critchley and Gowing, 2012). Water harvesting has delivered the largest gains in areas with low rainfall (Mazvimavi et al., 2008).

9.2.6 Synergies

As none of the techniques discussed here can be considered on their own, synergistic approaches are recommended for the multiple challenges smallholders face amidst climate change. As an example, traditional activities in the rural communities create competition for biomass resources that are also needed for ground cover in conservation agriculture. Integrating agroforestry on cropland may lessen that competition (Scopel et al., 2013). However, Hassan and Nhemachena (2008) found that in most cases adaptation strategies embodied a menu of measures implemented in conjunction with one another, rather than in isolation. For example, combining conservation agriculture with agroforestry supports the natural creation and deposit of ground cover, compounding its benefits and increasing efficiency in resource use. In Zimbabwe, combining water harvesting and conservation agriculture yielded increases in returns to labour between two and three times and to gross margins between four and seven times those of traditional techniques (Mazvimavi et al., 2008).

9.3　FROM CLIMATE-RESILIENT AGRICULTURE TO GREEN GROWTH

The techniques discussed in the previous section, when implemented at the right scale, can support a third objective, the transition to a low carbon economy (Winterbottom et al., 2013; New Climate Economy, 2014). This section looks at the challenges of supporting sustainable and climate resilience development with a view to achieving 'green growth' in agriculture.

9.3.1　Scaling Up

While 'islands of success' have been identified regarding adaptation measures (Cooper et al., 2008, p. 26), in order to make a significant impact projects will need to be scaled up. This entails substantial challenges that require significant planning and strong policies. In order to maximize green growth potential, green objectives should not obstruct development goals. Supporting the productive capacity and income level of the poor is essential in order to support a genuine and all-encompassing economic development. As such, policies aimed at achieving green growth must have a triple focus: supporting resilience to the climate change; improving living standards of the targeted population; as well as mitigating climate change as efficiently as possible. Pagiola and Platais (2007) reason that green policies should focus on populations where the potential to reach environmental objectives is highest. However, this approach does not prioritize the poor and so may not deliver developmental outcomes if the policy space is restricted by limited budgets, as is usually the case. It therefore becomes essential to appropriately target policies so that they are capable of delivering on all the three goals.

Although poverty and land degradation are often coupled together, failing to properly target policies such as payments for environmental services will not necessarily address issues of poverty. Even within poor areas income distribution can vary substantially (Pagiola et al., 2005). As noted by Pagiola et al. (2005), the degree to which a policy affects the poor is determined by the compatibility of the policy's design and implementation to the local context.

9.3.2   Challenges of Tri-fold Goals

As green growth in principle is a 'triple win', its achievement presents a challenge of balancing pursuit of the three goals, with inherent trade-offs requiring consideration. In looking to encourage increased participation, offering a menu of environmental services offers the poor the ability to choose the approaches that are most compatible with their circumstances as well as exploiting synergies (Lovo et al., 2015). For example, The N'hambita Project in Mozambique offers participants the possibility to choose from a variety of agroforestry systems including tree planting, orchards or intercropping (Jindal et al., 2012), while Nicaragua's Silvopastoral Ecosystem Management Project allows participants to choose the level of their investment in land use changes, ranging from relatively cheap alterations such as sowing improved grasses, to relatively more expensive ones such as fodder banks (Pagiola et al., 2008).

However, this flexibility may compromise the economic efficiency of the projects and potentially limit their environmental effectiveness. Transaction and supervision costs are likely to be higher when a range of environmental services need to be monitored (Jindal et al., 2012). In other instances, flexibility may hamper efficient adoption. Farmers may opt for partial implementation (Scopel et al., 2013), which may be detrimental where interactions between the techniques propel the gains in productivity and environmental resilience.

An additional challenge is the need to grasp the interactions between the local setting and the green-inspired project in implementing the different interventions. Given the substantial amount of resources, monetary and otherwise entailed with these projects, piloting projects is recommended to increase the likelihood that the intervention is a success. Doing so allows for adjustments to be made before implementation should the project require tweaking to suit a particular context. Furthermore, it allows the would-be administrators of the programme to become familiar with the arrangements in practice and address unforeseen outcomes. To ensure the results of the pilot are as accurate as possible, guidelines for policy analysis would be advisable to provide the most accurate initial assessment of the programme.

9.3.3 Financial Considerations and Limitations

Like any other investment project, agricultural adaptation efforts are characterized by the time frame for flow of costs and benefits, such that costs are incurred in the initial phases and the full benefits of investing in soil improvements are realized years later (Hobbs, 2007; Yesuf and Bluffstone, 2007). Further, conservation agriculture is noted for having a transitionary period during which adverse effects, such as initial weed issues, may lead to abandonment of the techniques before benefits are realized (Hobbs, 2007). Therefore, policies should look to reflect the time preference of their targeted populations and increase awareness of the full extent of both short- and long-term benefits.

At times, seemingly attractive investment options could be adversely affected by the asset constrained situation of many smallholders and the long-term nature of such investments. In line with this, between 66 and 83 per cent of farmers surveyed in Malawi, Mozambique and Zambia were reported to have been aware of the benefits of agroforestry, despite very low adoption rates (Akinnifesi et al., 2008).

For externally funded project-based interventions, sustainability and coverage are critical issues. Even well-funded projects may see limited and unsustainable success. For instance, while projects such as the N'hambita Community Carbon Project in Mozambique were effective in reaching the poor – many of their participants were in the poorest demographic – the income effect was found to be small (Jindal et al., 2012). Participants had little to say about the impact of agroforestry, but instead emphasized the importance of cash payments. Meanwhile unexpected increases in carbon emissions as a consequence of payments increasing the purchasing power of participants were found to threaten the programme's effectiveness regarding environmental objectives (Jindal et al., 2012).

Cash-in-hand payments, considered effective by some (e.g. Pagiola and Platais, 2007), may pose a challenge in terms of financial sustainability. Programmes often require sustainable, stable funding in order to be successful in the long run (Swallow and Goddard, 2013). Increasing the link between the beneficiaries of environmental services and their providers can help, as seen in the case of the Mexican Payment for Hydrological Environmental Services Project whereby partial financing came from water use fees (García-Amado et al., 2011). Wunder et al. (2008) find that projects are more effective and efficient when user financed, as opposed to government financed. However, this is not always feasible, particularly where public benefits exceed private ones, leading to suboptimal incentives to invest in the resource, as is often the case, for example, with biodiversity and water services.

A common way of correcting for insufficient financing that restricts efficient implementation of an intervention is subsidization (New Climate Economy, 2014). However, it should be noted that when the problems exceed narrow finance-related difficulties, subsidization cannot be expected to support an efficient outcome. Indeed, merely increasing financial subsidization fails to account for the multiple facets and interactions contributing to low productivity and poverty in such settings.

Further, the use of subsidies to poor households to encourage greater participation may not be widely utilized given their expense. While the targeting of the desired populations may lower the costs of the subsidies themselves, the added expenses for targeting, investigating and selecting the households is likely to partly offset such gains. In order to effectively and efficiently target households, Groom et al. (2009) suggest land endowments, education level, household structure and the institutional constraints, such as those pertaining to land tenure, as indicators for identification of households appropriate for targeting. In some cases, a stratified subsidy system can allow for regional diversity to be taken into account to better match the unique needs of participants. This was seen with the land conservation programme in China (Xu et al., 2010). By accounting for variations in the local context of potential participants, targeting, while an expense, holds the potential to support more effective programmes and may be more cost-effective in the long run.

When it comes to compensation, the design of the payment schemes should reflect the financial requirements of poor households. Failure to do so not only inhibits the poor from upward mobility but disincentivizes participation in such environmental programmes, therein derailing all the objectives of green growth. While seemingly logical, regular payments of the same denomination are not necessarily compatible with participating households' liquidity constraints. This was found to be the case in western Uganda, where regular payments from a payment for environmental services programme were only found suitable for participants who already had consistent income streams (Jayachandran, 2013). Thus, conditional payments in arrears may prove more suitable for the liquidity constrained, as may upfront payments in order to support reserves in case of emergency.

9.3.4 Institutions and their Functionality

The adoption of climate adaptation and mitigation interventions is highly dependent on the conditioning institutional environment. For instance, the uptake of soil conservation activities, a key climate adaptation tool (Kato et al., 2009), is highly influenced by the property rights regime (e.g. Besley, 1995; Di Falco et al., 2011). For example, the success of Niger's agroforestry experience has been primarily attributed to a shift in legislation that recognized smallholder tree ownership, creating incentives to invest in the long-term success of the resource (Winterbottom et al., 2013). Further, power and resource access imbalances associated with land access are shown to negatively impact the distribution of benefits, and hence the likelihood of participation of poorer and landless communities in watershed development activities (Kerr, 2002). Related to this, credible enforcement of the legal framework is an important aspect of institutional functionality as seen in Zimbabwe's Communal Areas Management Programme for Indigenous Resources initiative where district authorities retained a majority of benefits intended for participants of the initiative (Frost and Bond, 2008). Other types of institutional improvements were also found to be critical in the development of a climate resilient economy in Africa. For instance, Hassan and Nhemachena (2008) show that improved access to extension and credit services has a positive impact on farmers' probabilities of adopting adaptation strategies.

9.3.5 Education and Extension Services

Education plays an important role in the adoption of adaptation measures by, first and foremost, improving knowledge of climate change impacts. While experience was found to influence the correct perception of climate change, in assessing whether those who correctly perceived climate change adapted to it, Maddison (2007) found education to be the decisive attribute across ten African countries examined.

Training schemes and technical assistance can increase the technical knowledge and skills necessary to make the greatest environmental and welfare gains possible through a given green agricultural programme. This was found in the cases of the Pimampiro payment for ecosystem services programme and the PROFAFOR scheme in Ecuador (Wunder and Albán, 2008).

A number of studies have found that the rates of adoption of soil and water conservation practices were improved when extension services were made accessible (Anderson and Thampapillai, 1990; Baidu-Forson, 1999; Bekele and Drake, 2003; Maddison, 2007; Tizale, 2007; Hassan and

Nhemachena, 2008). It is not enough for these services to be made available. Because of the seasonal nature of agriculture, the timing in which these services are provided is crucial for getting substantial participation (Feder et al., 2004). Different agro-climatic zones, even within a country or region, will have different timings regarding agricultural seasons and as such a standard roll out of programmes will not be as effective as those that match the seasonal experience of the zone. Furthermore, courses should present season-specific information to be as relevant to the current needs of the farmers as possible.

In the case of conservation agriculture, the practices associated with a no-tillage approach vary substantially from the traditional plough-based systems (Scopel et al., 2013). Adoption of conservation agriculture amongst small-scale farmers becomes primarily an issue of knowledge gaps at various levels. Because these practices differ so greatly from what has been traditionally relied upon, farmers must understand what the practice truly entails in terms of investment, timing and correct application. These include understanding the ecological concepts underpinning the practice, the new crop management techniques required to maximize the benefits and address the new challenges and the necessary changes in the application of production inputs, for example, water inputs (Scopel et al., 2013). While these knowledge gaps are important to address, it is also necessary to address the risks perceived by farmers in making such a significant shift (Scopel et al., 2013), which may require support in terms of education on the yield expectations and timing. This again highlights the need for research on the outcomes of such climate-resilient agricultural practices in order to better inform understanding of the potential, both at the policy level and at the small-scale farmer level.

9.3.6 Complementary Policies

As discussed in the introduction, climate-resilient development in agriculture is multi-faceted, expected to address mainstream economic objectives, with consideration of the natural resource base (protecting the environment) and with credible actions towards climate change adaptation and mitigation. Such multidimensionality calls for a holistic approach with synchronization of complementary policies that look to address the wider inhibiters of participation, such as credit and insurance market imperfections, as well as tenure insecurity.

The advantage of complementing climate adaptation initiatives with other policies is demonstrated, for example, by insurance schemes paired with climate-adaptive technology adoption interventions (Graff-Zivin and Lipper, 2008); off-farm work provision paired with labour saving agroforestry practices (Groom et al., 2009); and environmental awareness training combined with afforestation projects (Schwartzman, 2005). Similarly, Pagiola et al. (2005) note that when property rights are insecure, initiatives to support increased conservation and reductions in poverty will not reach their potential.

However, implementing seemingly complementary policies that promote climate-resilient development may not always be feasible. In some cases, if climate-resilient policies are not structured to reflect the local land ownership context, the many poor, small-scale farmers who lack formal entitlement could be unnecessarily excluded from initiatives that would benefit both themselves and the environmental goals. This was found to be the case in Costa Rica, where the number of poor farmers participating in the payments for ecosystem services increases substantially once formal land titles were no longer considered a prerequisite (Pagiola, 2008). A study of a payment for environmental services programme in Indonesia found that the initiative itself may have improved both the property rights present and their enforceability, and consequently provided the community with enhanced bargaining power against external commercial interests, in this case the logging companies (Engel and Palmer, 2008).

9.3.7 Equity and Inclusion

The degree of achievement of climate-resilient development, like any other intervention, is heavily influenced by the local economic, social and cultural context. Supporting its success therefore necessitates that barriers to participation within these realms are addressed. Participatory approaches are heavily recommended to promote programme sustainability and a strong impact (Axinn, 1988; Braun et al., 2000).

The effectiveness of climate-resilient interventions in agriculture to deliver their goals is as crucial as their applicability at a larger scale. Without the potential for economies of scale, projects that invoke meaningful reductions in poverty and climate vulnerability through lower carbon practices are unlikely to be adopted more widely as projects compete for scarce financial resources. Consequently, the notion of transaction costs and scaling is of great relevance. Poor farmers tend to own or work on relatively small plots, and while their collective behaviour may have significant environmental implications, implementing green agricultural policies will often be more expensive per hectare when targeting a large number of small plots. As a result, as in cases such as the PROFAFOR project in Ecuador, green agricultural policies may set minimum plot size requirements, in this case 50 ha, in order to achieve environmental goals with least cost, however, in doing so, they restrict their ability to reach the poorest populations (Engel and Palmer, 2008).

In order to accommodate the restrictions of limited funds, policies should be designed to reflect the specifics of the local setting to capitalize on context-specific opportunities; often this will entail integrating greater flexibility. To combat high transaction costs, projects can promote small-scale farmers to group together to participate in programmes, as was found across 23 carbon sequestration projects in 11 African countries (Jindal et al., 2008). Providing the flexibility for both individual and group participants can broaden the coverage of various programmes (Dasgupta and Beard, 2007).

Even if programmes look to support greater inclusion of the poor there still may be an inequitable distribution of participation and benefits. Corbera et al. (2007) argue that existing inequities may be reinforced by the introduction of community contracts. In these cases, rectifying these imbalances for a sustainably fair outcome requires meaningful involvement of all stakeholders and recognition of customary rights and compensation in accordance (Ostrom, 1990).

9.3.8 Gender

The status of women holds substantial implications for the success of initiatives over the long term. In the realm of climate-resilient development, gender equity has a reinforcing relationship with its success. Despite women carrying out 80 per cent of agricultural work and exceeding their male counterparts' weekly hours dedicated to food production by 10–12 hours, in rural sub-Saharan Africa 95 per cent of external resources and assistance goes to males (Winterbottom et al., 2013). At the same time, women in developing countries are considered to feel most profoundly the impacts of environmental degradation (Denton, 2002). This misallocation has resulted in an important missed opportunity. Should the gender gap be narrowed, it is estimated that agricultural productivity would increase by over 20 per cent in the region (Quisumbing, 2003).

Kerr (2002) points out that in the Watershed Development Project, ensuring the inclusion of marginalized women throughout the process was crucial to both social and environmental objectives. In order for policies to effectively address issues of poverty and ensure environmental sustainability, communal laws and rights should be examined through gender-sensitive evaluation criteria (Besley and Burgess, 2000; Lovo et al., 2015). Following investigation of the gender context, including differences in perceptions, strategies would be prudent to incorporate a gender-specific focus to their education and extension services (Kanesathasan, 2012).

Moreover, strategies could support women's empowerment for long-term improvements in equity in broad terms that will serve to benefit the more specific agricultural development goals. Of course, altering gender norms is a momentous task and is certainly not restricted to agriculture, nor easily addressed.

However, improving the productive capacity of women and bridging the gender gaps in agriculture, with specific emphasis on increasing communication of gender equity oriented goals and the inclusion of both male and female participants (Kanesathasan, 2012) could go a long way in contributing towards the achievement of economic empowerment of women.

There are a number of effective steps that can be taken in the short term. For instance, previously formalized land rights tended to take a patrilineal shape, with poor and vulnerable household groups, particularly women, losing out in the process (Besley and Burgess, 2000; Platteau, 2000; Deininger et al., 2008). Accordingly, there has been increasing interest in new ways of strengthening both individual and communal land rights in Africa. These include strengthening customary land rights, recognizing occupancy short of full title, improving female land ownership and decentralizing land administration (Deininger et al., 2008).

9.4 CONCLUSIONS

In poor, agriculture-based economies, the threat of climate change coupled with deepening poverty make climate-resilient development less of an optional policy path and more of an imperative one. With the adoption of climate-resilient development as a mainstream development path, understanding the associated constraints and opportunities is crucial for successful growth of the agricultural sector. The objective of this chapter has been to provide an assessment of these opportunities and constraints, through the evaluation of related programmes and projects.

The analysis is based on a review of theoretical and empirical studies that evaluate interventions regarded as leading to climate-resilient development or green growth in some cases. This assessment led to three major findings. First, the success of interventions contributing towards climate-resilient development is heterogeneous and largely reliant on the institutional and policy environment. Second, among successful interventions, wider applicability depends on the possibility of scaling up. Third, complementarities of policies and projects for a holistic approach, while essential, may not always be guaranteed.

Overall, the key message is one of interactions. On the one hand, interactions between initiatives can offer significant gains to all objectives. On the other hand, the interactions between policies and socio-economic factors can either support or hinder the successes of the policies in scaling up and sustaining such initiatives. Well-informed policy design will support the greatest gains towards achieving the elusive 'triple win' of green growth. The varying local contexts, including the social, economic and political, create constraints on policies. Flexibility and forethought is key. Supporting participation by all relevant stakeholders will allow for their local knowledge to be put to use and for initiatives to reflect their needs accurately, as well as ensure important segments of the population are not left out. Policies cannot operate on their own, and corrective measures to address market failures and improve institutions will go a long way in supporting the long-term effectiveness of green agricultural policies.

While these findings are indicative of the potential performance of climate-resilient development paths in such environments, further research is required for a fuller understanding. One area that requires further focus is on the prospects for scaling up successful schemes. This could face numerous challenges as the projects are rarely implemented at large scale and there may not be sufficient research on their applicability at a wider scale. Hence, more research on the feasibility of alternative interventions in heterogeneous environments is required. In addition, many of the studies reviewed in this chapter leave vulnerable and marginalized household groups out of their analyses. Since such households are likely to be the most affected by the vagaries of climate change, a deeper understanding of their role in climate-resilient development is likely to add to the credibility of the intervention as a genuinely inclusive development path.

REFERENCES

Akinnifesi, F.K., Chirwa, P.W., Ajayi, O.C. et al., 2008. 'Contributions of agroforestry research to livelihood of smallholder farmers in Southern Africa: 1. Taking stock of the adaptation, adoption and impact of fertilizer tree options', *Agricultural Journal*, 3(1), 58–75.

Allison, F.E., 1973. *Soil Organic Matter and its Role in Crop Production*, Vol. 3. New York: Elsevier.

Anderson, J.R. and Thampapillai, J., 1990. *Soil Conservation in Developing Countries: Project and Policy Intervention*, Vol. 8. Washington, DC: World Bank.

Asfaw, S., Shiferaw, B., Simtowe, F. and Haile, M.G., 2011. 'Agricultural technology adoption, seed access constraints and commercialization in Ethiopia', *Journal of Development and Agricultural Economics*, 3(9), 436–77.

Axinn, G.H., 1988. *Guide on Alternative Extension Approaches*. Rome: Food and Agriculture Organization of the United Nations.

Baidu-Forson, J., 1999. 'Factors influencing adoption of land-enhancing technology in the Sahel: lessons from a case study in Niger', *Agricultural Economics*, **20**(3), 231–9.

Bekele, W. and Drake, L., 2003. 'Soil and water conservation decision behavior of subsistence farmers in the Eastern Highlands of Ethiopia: a case study of the Hunde-Lafto area', *Ecological Economics*, **46**(3), 437–51.

Benhin, J.K., 2006. 'Climate change and South African agriculture: impacts and adaptation options', CEEPA Discussion Paper No. 21.

Berry, L., Olson, J. and Campbell, D., 2003. *Assessing the Extent, Cost and Impact of Land Degradation at the National Level: Findings and Lessons Learned from Seven Pilots*. Washington, DC: World Bank.

Besley, T., 1995. 'Property rights and investment incentives: theory and evidence from Ghana', *Journal of Political Economy*, **103**(5), 903–37.

Besley, T. and Burgess, R., 2000. 'Land reform, poverty reduction, and growth: evidence from India', *Quarterly Journal of Economics*, **115**(2), 389–430.

Bezabih, M. and Gaeback, T., 2010. 'Environmental change, species coping ability and the insurance value of biodiversity: a stochastic dynamic optimization approach', *Natural Resource Modelling*, **23**(2), 253–84.

Bezabih, M., Holden, S. and Mannberg, A., 2016. 'The role of land certification in reducing gaps in productivity between male- and female-owned farms in rural Ethiopia', *Journal of Development Studies*, **52**(3), 360–76.

Boardman, J. and Favis-Mortlock, D.T. 1993. 'Climate change and soil erosion in Britain', *Geographical Journal*, **159**(2), 179–83.

Braun, A.R., Thiele, G. and Fernández, M., 2000. *Farmer Field Schools and Local Agricultural Research Committees: Complementary Platforms for Integrated Decision-making in Sustainable Agriculture*. London: Overseas Development Institute.

Bryan, E., Ringler, C., Okoba, B., Koo, J., Herrero, M. and Silvestri, S. 2011. *Agricultural Management for Climate Change Adaptation, Greenhouse Gas Mitigation, and Agricultural Productivity: Insights from Kenya* (No. 1098). Washington, DC: International Food Policy Research Institute (IFPRI).

Caldwell, M.M., Dawson, T.E. and Richards, J.H., 1998. 'Hydraulic lift: consequences of water efflux from the roots of plants', *Oecologia*, **113**(2), 151–61.

Cooper, P.J.M., Dimes, J., Rao, K.P.C., Shapiro, B., Shiferaw, B. and Twomlow, S., 2008. 'Coping better with current climatic variability in the rain fed farming systems of sub-Saharan Africa: an essential first step in adapting to future climate change?', *Agriculture, Ecosystems & Environment*, **126**(1), 24–35.

Corbera, E., Brown, K. and Adger, W.N., 2007. 'The equity and legitimacy of markets for ecosystem services', *Development and Change*, **38**(4), 587–613.

Critchley, W. and Gowing, J.W. (eds), 2012. *Water Harvesting in sub-Saharan Africa*. London: Routledge.

Dasgupta, A. and Beard, V.A., 2007. 'Community driven development, collective action and elite capture in Indonesia', *Development and Change*, **38**(2), 229–49.

Dasgupta, P. and Mäler, K.G., 1994. *Poverty, Institutions, and the Environmental-resource Base*. Washington, DC: World Bank.

Deininger, K., Ali, D.A. and Yamano, T., 2008. 'Legal knowledge and economic development: the case of land rights in Uganda', *Land Economics*, **84**(4), 593–619.

Denton, F., 2002. 'Climate change vulnerability, impacts, and adaptation: why does gender matter?', *Gender & Development*, **10**(2), 10–20.

Derpsch, R., Friedrich, T., Kassam, A. and Li, H., 2010. 'Current status of adoption of no-till farming in the world and some of its main benefits', *International Journal of Agricultural and Biological Engineering*, **3**(1), 1–25.

Di Falco, S. and Bulte, E., 2013. 'The impact of kinship networks on the adoption of risk-mitigating strategies in Ethiopia', *World Development*, **43**(2), 100–10.

Di Falco, S. and Chavas, J.-P., 2009. 'On crop biodiversity, risk exposure and food security in the Highlands of Ethiopia', *American Journal of Agricultural Economics*, **91**(3), 599–611.

Di Falco, S., Bezabih, M. and Yesuf, M., 2010. 'Seeds for livelihood: biodiversity and food production in multicropping farms in Ethiopia', *Ecological Economics*, **69**, 1695–702.

Di Falco, S., Veronesi, M. and Yesuf, M., 2011. 'Does adaptation to climate change provide food security? A micro-perspective from Ethiopia', *American Journal of Agricultural Economics*, **93**(3), 829–46.

Dinar, A., Hassan, R., Mendelsohn, R. and Benhin, J., 2012. *Climate Change and Agriculture in Africa: Impact Assessment and Adaptation Strategies*. London: Routledge.

Dumanski, J., Peiretti, R., Benites, J.R., McGarry, D. and Pieri, C., 2006. 'The paradigm of conservation agriculture', *Proceedings of the World Association of Soil and Water Conservation*, **1**, 58–64.

Engel, S. and Palmer, C., 2008. 'Payments for environmental services as an alternative to logging under weak property rights: the case of Indonesia', *Ecological Economics*, **65**(4), 799–809.

Feder, G., Murgai, R. and Quizon, J.B., 2004. 'Sending farmers back to school: the impact of farmer field schools in Indonesia', *Applied Economic Perspectives and Policy*, **26**(1), 45–62.

Frost, P.G. and Bond, I., 2008. 'The CAMPFIRE programme in Zimbabwe: payments for wildlife services', *Ecological Economics*, **65**(4), 776–87.

García-Amado, L.R., Pérez, M.R., Escutia, F.R., García, S.B. and Mejía, E.C., 2011. 'Efficiency of payments for environmental services: equity and additionality in a case study from a biosphere reserve in Chiapas, Mexico', *Ecological Economics*, **70**(12), 2361–8.

Graff-Zivin, J. and Lipper, L., 2008. 'Poverty, risk, and the supply of soil carbon sequestration', *Environment and Development Economics*, **13**(3), 353–73.

Groom, B., Grosjean, P., Kontoleon, A., Swanson, T. and Zhang, S., 2009. 'Relaxing rural constraints: a "win-win" policy for poverty and environment in China?', *Oxford Economic Papers*, gpp021.

Hassan, R. and Nhemachena, C., 2008. 'Determinants of African farmers' strategies for adapting to climate change: multinomial choice analysis', *African Journal of Agricultural and Resource Economics*, **2**(1), 83–104.

Henao, J. and Baanante, C., 2006. *Agricultural Production and Soil Nutrient Mining in Africa: Implications for Resource Conservation and Policy Development*. Alabama: IFDC, International Center for Soil Fertility and Agricultural Development.

Hobbs, P.R., 2007. 'Conservation agriculture: what is it and why is it important for future sustainable food production?', *Journal of Agricultural Science*, **145**(2), 127–37.

Hobbs, P.R., Sayre, K. and Gupta, R., 2008. 'The role of conservation agriculture in sustainable agriculture', *Philosophical Transactions of the Royal Society B: Biological Sciences*, **363**(1491), 543–55.

Howden, S.M., Soussana, J.F., Tubiello, F.N., Chhetri, N., Dunlop, M. and

Meinke, H., 2007. 'Adapting agriculture to climate change', *Proceedings of the National Academy of Sciences*, **104**(50), 19691–6.

Jayachandran, S., 2013. 'Liquidity constraints and deforestation: the limitations of payments for ecosystem services', *American Economic Review*, **103**(3), 309–13.

Jindal, R., Swallow, B. and Kerr, J., 2008. 'Forestry-based carbon sequestration projects in Africa: potential benefits and challenges', *Natural Resources Forum*, **32**(2), 116–30.

Jindal, R., Kerr, J.M. and Carter, S., 2012. 'Reducing poverty through carbon forestry? Impacts of the N'hambita community carbon project in Mozambique', *World Development*, **40**(10), 2123–35.

Kanesathasan, A., 2012. 'Cultivating women's participation: strategies for gender-responsive agriculture programming', Technical Brief, International Center for Research on Women (ICRW), Washington, DC.

Kassie, M., Zikhali, P., Pender, J. and Köhlin, G., 2010. 'The economics of sustainable land management practices in the Ethiopian highlands', *Journal of Agricultural Economics*, **61**(3), 605–27.

Kato, E., Ringler, C., Yesuf, M. and Bryan, E., 2009. *How Can African Agriculture Adapt to Climate Change: Are Soil and Water Conservation Technologies a Buffer Against Production Risk in the Face of Climate Change?* (No. 15(17). Washington, DC: International Food Policy Research Institute (IFPRI).

Kennedy, A.C., 1999. 'Soil microorganisms for weed management', *Journal of Crop Production*, **2**, 123–38.

Kerr, J., 2002. 'Watershed development, environmental services, and poverty alleviation in India', *World Development*, **30**(8), 1387–400.

Kumar, A., Dixit, S. T. Ram, R.B., et al., 2014. 'Breeding high-yielding drought-tolerant rice: genetic variations and conventional and molecular approaches', *Journal of Experimental Botany*, **67** (7): 2–14.

Kurukulasuriya, P. and Mendelsohn, R., 2008. 'A Ricardian analysis of the impact of climate change on African cropland', *African Journal of Agricultural and Resource Economics*, **2**(1), 1–23.

Kurukulasuriya, P., Mendelsohn, R., Hassan, R. et al., 2006. 'Will African agriculture survive climate change?', *The World Bank Economic Review*, **20**(3), 367–88.

Lin, B.B., 2011. 'Resilience in agriculture through crop diversification: adaptive management for environmental change', *BioScience*, **61**(3), 183–93.

Lovo, S., Bezabih, M. and Singer, G., 2015. 'Green agricultural policies and poverty reduction', Policy brief, The Grantham Research Institute on Climate Change and the Environment, London.

Maddison, D.J., 2007. 'The perception of and adaptation to climate change in Africa', World Bank Policy Research Working Paper No. 4308, World Bank, Washington, DC.

Mano, R. and Nhemachena, C., 2007. 'Assessment of the economic impacts of climate change on agriculture in Zimbabwe: a Ricardian approach', Policy Research Working Paper No. 4292, Development Research Group, Sustainable Rural and Urban Development Team, World Bank, Washington, DC.

Marenya, P.P. and Barrett, C.B., 2009. 'State-conditional fertilizer yield response on western Kenyan farms', *American Journal of Agricultural Economics*, **91**(4), 991–1006.

Mazvimavi, D., Hoko, Z., Jonker, L., Nhapi, I. and Senzanje, A., 2008. 'Integrated water resources management (IWRM) – from concept to practice', *Physics and Chemistry of the Earth, Parts A/B/C*, **33**(8), 609–13.

Mellor, J.W. 1988. 'The intertwining of environmental problems poverty', *Environment: Science and Policy for Sustainable Development*, **30**(9), 6–30.

Moser, C. and Barrett, C.B., 2003. 'The disappointing adoption dynamics of a yield increasing, low external input technology: the case of SRI in Madagascar', *Agricultural Systems*, **76**(3), 1085–100.

New Climate Economy, 2014. *Land Use. Better Growth, Better Climate: The New Climate Economy Report*. Available at http://2014.newclimateeconomy.report/wp-content/uploads/2014/08/NCE_Chapter3_LandUse.pdf (accessed 2 April 2015).

O'Neal, M.R., Nearing, M.A., Vining, R.C., Southworth, J. and Pfeifer, R.A. (2005). 'Climate change impacts on soil erosion in Midwest United States with changes in crop management', *Catena*, **61**(2), 165–84.

Ostrom, E.,1990. *Governing the Commons: The Evolution of Institutions for Collective Action*. Cambridge: Cambridge University Press.

Pagiola, S., 2008. 'Payments for environmental services in Costa Rica', *Ecological Economics*, **65**(4), 712–24.

Pagiola, S. and Platais, G., 2007. *Payments for Environmental Services: From Theory to Practice*. Washington, DC: World Bank.

Pagiola, S., Arcenas, A. and Platais, G., 2005. 'Can payments for environmental services help reduce poverty? An exploration of the issues and the evidence to date from Latin America', *World Development*, **33**(2), 237–53.

Pagiola, S., Rios, A.R. and Arcenas, A., 2008. 'Can the poor participate in payments for environmental services? Lessons from the Silvopastoral Project in Nicaragua', *Environment and Development Economics*, **13**(3), 299–325.

Platteau, J.P., 2000. 'Allocating and enforcing property rights in land: informal versus formal mechanisms in Subsaharan Africa', *Nordic Journal of Political Economy*, **26**(1), 55–81.

Quisumbing, A.R., 2003. *Household Decisions, Gender, and Development: A Synthesis of Recent Research*. Washington, DC: International Food Policy Research Institute.

Schwartzman, S., 2005. 'Education-oriented social programs in Brazil: the impact of Bolsa Escola', Instituto de Estudos do Trabalho e Sociedade, Rio de Janeiro, Paper presented at Global Conference on Education Research in Developing Countries, Global Development Network, 30 March–2 April 2005, Prague.

Scopel, E., Triomphe, B., Affholder, F. et al., 2013. 'Conservation agriculture cropping systems in temperate and tropical conditions, performances and impacts. A review', *Agronomy for Sustainable Development*, **33**(1), 113–30.

Swallow, B.M. and Goddard, T.W., 2013. 'Value chains for bio-carbon sequestration services: lessons from contrasting cases in Canada, Kenya and Mozambique', *Land Use Policy*, **31**, 81–9.

Tizale, C.Y., 2007. 'The dynamics of soil degradation and incentives for optimal management in the Central Highlands of Ethiopia', Doctoral dissertation, University of Pretoria.

USAID (2014). *Climate-resilient Development: A Framework for Understanding and Addressing Climate Change*. Washington, DC: USAID.

Winterbottom, R., Reij, C., Garrity, D. et al., 2013. 'Improving land and water management', World Resources Institute Working Paper, Installment 4 of Creating a Sustainable Food Future, World Resources Institute, Washington, DC.

Wunder, S. and Albán, M., 2008. 'Decentralized payments for environmental services: the cases of Pimampiro and PROFAFOR in Ecuador', *Ecological Economics*, **65**(4), 685–98.

Wunder, S., Engel, S. and Pagiola, S., 2008. 'Taking stock: a comparative analysis of payments for environmental services programs in developed and developing countries', *Ecological Economics*, **65**(4), 834–52.

Xu, J., Tao, R., Xu, Z. and Bennett, M.T., 2010. 'China's sloping land conversion program: does expansion equal success?', *Land Economics*, **86**(2), 219–44.

Yesuf, M. and Bluffstone, R., 2009. 'Poverty, risk aversion and path dependence in low income countries: experimental evidence from Ethiopia', *American Journal of Agricultural Economics*, **91**(4), 1022–37.

10. Insurance instruments for climate-resilient development

Swenja Surminski

10.1 INSURANCE AND CLIMATE-RESILIENT DEVELOPMENT

An important aspect of climate-resilient development is managing the risks from growing climatic extremes, which pose a threat to both short-term economic stability and long-term sustainable development (Benson and Twigg, 2007). From 1995 to 2010,[1] natural disasters affected 3.6 billion people and created $900 billion in damages in non-Organisation for Economic Co-operation and Development (OECD) member countries. Damages are rising further due to high population growth, an increase in assets in risk areas as well as the influence of climate change (World Bank, 2013). In its *Fifth Assessment Report*, the Intergovernmental Panel on Climate Change (IPCC) finds growing evidence of climate change as a 'threat multiplier', which together with a significant adaptation deficit in both developing and developed countries means that the magnitude of impacts and consequences of climate change is expected to increase significantly (IPCC, 2014).

An important example of how climate change and other risk drivers interact is population growth. About 800 million people are currently living in flood-prone areas, of which on average about 70 million people are experiencing floods each year (UNISDR, 2011). Even without any climatic changes, the exposure of flood risk is expected to increase with population growth. A World Bank study into impacts of sea-level risk and storm surges for 393 cities in 31 developing countries found high asymmetries in projected impacts, when taking into account population growth and economic development: 'Our results suggest gross inequality in the heightened impact of future disasters, with 50 per cent of the burden falling on the residents of ten Asian cities and over 40 per cent falling on Manila, Karachi, and Jakarta alone' (Brecht et al., 2012 p. 120).

Policies and investment in disaster risk management and climate adaptation measures are needed to manage those risks. This can only succeed if governments and individuals steer towards development pathways that are compatible with climate change and do not reinforce vulnerability and exposure (UNISDR, 2011). Achieving this requires an anticipatory view of risk, rather than a reactive 'wait and see' approach. However, despite some progress over the last decade global efforts to deal with disaster are still heavily focused on *ex post* relief and reconstruction, rather than *ex ante* investments. The current split of 87 per cent versus 13 per cent (Kellet and Caravani, 2013) signals a need for further efforts away from unplanned and ad hoc responses to proactive and systematic risk management (World Bank, 2013). This is echoed in recent IPCC reports (IPCC, 2012, 2014), which underline the need for risk-based assessment and careful management planning before disasters strike.

One proactive instrument, which is highlighted by climate adaptation, disaster risk reduction and development experts alike, is insurance. Insurance has been used for centuries as a tool to manage the risk of extreme weather and other uncertain losses. In its most basic form it is a mechanism where risks or part of a risk are transferred from one party (the insured) to another (the insurer) in return for a premium payment. Such risk sharing is an important mechanism driving our economic systems: without insurance many activities and processes would be deemed too risky and would not be undertaken, and those affected by a loss might struggle to recover.[2]

Risk management and insurance is widely used in most developed countries, albeit with significant local differences in uptake and utilization,[3] but it remains far less established in low-income countries. Latin America, Africa and Oceania account for only 6 per cent of the global insurance premium (CEA, 2011). Reliance on post-disaster aid and informal safety nets forms the largest part of disaster funding in those countries (GFDRR, 2011; World Bank, 2013).

The associated lack of financial resources is a key constraint in the efforts of low-income countries to increase their climate resilience and they often struggle to invest in proper risk reduction measures. Linked to this are gaps in technical expertise and data, which influence the way a country can respond to natural disaster risks (UNISDR, 2009, 2011). Post-disaster aid often turns out to be insufficient and delayed, as highlighted by the example of Honduras. In the aftermath of Hurricane Mitch in 1998, 'Honduras only received about 50 per cent of the funds necessary for relief and reconstruction, and experienced extreme difficulties in repairing public infrastructure and assisting the recovery of the private sector following Hurricane Mitch in 1998. Five years after Mitch's devastation the GDP of Honduras was 6 per cent below pre-disaster projections' (Mechler et al., 2010, p. 9).

Individuals and households in low-income countries often have no other option than to cope with disaster through the liquidation of productive assets, for example, selling livestock, and a reduction in (food) consumption. This can inhibit their future earning potential (see, for example, Fafchamps and Gavian, 1997; Dercon, 2002) as well as lead to permanent health impacts, especially for children.

The rapid increase in global economic losses from climate-related disasters has triggered discussions among private insurers, governments and international organizations. This discourse has considered the role of insurance in addressing these risks and supporting climate-resilient development through a more anticipatory risk view. Insurance does not provide a solution to all climate risks – for example, the use of insurance is not suitable for changes in 'average' conditions or slow onset events such as sea-level rise (Ranger et al., 2011).

However, insurance can play a cost-effective role in a country's efforts to increase its disaster resilience, especially when compared to *ex post* disaster aid (Collier et al., 2009). It has been the cornerstone for new risk management initiatives, such as the African Risk Capacity (ARC), which aims to reduce the impact of droughts and floods by speeding up response mechanisms, move away from post-disaster aid towards anticipatory action and ensure timely, predictable pay-outs. Helping people quickly before they sell assets creates five times more value to vulnerable populations than traditional aid, which is raised after the disaster strikes, and arrives much later. According to the ARC, 'using an indicative but conservative model, estimates show that a contingency fund of $250 million could save African countries and donors nearly $1 billion in cash over 20 years' (African Union and WFP, 2013).

The use of risk management and financing is thus an important element that can determine the ability of an individual or government to maintain stability after a natural disaster. This in turn increases the capacity to reduce loss as well as improving and benefitting the experience that people have in conducting their lives and pursuing development opportunities (World Bank, 2014).

Designing and implementing insurance faces significant barriers, particularly in countries with insufficient financial infrastructure. Recent pilots and trials in several developing countries are attempting to address those barriers, indicating a degree of innovation and progress that could possibly lead to a broader application of insurance. However, insurance can also increase the potential for moral hazard and reduction of incentives for risk reduction, particularly if poorly designed and implemented (Surminski, 2014).

This chapter considers if and how insurance can support climate-resilient development. It reviews existing concepts and considers the current application 'on the ground', before concluding with recommendations for those involved in the climate-resilient development discourse.

10.2   WHAT INSURANCE CAN OFFER

The economic justification for insurance is derived from a social welfare function, where the sharing of risk through insurance can increase the expected utility of individuals and companies and thus the overall welfare of society as a whole. Sharing risk increases individual utility through risk aversion as individuals are willing to pay a premium to avoid risk; they can achieve this through the purchase of insurance.

Insurance can buffer and smooth the effects of losses, thus avoiding the prospect of severe financial consequences. This makes it possible to undertake higher risk activities that would otherwise not go ahead, therefore stimulating productivity and growth as well as promoting an efficient mix of activities that would not have been possible in the absence of such instruments (Brainard, 2008).

If properly designed and implemented this wider role of insurance can be harnessed for climate-resilient development. The main focus of this discourse has been on the role of insurance in response to natural disaster risks, where the provision or absence of natural disaster insurance can have implications on the scale and duration of the economic impact of disasters, the resilience of businesses, governments and individuals as well as the speed of recovery (see, for example, Hallegatte, 2014). Insurance offers a shift in the mobilization of financial resources away from an ad hoc post-event scenario, where funding is often unpredictable and delayed, towards a more strategic, and in many cases more efficient, pre-disaster set-up.

While not stopping disasters, insurance is designed to address liquidity needs in their immediate aftermath and help fund the recovery process. Purchased and implemented prior to an event, risk financing can be applied to address the financial needs of governments (sovereign insurance, reserve funds, contingent credit lines), businesses (property and business insurance), farmers (agricultural insurance) and individuals (property and micro-insurance). This is illustrated in Figure 10.1.

Hallegatte (2011) categorizes the potential for insurance in the context of disaster risk under five headings: risk spreading over space and time; risk smoothing; faster and more efficient reconstruction; certainty about post-disaster support; and reducing immediate welfare losses and consumption reductions. Surminski (2014) argues that insurance allows households, firms and governments to offset losses and consequential costs and thus maintain stability after an event. In other words, insurance can protect government budgets in case of disaster, allowing the continuation of other important functions such as in schools and hospitals. It also enables individuals and businesses to recover quickly, helping them to

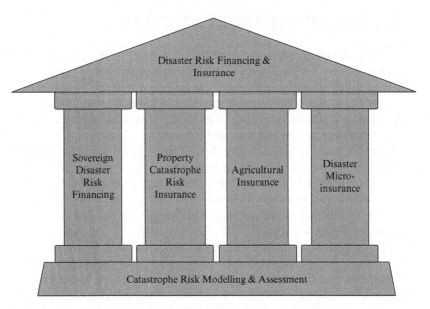

Source: World Bank (2011).

Figure 10.1   Disaster risk financing and insurance pillars

cope with disasters and avoid falling into a poverty trap (Hallegatte, 2014; Ranger et al., 2011).

As argued above, insurance encourages the 'positive risk taking' that is fundamental to any development process: it can make investments less risky and therefore foster innovation and growth. However, this may also lead to an increased vulnerability to exceptional events, if resilience measures encourage investment in at-risk areas. This points to a potential flipside of using insurance in support of climate-resilient development – where insurance can create a false sense of security or encourage development in high-risk areas.

Such moral hazard[4] can affect individuals, businesses and even governments. Fankhauser and McDermott (2014) find a negative relationship between the extent of insurance cover and the demand for adaptation, with 'insurance acting as a substitute for adaptation' (p. 13).

This highlights the need to consider if and how insurance can influence the underlying risk-decisions. Purchasing insurance cover can lead to more risky behaviour, or it can work as an incentive, triggering risk reduction investments or the implementation of prevention measures (see Kunreuther, 1996; Kunreuther and Pauly, 2006; Kunreuther and Michel-Kerjan, 2009;

Linnerooth-Bayer and Mechler, 2009; Linnerooth-Bayer et al., 2011; Kunreuther et al., 2013).

A potential side-benefit of insurance relates to the need to assess and analyse risks, which can lead to increased knowledge and understanding as well as a more strategic response to risk. This aspect may be particularly relevant in the context of climate change, as stated by Ranger and Surminski (2011). They show how risk data collected for insurance purposes can support the general understanding of risks and provide information for the design of climate adaptation measures. This can go as far as signalling the uninsurabilty of a certain risk – for example, in areas where floods occur very frequently, which may in turn lead to the employment of other disaster risk management (DRM) and adaptation measures. However, this risk signalling function of insurance is often obscured, mainly because concerns about affordability lead to subsidization approaches or because of a lack of data and technical know-how (Stahel et al., 2009; Surminski, 2014).

Determining if and where insurance offers an effective solution is not straightforward. Insurance theory and recent cost-benefit assessments indicate that risk financing is only viable for large and residual risks that cannot be reduced or managed otherwise (Mechler et al., 2014). The large majority of those who buy insurance will not experience a loss and therefore not receive a pay-out. This implies a need to integrate insurance (risk financing) with adaptation and DRM measures (risk reduction). Establishing the best combination of the different tools requires a comprehensive risk assessment and an understanding of the economic and fiscal implications of disasters (World Bank, 2011; Mechler et al., 2014). This can be achieved through risk layering – a method that considers the different DRM and risk financing tools and mechanisms as complementary and allows for a combination of hard and soft DRM measures, as illustrated in Figure 10.2 (GFDRR, 2013; World Bank et al., 2013).

Risk layering can help to establish an appropriate balance between *ex post* and *ex ante* measures, including insurance. Risk is defined by its return period and frequency, which determines the appropriate risk management application to implement. This method is based on a distinction between low, medium and high probability events as well as taking into account the level of risk that can be borne by the stakeholder in question, whether that is a community or organization. For example, small and frequent losses are best addressed by changes to operations and practice – for example, irrigation or change in crop selection. More severe but low probability events such as a flooding disaster or prolonged drought are most suitable for risk financing, including insurance. Beyond a certain risk threshold, such as a return period of 1 in 500 or 1 in 1,000 years, risk financing tools are often too expensive, creating residual risk with individuals or the government.

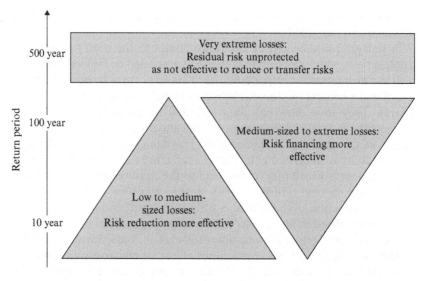

Source: Mechler et al. (2014).

Figure 10.2   The layering approach for risk reduction and risk financing

In the context of climate change it is important to reflect how future climatic impacts may change the suitability of those response strategies. Theory and evidence from existing insurance markets suggests that a 'riskier and more uncertain world would be associated with an increase in insurance demand, at least until some local threshold were reached where the affordability of insurance or the insurability of risk were threatened' (Ranger and Surminski, 2011).

Maintaining insurability and securing affordable premiums in the wake of rising losses from extreme weather events may become a challenge. Several private insurers have initiated projects to explore this issue through collaboration with scientists, engagement in policy debates and assessment of their own products.

10.3   THE CURRENT APPLICATION OF INSURANCE FOR CLIMATE-RESILIENT DEVELOPMENT

The penetration of insurance is to a large extent dependent on income levels, with rising income linked to increasing insurance penetration (Ibarra and Skees, 2007). This is one explanation for the low usage of insurance in developing countries.

In addition to income, a range of other factors are at play in driving insurance penetration (Ranger and Surminski, 2011), such as stable and effective institutions, law enforcement and the availability of risk data (Hussels et al., 2005; Brainard, 2008). Other driving factors include education and financial literacy levels (Masci et al., 2007) and specific market characteristics, such as distribution channels, a functioning financial sector, access to global markets and the appetite for innovation in terms of products and services (UNCTAD, 2012; see also Freeman and Kunreuther, 1997 for an overview).

The generally low usage of insurance in developing countries is also visible in the context of natural disasters: while 46 per cent of disaster losses in the USA are covered by insurance, in the developing world the figure is below 1 per cent. Market players such as Lloyds of London warn of a growing under-insurance challenge (Lloyds, 2012) and identify emerging markets as strategic growth targets.

When entering developing country markets, (re)insurers have to contend with their poor understanding of natural catastrophes in these areas, the problems of pricing business correctly and the need to monitor exposure growth without suitable risk modelling tools. In many developing countries the data needed to underwrite flood risk is often not readily available, and there is no commercial case for private sector actors to develop such models on their own.

This has led to an increased focus on public-private partnerships: ClimateWise, the industry-led climate initiative launched in 2008, points to the need for public-private partnerships in order to exhaust the full potential of 'what is possible in building resilience to climate change impacts' (ClimateWise, 2011a, p. 2). ClimateWise refers to pilot projects and initiatives where its members are engaged and 'where national governments have come together with other relevant organisations such as private (re)insurers, non-governmental organisations and community groups to develop and implement new climate risk management and insurance partnerships' (ClimateWise, 2011a, p. 3). The Munich Climate Insurance Initiative (MCII), set up in April 2005 and particularly active at the UN level, promotes the use of insurance as a tool supported by both the private and public-private sectors in the quest to develop new insurance solutions. The initiative suggests that such a partnership could 'offer the market sustainability of private sector approaches, and the flexibility and innovation of public sector approaches (and that) subsidiarity means that each partner will have clearly defined, distinct roles to play' (MCII, 2012, p. 15).

Over the past few years a range of new risk transfer schemes has been implemented, often in response to demand and supply challenges, testing innovative risk transfer forms such as micro-insurance or index-based risk transfers. Regional risk financing facilities and platforms, which aim to create economies of scale for managing risks financially and supporting disaster risk management more broadly, have been set up, for example, in Colombia, Mexico, the Caribbean countries and Pacific Small Island Developing States (SIDS). However, the amounts covered by those schemes often remain small and may not be adequate to safeguard public budgets from disaster risk (GFDRR, 2012).

At the household level, new products, such as micro-insurance, have been developed to overcome existing barriers. As of the end of 2011, micro-insurance was accessed by 4.4 per cent of all Africans, covering 44.4 million lives and properties (Munich Re and GIZ, 2013). Figure 10.3 shows the global coverage of micro-insurance provision by continent.

Another innovation is the use of parametric cover. This refers to schemes where pay-out is not triggered by a loss event, but by the occurrence of a pre-agreed objective measure of the disaster, such as an amount of excess rainfall measured by weather station and satellite data.

The ClimateWise Compendium (ClimateWise, 2011b) on disaster risk transfer documents 123 existing initiatives in middle-income and lower-income countries that involve the transfer of financial risk associated with the occurrence of natural hazards such as flooding (Surminski and Oramas-Dorta, 2011; Figure 10.4).

The Compendium indicates an increasing potential for risk transfer instruments in developing countries. The documented insurance schemes show a wide diversity, with application of schemes to specific needs or communities, a range of stakeholders and the accommodation of differing levels of risk transfer. Provision varies from private insurers, government to public-private partnerships. The most common example of insurance scheme across all countries is agricultural insurance, although specific geographical preferences are visible, for example, micro-insurance for natural disasters in Asia. This may reflect cultural difference or local traditions and may also be linked to the availability of financing tools such as micro-finance (Surminski and Oramas-Dorta, 2014).

If and how insurance instruments play a supporting role in fostering risk reduction and triggering climate resilience beyond financial transfers is not clear. Surminski (2010) provides an overview of how insurers in developed markets are incentivizing adaptation activities from raising awareness, to promoting public and private action through information provision, financial means and action on incentivization. However, establishing the effectiveness of these measures is only now becoming a topic for researchers and practitioners.

Growing concerns about climate change and affordability of insurance cover have led to efforts in harnessing the 'risk signalling' role of insurance.

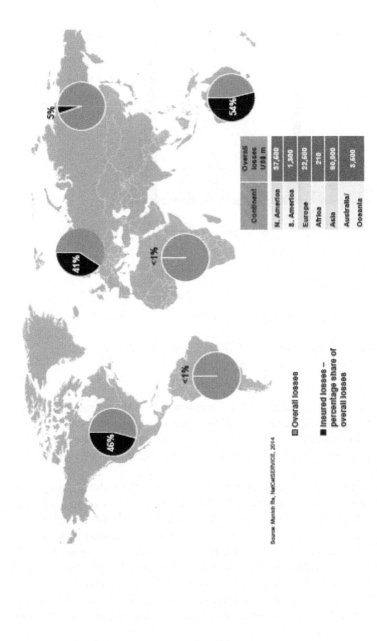

The following table appears within the figure:

Continent	Overall losses US$ m
N. America	37,500
S. America	1,300
Europe	22,600
Africa	210
Asia	90,000
Australia/ Oceania	3,500

☒ Overall losses

■ Insured losses – percentage share of overall losses

Source: Munich Re, NatCatSERVICE, 2014

Source: MIN (2015).

Figure 10.3 The coverage of micro-insurance

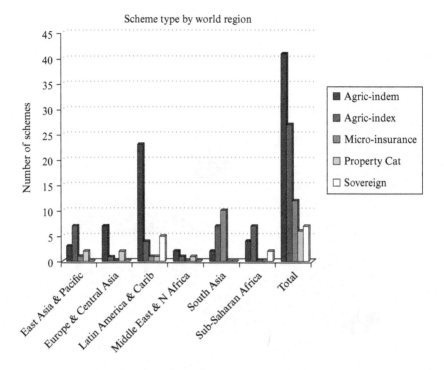

Source: Surminski and Oramas-Dorta (2011).

*Figure 10.4   Natural disaster risk financing schemes in low- and
middle-income countries*

Although still only considered for a small number of insurance schemes
(Surminski and Oramas-Dorta, 2011), there is a growing recognition of
this potential benefit of insurance such as information about drought-
resilient crop strategies and support for longer-term adaptation efforts
(Box 10.1).

A product that has received particular attention from those engaged in
developing new types of insurance for low-income countries is index-based
insurance. Index-based insurance is insurance that indemnifies all policy
holders in a defined geographic area against events beyond a particular
impact threshold, based on agreed criteria. These may be crop or livestock
losses or weather-related indices, such as a particular temperature threshold or level of rainfall. The index is often based on aggregated criteria.

The cost of setting up and administering an index-based scheme is often
much lower and it is easier to avoid issues of moral hazard and adverse

---

BOX 10.1   INNOVATIVE INSURANCE SCHEMES

Mexico's Fund for Natural Disasters (FONDEN) links risk financing to direct DRM action. Identified as early as 1990, DRM was used to identify sovereign insurance by Mexico's Finance Ministry, primarily for fiscal stability. FONDEN was established in 1996 with the objective of preventing imbalances in federal government finances due to natural catastrophes. This subsequently led to innovative risk financing arrangements, such as catastrophe bonds. Risk reduction has also stemmed from the information collected by the approach and about 25 per cent of FONDEN resources are used post-event to protect against future disasters. Another innovative measure includes relocation of housing in high-risk areas (World Bank, 2012b).

Climate Corporation is a global business that provides weather information and offers insurance to farmers worldwide. Offering data, modelling and weather simulations, the Climate Corporation aims to protect and improve farming operations (Climate Corporation, 2014). Coupled with insurance provision that automatically pays out in the event of a loss, the scheme demonstrates the potential for more climate-linked measures to aid knowledge, awareness and financial protection.

The Peruvian Flood Index (ENSO) insurance scheme is an index-based scheme aimed at businesses in an effort to prevent business interruption (GlobalAgRisk, 2013). It also addresses risk awareness through capacity building initiatives. The scheme has been developed by GlobalAgRisk and sold by La Positiva, a Peruvian insurer. The index is based on sea surface temperature as a proxy for loss. Different contracts are available with different threshold losses, with a maximum pay-out at a temperature of 27 degrees (ClimateWise, 2011b).

---

selection. However, one limitation is basis risk, whereby any risk not reflected in the index results in loss. This may occur for several reasons. One issue is measurement, if the way the index threshold is assessed by the insurer differs from that of the policy holders. Another possibility is that the index does not cover a 'useful' risk or does not fully reflect the risk in question. Managing this basis risk is essential when scaling up index insurance schemes to prevent policy holders being exposed to risks not covered in the index and in fact increasing their risk overall (IFAD, 2011).

A recent example of a scheme designed with climate-resilient development in mind is the introduction of index-based flood insurance in Peru, called the Extreme El Nino Insurance Product (EENIP). EENIP uses US National Oceanic and Atmospheric Administration (NOAA) data of sea surface temperatures, which can be used months in advance for a pay-out (see Box 10.1).

Another example aimed at fiscal risks arising from disasters is the African Risk Capacity (ARC), an index based insurance scheme that aims to insure national governments against losses from sub-Saharan drought

---

BOX 10.2   THE AFRICAN RISK CAPACITY FACILITY

The African Risk Capacity Facility (ARC) is a specialized agency proposed and led by the African Union. It aims to manage extreme weather events and natural disaster risks through establishing a risk pool into which donors and member countries pay an annual premium. The scheme is supported throughout the whole of Africa and aims to insure the risk of drought in the sub-Saharan area. Currently at design stage and subject to change, the ARC represents a solidarity approach to providing governments with disaster financing and the capacity to rapidly distribute funds for post-emergency services (ARC, 2014).

The ARC Ltd was launched in May 2014, and is based around a mutual 'Africa owned' insurance company, capitalized with donor commitments from Germany and the UK (DFID, 2014). The World Food Programme has been involved alongside the ARC in developing Africa RiskView, an advanced satellite weather surveillance programme and software modelling system, which is crucial for identifying the index-based threshold.

The scheme has a parametric trigger for pay-outs, based on rainfall levels and derived from Africa RiskView. This reduces the time taken for on the ground verification and thus a potentially lengthy pay-out process. The speed of pay-out will be a key indicator of success for the ARC, with a view to reduce the macroeconomic impacts of disasters by avoiding reductions in income and budget reallocations.

The ARC requires compulsory contingency planning by member governments as a condition for granting cover and imposes clear rules on how pay-outs can be used. Risk awareness and knowledge sharing is fostered through members' participation in Africa RiskView.

(Box 10.2). The ARC responds to one of the fundamental challenges for many African countries wishing to adopt insurance solutions, which is a lack of access to commercial markets (DFID, 2014). External governmental support from bilateral or multilateral donors is often unreliable and with the threat of growing macroeconomic impacts[5] a more integrated approach coupled with adaptation and contingency planning is required.

The ARC aims to increase the financial response capacity of a government in the aftermath of a natural disaster by speeding up response mechanisms, away from post-disaster aid towards anticipatory action and timely predictable pay-outs. It operates in a framework determined by African states and anchored in the African Union. ARC is designed to address some of the typical difficulties of insurance schemes in low-income countries, such as the need to maintain transparency, the use of risk data and know-how, demand and political buy-in. However, the sustainability of the scheme in light of climate change remains unclear (Surminski et al., 2016).

10.4 CONCLUSIONS

Using insurance as part of a wider approach towards climate resilience offers clear benefits. It supports the move away from a highly ineffective post-disaster perspective towards a more forward looking *ex ante* approach. It smooths losses and helps governments, businesses and individuals to cope with disasters, reducing the threat of a poverty trap after a disaster. In addition, insurance can support a more strategic and information-based approach to adaptation and disaster risk management and increase risk understanding while fostering knowledge sharing between different stakeholders.

However, insurance can also lead to a 'business as usual' approach, providing disincentives for governments, businesses or individuals to act, which could jeopardize efforts of climate-resilient development. This underlines the importance of design and operation of insurance in close reflection on the underlying risks and risk behaviour. Experience with flood and windstorm insurance schemes suggests three principles that need to be met to harness the risk reduction potential of insurance (Surminski, 2014):

1. Risk levels should drive the pricing of insurance cover (risk-based pricing rather than cross-subsidization).
2. Granting of cover should be conditional on certain measures of risk reduction (such as business continuity plans or strengthened roofs in exposed coastal areas; existence of contingency plans).
3. Insurance pay-outs after a loss must increase resilience (for example, through resilient repair after a flood).

In practice, those designing insurance schemes are often confronted with (real or apparent) trade-offs between affordability, availability and risk reduction. Insurance premiums that reflect risk levels are likely to be unaffordable for poor households, while the absence of any risk reduction and contingency plans might make a risk uninsurable for private insurers. One important conclusion is to avoid, as far as possible, a situation where risk reduction is seen as a trade-off with affordability and availability. Considering these aspects as mutually reinforcing seems to be a more sensible approach. Risk reduction efforts are essential in maintaining the insurability of climate risks and effective adaptation may actually become a condition for granting insurance cover in the future (Surminski, 2014).

While the complex interactions and uncertainties mean that it is impossible to forecast quantitatively the future impacts of climate change on insurance demand, Ranger and Surminski (2013) conduct a preliminary evaluation of the relative scale and directions. Mapping the influence and trends through the use of scenarios, the study shows that the influence of climate change on insurance demand to 2030 is likely to be small but not insignificant when compared with the expected growth due to rising incomes. This effect could intensify, however, if policy makers introduce regulatory mechanisms to counter climate change, such as obligatory insurance and state-subsidized insurance products. The same also applies if new business opportunities arise following measures designed to reduce greenhouse gas emissions or adapt to climate change (Ranger and Surminski, 2013).

Risk transfer alone, without consideration of risk reduction efforts, is not a sustainable solution in the context of a changing climate. This is particularly important as insurance does not offer a 'silver bullet' and has several limitations (Warner et al., 2009). Insurance is not suitable to deal with changes in 'average' conditions or slow onset events such as sea-level rise. While some risks such as flooding can be reduced through better preparedness, there will always be residual risks that leave those exposed with significant financial gaps and an increased risk of poverty. This residual loss – beyond insurance and adaptation – is starting to be addressed as part of the Loss and Damage discourse within the international climate change negotiations (see UNFCCC, 2010). While elements of risk transfer can provide a supporting role, it highlights the importance of implementing insurance as one component of an integrated climate adaptation approach. The extent to which insurance can feature in this mix is risk and country-specific and dependent on local risk appetite, as well as societal values.

Insurance can play an important role in increasing the capacity to reduce losses as well as improving and benefitting the experience that people have in conducting their lives and pursuing development opportunities (World Bank, 2014). Many crises and development setbacks are the result of mismanaged risks. Therefore, as climate change is becoming central to the development agenda, effective risk financing and insurance tools play a crucial role to support financial resilience. Developing countries also need to progress their own potential for financial infrastructure that will aid development. This may be through improving resource mobilization, strengthening tax administration, improving the incoming revenue from natural resources and reducing illegitimate financial flows (World Bank, 2013).

Recent innovations in disaster insurance attempt to harness insurance for climate-resilient development – where risk transfer offers governments and individuals financial resilience and motivates climate change adaptation. Achieving this will not be immediate but an increased understanding of when and where insurance can work and how it can be designed to support adaptation is important. Rather than exploring potential trade-offs between support for insurance market development versus other adaptation investments the focus has to be on integrated approaches that combine all aspects of climate risk management.

NOTES

1. Developed using EM-DAT, a database from the Centre on Research on the Epidemiology of Disasters (CRED) developed using data from United Nations (UN) agencies, non-governmental organizations (NGOs), insurers, research institutions and the press.
2. Insurance encompasses two kinds of activities: providing insurance risk transfer (liability side) and investing insurance funds (asset side). This chapter only considers the liability side of insurance.
3. The use of insurance varies significantly across the world and is subject to varying degrees of regulation, attitudes to risk as well as cultural influences in the form of local traditions and customs.
4. Moral hazard occurs when a party acts conversely to the principles set out in an agreement between two parties. For example, in an insurance contract, individuals' motives and behaviour to prevent loss may be reduced if they are financially protected through a policy, thus resulting in an increased probability of loss. For more detail on moral hazard, see Arrow (1968) and Pauly (1968).
5. For example, macroeconomic impacts can include budget reallocation, loss of consumption and poverty traps.

REFERENCES

African Union and WFP, 2013. 'African risk capacity – sovereign disaster risk management for Africa', Paper presented at the International Disaster and Risk Conference (IDRC) 2012, 26–30 August, Davos, Switzerland. Available at http://www.slideshare.net/GRFDavos/african-risk-capacity-sovereign-disaster-risk-management-for-africa (accessed 27 May 2015).

ARC, 2014. *African Risk Capacity*. Available at http://www.africanriskcapacity.org/home (accessed 1 July 2014).

Arrow, K.J., 1968. 'The economics of moral hazard: further comment', *American Economic Review*, **58**(3) 537–9.

Benson, C. and Twigg, J., 2007. *Tools for Mainstreaming Disaster Risk Reduction: Guidance Notes or Development Organisations*. Geneva: ProVention Consortium. Available at http://www.preventionweb.net/files/1066_toolsformainstreaming-DRR.pdf (accessed 25 February 2014).

Brainard, L., 2008. 'What is the role of insurance in economic development?', Working Paper No. 2, Zurich Government and Industry Thought Leadership Series.

Brecht, H., Dasgupta, S., Laplante, B., Murray, S. and Wheeler, D., 2012. 'Sea-level rise and storm surges: high stakes for a small number of developing countries', *Journal of Environment and Development*. doi: 1070496511433601

CEA, 2011. *European Insurance – Key Facts*. Available at http://www.insuranceeurope.eu/uploads/Modules/Publications/key-facts-2011.pdf (accessed 21 July 2015).

ClimateWise, 2011a. *Submission by ClimateWise – the Global Collaboration of Leading Insurers Focused on Reducing the Risks of Climate Change*. Available at http://unfccc.int/resource/docs/2011/smsn/ngo/249.pdf (accessed 30 March 2015).

ClimateWise, 2011b. *Compendium of Disaster Risk Transfer Initiatives in the Developing World*. Available at http://www.climatewise.org.uk/climatewise-compendium/ (accessed 27 February 2015).

Climate Corporation, 2014. Website of the Climate Corporation. Available at http://www.climate.com/ (accessed 4 June 2014).

Collier, W.M., Jacobs, K.R., Saxena, A., Baker-Gallegos, J., Carroll, M. and Yohe, G.W., 2009. 'Strengthening socio-ecological resilience through disaster risk reduction and climate change adaptation: identifying gaps in an uncertain world', *Environmental Hazards*, **8**(3), 171–86.

Dercon, S., 2002. 'Income risk, coping strategies, and safety nets', *The World Bank Research Observer*, **17**(2), 141–66.

DFID, 2014. *Business Case Intervention Summary African Risk Capacity*. London: Department for International Development. Available at http://iati.dfid.gov.uk/iati_documents/4643483.doc (accessed 2 June 2015).

Fafchamps, M. and Gavian, S., 1997. 'The determinants of livestock prices in Niger', *Journal of African Economies*, **6**(2), 255–95.

Fankhauser, S. and McDermott, T.K., 2014. 'Understanding the adaptation deficit: why are poor countries more vulnerable to climate events than rich countries?', *Global Environmental Change*, **27**, 9–18.

Freeman, P.K. and Kunreuther, H., 1997. *Managing Environmental Risk through Insurance*. Boston, MA: Kluwer Academic, pp. 159–89.

GFDRR. 2011. *Sovereign Disaster Risk Financing. Global Facility for Disaster Reduction and Recovery*. Available at http://www.gfdrr.org/sites/gfdrr.org/files/documents/DRFI_SDRF_Concept_Jan11.pdf (accessed 16 July 2014).

GFDRR, 2012. *Improving the Assessment of Disaster Risks to Strengthen Financial Resilience*. Washington, DC: International Bank for Reconstruction and Development/International Development Association of the World Bank. Available at http://www.gfdrr.org/sites/gfdrr.org/files/GFDRR_G20_Low_June13.pdf (accessed 16 July 2015).

GFDRR, 2013. *Financing Post-disaster Recovery and Reconstruction Operations: Developing an Institutional Mechanism to Ensure the Effective Use of Financial Resources*. Washington, DC: Disaster Risk Financing and Insurance Program, FCMNB and GFDRR, World Bank. Available at http://siteresources.worldbank.org/EXTDISASTER/Resources/8308420-1342531265657/Central-Note-on-Reconstruction-Process_04Nov2013.pdf (accessed 27 May 2015).

GlobalAgRisk, 2013. *First-ever 'Forecast Insurance' Offered for Extreme El Nino in Peru*. Available at http://globalagrisk.com/Pubs/2013%20Press%20Release_First_Ever%20_Forecast%20Insurance%20Peru.pdf (accessed 4 June 2015).

Hallegatte, S., 2011. 'How economic growth and rational decisions can make disaster losses grow faster than wealth', World Bank Policy Research Working Paper No. 5617, World Bank, Washington, DC.

Hallegatte, S., 2014. 'The indirect cost of natural disasters and an economic definition of macroeconomic resilience', Impact Appraisal for Sovereign Disaster Risk

Financing and Insurance Project: Phase 1 Public Finance and Macroeconomics, Paper 3. Available at https://www.gfdrr.org/sites/gfdrr.org/files/documents/Public%20finance%20and%20macroeconomics,%20Paper%203.pdf (accessed 17 February 2016).

Hussels, S., Ward, D. and Zurbruegg, R., 2005. 'Stimulating the demand for insurance', *Risk Management and Insurance Review*, **8**(2), 257–78.

Ibarra, H. and Skees, J., 2007. 'Innovation in risk transfer for natural hazards impacting agriculture', *Environmental Hazard*, **7**, 62–9.

IFAD, 2011. *Weather Index-based Insurance in Agricultural Development: A Technical Guide*. Rome: International Fund for Agricultural Development (IFAD). Available at http://www.ifad.org/ruralfinance/pub/WII_tech_guide.pdf (accessed 1 July 2014).

IPCC, 2012. *Managing the Risks of Extreme Events and Disasters to Advance Climate Change Adaptation. A Special Report of Working Groups I and II of the Intergovernmental Panel on Climate Change*, edited by C.B. Field, V. Barros, T.F. Stocker et al. (eds). Cambridge and New York: Cambridge University Press.

IPCC, 2014. *Climate Change 2014: Impacts, Adaptation, and Vulnerability. Working Group II Contribution to the IPCC 5th Assessment Report*. Stanford, CA: IPCC Working Group II.

Kellet, J. and Caravani, A., 2013. *Financing Disaster Risk Reduction: A 20 Year Story of International Aid*. Washington, DC: Global Facility for Disaster Reduction and Recovery (GFDRR) and Overseas Development Institute (ODI).

Kunreuther, H., 1996. 'Mitigating disaster losses through insurance', *Journal of Risk and Uncertainty*, **12**, 171–87.

Kunreuther, H.C. and Michel-Kerjan, E.O., 2009. 'Managing catastrophes through insurance: challenges and opportunities for reducing future risks', Working Paper 2009-11-30, The Wharton School, University of Pennsylvania, PA.

Kunreuther, H. and Pauly, M., 2006. 'Rules rather than discretion: lessons from Hurricane Katrina', *Journal of Risk and Uncertainty*, **33**(1–2), 101–16.

Kunreuther, H., Heal, G., Allen, M., Edenhofer, O., Field, C.B. and Yohe, G., 2013. 'Risk management and climate change', *Nature Climate Change*, **3**(5), 447–50.

Linnerooth-Bayer, J. and Mechler, R., 2009. 'Insurance against losses from natural disasters in developing countries', DESA Working Paper No. 85 ST/ESA/2009/DWP/85, Department of Economic and Social Affairs, United Nations. Available at http://www.un.org/esa/desa/papers/2009/wp85_2009.pdf (accessed 1 July 2014).

Linnerooth-Bayer, J., Mechler, R. and Hochrainer, S., 2011. 'Insurance against losses from natural disasters in developing countries. Evidence, gaps and the way forward', *IDRiM Journal*, **1**(1), 2011, 59–81. Available at http://www.idrim.net/index.php/idrim/article/view/13/pdf_4 (accessed 17 February 2016).

Lloyds, 2012. *Lloyds' Global Underinsurance Report*. London: Lloyds. Available at http://www.lloyds.com/~/media/Files/News%20and%20Insight/360%20Risk%20Insight/Global_Underinsurance_Report_311012.pdf (accessed 16 July 2014).

Masci, P., Tejerina, L. and Webb, I., 2007. 'Insurance market development in Latin America', Insurance Market Development in Latin America and the Caribbean Sustainable Development Department Technical Papers Series, Inter-American Development Bank, Washington, DC.

MCII, 2012. *Submission by the Munich Climate Insurance Initiative (MCII) SBI Work Programme on Loss and Damage. Insurance Solutions in the Context* of Climate Change-related Loss and Damage: Needs, Gaps, and Roles of the Convention in Addressing Loss and Damage. Available at http://unfccc.int/resource/docs/2012/smsn/ngo/276.pdf (accessed 13 August 2015).

Mechler, R., Hochrainer, S., Pflug, G., Lotsch, A. and Williges, K., 2010. 'Assessing the financial vulnerability to climate-related natural hazards', Policy Research Working Paper No. 5232, World Bank, Washington, DC. Available at https://openknowledge.worldbank.org/bitstream/handle/10986/3718/WPS5232.pdf?sequence=1 (accessed 13 August 2014).

Mechler, R., Bouwer, L.M., Linnerooth-Bayer, J. et al., 2014. 'Managing unnatural disaster risk from climate extremes', *Nature Climate Change*, **4**(4), 235–7.

MIN, 2015. *The World Map of Microinsurance*. Luxembourg: Micro Insurance Network. Available at http://www.microinsurancenetwork.org/world-map-microinsurance (accessed 27 May 2015).

Munich Re and GIZ, 2013. *The Landscape of Microinsurance in Africa 2012. Munich Re Foundation and GIZ-Program Promoting Financial Sector Dialogue in Africa: 'Making Finance Work for Africa'*. Available at http://www.munichre-foundation.org/dms/MRS/Documents/Microinsurance/2012MILandscape/2013LS_MI_AfricaFull_E_web.pdf (accessed 4 June 2015).

Pauly, M.V., 1968. 'The economics of moral hazard: comment', *American Economic Review*, **58**(3), 531–7.

Ranger, N. and Surminski, S., 2011. 'A preliminary assessment of the impact of climate change on non-life insurance demand in the BRICS economies', Working Paper No. 72, Centre for Climate Change Economics and Policy. Available at http://www.cccep.ac.uk/Publications/Working-papers/Papers/70-79/WP72_climate-change-non-life-insurance-brics.pdf (accessed 17 January 2012).

Ranger, N. and Surminski, S., 2013. 'A preliminary assessment of the impact of climate change on non-life insurance demand in the BRICS economies', *International Journal of Disaster Risk Reduction*, **3**(1), 14–30.

Ranger, N., Hallegatte, S., Bhattacharya, S. et al., 2011. 'An assessment of the potential impact of climate change on flood risk in Mumbai', *Climatic Change*, **104**(1), 139–67.

Stahel, W.R., 2009. 'In favour of a proactive insurance approach to climate change', *The Geneva Papers on Risk and Insurance – Issues and Practice*, **34**(3), 319.

Surminski, S., 2010. *Adapting to the Extreme Weather Impacts of Climate Change – How can the Insurance Industry Help?* Available at http://www.climate wise.org.uk/storage/_website-2012/collaborations/adaptationrisk-management/ClimateWise%20Adaptation%20Report.pdf (accessed 31 May 2014).

Surminski. S., 2014. 'The role of insurance in reducing direct risk – the case of flood insurance', *International Review of Environmental and Resource Economics*, **7**(3–4), 241–78.

Surminski, S. and Oramas-Dorta, D., 2011. 'Building effective and sustainable risk transfer initiatives in low- and middle-income economies: what can we learn from existing insurance schemes', Policy Paper, Centre for Climate Change Economics and Policy, Grantham Research Institute on Climate Change and the Environment, London. Available at http://www.cccep.ac.uk/Publications/Policy/docs/PP_sustainable-risk-transfer-initiatives.pdf (accessed 27 February 2012).

Surminski, S. and Oramas-Dorta, D., 2014. 'Flood insurance schemes and climate adaptation in developing countries', *International Journal of Disaster Risk Reduction*, **7**, 154–64.

Surminski, S, Bouwer, L, Lynnerooth-Bayer, J. 2016. How insurance can support climate resilience, *Nature Climate Change*, April 2016.

UNCTAD, 2012. *Trade and Development Report*. United Nations Conference on Trade and Development. Available at http://unctad.org/en/PublicationsLibrary/tdr2012_en.pdf (accessed 11 March 2014).

UNFCCC, 2010. *The Cancun Agreements: Outcome of the Work of the Ad Hoc Working Group on Long-term Cooperative Action under the Convention, 15 March 2011*, FCCC/CP/2010/7/Add. Available at http://unfccc.int (accessed 11 March 2012).

UNISDR, 2009. *Global Assessment Report on Disaster Risk Reduction. Risk and Poverty in a Changing Climate*. Geneva: United Nations International Strategy for Disaster Reduction Secretariat.

UNISDR, 2011. *Global Assessment Report on Disaster Risk Reduction: Revealing Risk, Redefining Development*. Geneva and Oxford: United Nations International Strategy for Disaster Reduction Secretariat and Information Press.

Warner, K., Ranger, N., Surminski, S. et al., 2009. *Adaptation to Climate Change: Linking Disaster Reduction and Insurance*. Geneva: United Nations International Strategy for Disaster Reduction Secretariat (UNISDR).

World Bank, 2011. *Innovation in Disaster Risk Financing for Developing Countries: Public and Private Contributions*. Washington, DC: World Bank. Available at https://www.gfdrr.org/sites/gfdrr.org/files/DRFI_WRC_Paper_FINAL_April 11.pdf (accessed 3 June 2015).

World Bank, 2012a. *World Bank Group Disaster Risk Financing Business Lines*. Washington, DC: World Bank, Global Facility for Disaster Reduction and Recovery.

World Bank, 2012b. Personal communication, World Bank, Washington, DC.

World Bank, 2013. *Financing for Development Post 2015*. Washington, DC: World Bank. Available at https://www.worldbank.org/content/dam/Worldbank/docu ment/Poverty%20documents/WB-PREM%20financing-for-development-pub-10-11-13web.pdf (accessed 21 July 2015).

World Bank, 2014. *World Development Report Risk and Opportunity Managing Risk for Development*. Washington, DC: World Bank. Available at http://siteresources. worldbank.org/EXTNWDR2013/Resources/8258024-1352909193861/8936935-1356011448215/8986901-1380046989056/WDR-2014_Complete_Report.pdf (accessed 21 July 2015).

World Bank, DRFIP, Schweizerische Eidgenossenschaft and GFDRR, 2013. *Guidance Note Financing Post-disaster Recovery and Reconstruction Operations: Developing an Institutional Mechanism to Ensure the Effective Use of Financial Resources*. Available at http://siteresources.worldbank.org/EXTDISASTER/Resources/8308420-1342531265657/Central-Note-on-Reconstruction-Process_04Nov2013.pdf (accessed 4 June 2015).

11. Migration and climate-resilient development

Maria Waldinger

11.1 INTRODUCTION

Most strategies for climate resilience focus on *in situ* adaptation. That is, measures are put in place to enable people and economic activities to remain in their original location (Castells-Quintana et al., Chapter 4, this volume). In this scenario, migration is seen as a failure in adaptation, as a last-resort response when all else has failed. Such involuntary migration is associated with high economic, social and psychological costs. However, moving away from hazard zones in a planned and proactive way can also be an adaptation tool. In some cases it may be the most effective way of remaining climate resilient.

Migration has been a frequent and often effective response to climate variability and change in the past. However, the motivations to migrate are complex. The effect of climate on migration decisions also depends crucially on socio-economic, political and institutional conditions. These conditions affect vulnerability to climate risks and hence how important climate is in determining migration decisions.

People migrate for many reasons – economic, political or social. An economic migrant leaves his or her place of residence primarily in order to improve living standards and quality of life or to take up employment outside their original location. A political migrant migrates to locations of more political freedom, for example, where freedom of speech is guaranteed. Social causes for migration include migration for marriage or family reunion. Environmental migration is migration with the prime motive to move from environmentally poor to environmentally more benign conditions. It includes people moving away from places subject to gradual environmental degradation as well as places experiencing a sudden environmental shock, such as a natural disaster.

Typically, several of these reasons interact to form the basis for migration decisions. But the empirical evidence shows that environmental reasons often feature. People in developing countries frequently respond to climatic change by migrating internally. Evidence on the relationship between climate change and international migration is more limited, but suggests that international migration in response to climate hazards is less frequent.

The extent to which migration is an effective response to climate risks depends on certain preconditions. Access to information on the economic and social costs of migration, on the advantages and disadvantages of potential destination locations, and the absence of credit constraints and other barriers can help potential migrants to make better decisions that will improve livelihoods. Policy intervention is also required to reduce possible negative impacts in both the sending and receiving region.

This chapter reviews what is known about the effects of climate change on migration patterns within and out of developing countries, concentrating on the economic aspects of migration. The chapter starts with a discussion of the different forms of migration (Section 11.2). It then reviews the link between climate risks and migration, both conceptually (Section 11.3) and empirically, based on past experience (Section 11.4). Section 11.5 reviews the economic impact migration has on sending countries. Section 11.6 asks to what extent migration may be a tool to foster climate-resilient development. Section 11.7 concludes.

11.2   FORMS OF MIGRATION

Migration can take many forms (Table 11.1). Depending on a migrant's destination it can be international (crossing a country border) or internal migration (staying within home country borders). Migrants can decide to stay temporarily (for example, seasonal or circular migration) or permanently in the destination location. The literature on migration also distinguishes between forced and voluntary migration. Forced migration includes situations where 'the migrants are faced with death if they remain in their present place of residency' (Hugo, 1996, p. 107); voluntary

Table 11.1   Alternative migration classifications

Criterion	Forms of migration
Destination	international, internal
Duration	seasonal, medium term, permanent
Motivation	economic, political, social, environmental, climate
Choice	forced, voluntary
Outcome	productive, unproductive

migration occurs where 'the choice and will of the migrant is the over-whelmingly decisive element encouraging people to move' (Hugo, 1996, p. 107).

Finally, migration can also be defined in terms of development out-comes. Migration is an important adaptation strategy in the face of spatial disparities in economic opportunities, political and environ-mental conditions. If people move to places that make them better off, then migration has a positive effect on economic development for the individual.

In the debate on the effects of climate change on migration, different terms are applied to those moving for environmental reasons, including environmental or climate refugee and environmental or climate migrant. Broadly speaking, the term 'environmental refugee' is used for people who 'are compelled to flee by sudden, drastic environmental change that cannot be reversed' (Keane, 2004, p. 214). The term is often applied to people affected by environmental disaster as opposed to people affected by gradual climate change.

The second category, that of environmental migrants, generally applies to people who leave their place of residency because of long-term, and often gradual, climatic changes that have negative effects on their present or future living conditions. The United Nations (UN) defines a migrant as an individual who has resided in a foreign country for more than one year irrespective of the causes, voluntary or involuntary, and the means, regular or irregular, used to migrate.

Until now, the status of people leaving their place of residency due to environmental reasons has remained undefined in international law. Legally speaking, the term 'environmental refugee' is a legal misnomer. According to Keane (2004, p. 215), 'refugee status results from the denial of human rights'. 'People forced from their homes by floods, earthquakes and other natural disasters are not in the same position. Their govern-ment is sympathetic towards them. It is not driving them away, and they still have rights ... There is no such thing as an environmental refugee' (Lubbers, 2004).

One reason for the lack of definition relating to migration caused by environmental degradation or change is linked to the difficulty of isolat-ing environmental factors from other drivers of migration. It may also not be in the political interest of developed countries to extend the range of acceptable reasons for immigration. Yet, scientists expect that climate change will lead to increased numbers of displaced people. Defining their legal status, in conjunction with sound migration policies, would increase the efficiency with which policy makers could plan and implement population movements due to climate change.

11.3   HOW CLIMATE RISKS AFFECT MIGRATION

There are various channels through which climate risks may affect migration decisions. The main channels are through the impact of climate events on income and conflict. However, the factors motivating migration decisions are invariably complex. The links are not automatic and socio-economic factors, such as the institutional context, play a crucial role.

11.3.1   Climate Effects Transmitted via Income

One of the most important drivers of migration patterns across the world are differences in income levels. If a person expects that her income or living standards more broadly would increase by moving elsewhere, she has a powerful incentive to do so (for example, Borjas, 2014).

Consequently, in cases where climate change affects people's current or future income or their living standards, climate change will affect people's decision to migrate. Generally speaking, one would expect that decreases in income lead to increases in migration. In the context of developing countries, however, where financial markets work imperfectly, decreases in income may also impose credit constraints and reduce the number of people able to migrate.

Empirical evidence shows strong effects of climatic variations on income in developing countries (Barrios et al., 2010; Dell et al., 2012), in particular in the agricultural sector (Deschenes and Greenstone, 2007, 2012). For India, Burgess et al. (forthcoming) show that excessive heat during the growing season decreased income from agriculture and increased mortality among the rural population. The authors point out that dependence on agriculture is the key factor shaping this strong income effect of climate. The same excessive heat does not affect people employed in the urban economy. Yet, people in the rural economy are not all equally affected. The effect is mitigated for people with access to credit, for example, through microcredit institutions. Flooding can also have important effects on productivity. Aguilar and Vicarelli (2011) find that during the 1998/99 El Nino Southern Oscillation (ENSO) event, extreme precipitation resulted in a severely decreased maize harvest and reduced agricultural income.

Adverse climatic conditions also reduce income through their effect on labour productivity. In the short term, heat decreases physical and cognitive abilities and hence labour supply (Heal and Park, 2013; Deryugina and Hsiang, 2014). In the medium and long term, a temporary reduction in income and food intake can have lasting effects on labour productivity, especially for those affected as children. Aguilar and Vicarelli (2011) show that households affected by the 1998/99 ENSO event decreased their intake of fruits, vegetables and animal proteins. For affected children this had long-lasting effects on cognitive development, for example, language development, working and long-term memory and visual-spatial thinking.

11.3.2 Climate Effects Transmitted through Conflict

The relationship between climate change and conflict remains controversial because the links are highly complex and heavily dependent on a country's socio-economic, institutional and political characteristics.

There is evidence of specific historical cases where changes in climatic conditions increased pressure on resources and led to violence. It has been argued that the European witch hunt and persecution of Jewish communities often coincided with times of economic distress (Oster, 2004; Anderson et al., 2013), and that rural uprisings in China increased during periods of higher drought frequency (Jia, 2014). However, with the introduction of the more drought-resistant sweet potato this relationship disappeared.

There is some (although contested) evidence on the link between climate, economic shocks and conflict today (Miguel et al., 2004; Burke et al., 2014). For example, the conflict in Syria has coincided with a record drought in the Fertile Crescent, made two to three times more likely by climate change (Kelley et al., 2015).

However, it is important to remember that 'climatic conditions are neither necessary nor sufficient for conflicts to occur' (Burke et al., 2014, p. 4). There is a relationship between resource scarcity and violence, but the effect of climatic conditions on resource scarcity must be understood in the socio-economic context. Climatic conditions cause resource scarcity if socio-economic conditions cannot mitigate its adverse effects.

11.3.3 Conditioning Factors

Specific weather shocks do not have an 'automatic' effect on living standards. Instead, the impacts of weather shocks are shaped by socio-economic, political and institutional conditions, which create differences in initial conditions and lead to different responses in the aftermath of the shock. In many cases, it is clear that these initial conditions, as well as responses to the shock, are decisive in shaping the magnitude of the damage. In other words, the effect of climate change on living standards and conflict risk depends on an individual's or a country's ability to adapt to these changes and to mitigate their outcomes.

In the Indian context, the strong effect of extreme temperature on mortality is also a consequence of the farmers' inability to react to extreme temperature, for example, by increasing irrigation, or to protect themselves from the outcomes, for example, by using savings. Areas with access to microcredit were significantly less affected as were people living in urban areas who did not depend on agriculture for their living (Burgess et al., forthcoming).

The effect of temperature on mortality is exacerbated in settings where credit constraints prevent investment in and use of adaptive measures. The strong relationship between hot temperature and mortality at the beginning of the twentieth century has since declined due to the use of air conditioning (Barreca et al., 2013).

Flooding often leads to destruction and hardship in the short term. As we have seen, it can also have adverse effects in the long term, for example, on cognitive skills (Aguilar and Vicarelli, 2011). However, the economic effects of flooding in the long run are less clear. One explanation for this phenomenon is that floods tend to attract considerable government attention. They are visually very powerful, attracting media attention as well as public funding for reconstruction (Mueller et al., 2014). Rebuilding the economic infrastructure gives people the opportunity of return to their work and to the pre-flooding state of affairs. On the other hand, these efforts also reduce the costs of flooding to the population and thereby reduce incentives to adapt to regular flooding, for example, by migrating to less flood-prone areas (Boustan et al., 2012).

11.4 EMPIRICAL EVIDENCE

The previous section examined channels through which climate change could affect migration decisions, in particular the effect of climate on income and conflict. This provides a structure to assess empirically what the relationship between climate change and migration has been in the past.

11.4.1 Climate Effects that Promote Migration

There are well-documented effects of climate on *internal migration* (Barrios et al., 2006; Marchiori et al., 2011). For example, a decline in precipitation in Africa has increased rural to urban migration within sub-Saharan African countries (Barrios et al., 2006; Henderson et al., 2014). Henry et al. (2004) find that inter-provincial migration in Burkina Faso is shaped by environmental as well as socio-demographic factors. Not all this migration is well ordered.

Compared with the significance of internal migration the number of people engaging in international migration is small. The relationship between climate change and international migration has nevertheless received considerable attention in public and policy debates. As Piguet et al. (2011, p. 15) observe, 'Debates on the climate change-migration nexus often seem to focus overwhelmingly on international migration, and particularly on flows from the "South" to the "North". But this bias tells more on Western fears than on actual trends.'

One prominent argument is that since climate change will affect income and livelihoods in developing countries particularly severely, the incentive of their people to migrate to rich countries will be especially strong. Beine and Parsons (2013) test this hypothesis empirically. They focus on the effect of long- and short-term temperature changes on migration, but also include other variables, such as incidences of conflict, in their model. This allows them to estimate how the effect of climate on migration compares with the effect of these other variables. They do not find evidence for an effect of climate on migration, but find strong evidence for conflict as a driver of migration.

This indicates that prevailing barriers to international migration, such as international laws, transportation costs and credit constraints, currently outweigh the effect of climate on international migration. Climate stress is only one factor among many that affect people's decisions to migrate and their choice of destination. Other factors include the costs of migration, both monetary (for example, transportation costs, set-up costs), practical (for example, learning a new language) and emotional (for example, losing a social network). International barriers to migration dramatically increase these costs and reduce the expected returns on migration.

These barriers will remain important in the future. However, it is difficult to extrapolate the effect of current climate stress to the impact that potentially much more dramatic climate risks might have in the future.

11.4.2 Climate Effects that Hinder Migration

Much of the debate on climate change and migration has discussed a model of migration where climate change potentially increases the number of migrants. Recent contributions, however, also emphasize the limits that credit constraints may impose on people's migration decisions. Dustmann and Okatenko (2014) find that credit constraints inhibit migration, especially in the poorest parts of the world in sub-Saharan Africa and parts of Asia.

As a result, the poorest and most vulnerable are often not those who migrate because they lack the necessary resources. For the relationship between climate change and migration this implies that climate risks may reduce migration if vulnerable population groups become too credit-constrained to migrate.

Gray and Mueller (2012) examine the effect of climate change on credit constraints and migration decisions and confirm that the poorest and most vulnerable are often not those who migrate, because they lack the necessary resources. They find that incidences of drought in rural Bangladesh increased mobility of households that were not directly affected while reducing mobility of the most affected households. Robalino et al. (2015) examine the effect of natural disasters on migration. Consistent with Gray and Mueller's (2012) finding, they conclude that the most severe disasters, through their effect on credit constraints, reduce migration (for other studies on the importance of credit constraints for migration, see McKenzie and Rapoport, 2007; Abramitzky et al., 2013).

11.4.3   Historical Migration Movements

Estimates of the effect of climate on modern-day population movements necessarily depend on contemporary changes in climate. These changes are small, relative to the dramatic impacts forecast under unmitigated climate change, and therefore an imperfect guide to future migration trends. Yet, in the history of humankind, human societies have already been exposed to some quite drastic climatic changes. It is instructive to explore how they were affected by these climatic changes and how it affected their migration behaviour.

Archaeological evidence indicates that periods of drastic climatic change often coincided with the collapse of past civilizations. Over the past millennia, 'whole empires collapsed [due to climatic factors] and their people were diminished to much lower subsistence levels, whereas in other cases, populations migrated and adapted to new subsistence modes' (de Menocal, 2001, p. 669).

It has also been shown that populations moved into more favourable areas in order to increase their chances of survival (Riehl et al., 2014, p. 12348). Urban centres of the Harrapan Society in the Indus Valley, now in Pakistan, were abandoned during a 200-year drought (Marris, 2014). During the African Humid Period (*c.* 9000 to 6000 years ago) the Sahara was home to lakes and vegetation (Claussen et al., 2003). This enabled inhabitants of the Sahel region to enter this area and to cross it, reaching the European and Asian continents. Wet conditions and increased vegetation in the Central Sahara/Sahel region in the pre-historic period (for example, 195,000 and 120,000–110,000 years ago) coincided with periods of human expansion into this region (Castaneda et al., 2009).

However, the observed relationship between societal collapse, outmigration and climate in the past should not be interpreted as a deterministic relationship, where changes in climate automatically led to societal collapse and outmigration. 'In all cases, the observed societal response reflects an interaction between human cultural elements (socioeconomic, political, and secular stresses) and persistent multi-century shifts in climate' (de Menocal, 2001, p. 669).

Like the recent empirical evidence, past episodes of climate change are not necessarily good guides to the future. Studies of climate change-induced migration forecast large streams of migrants (for example, Myers, 2002), although the underlying evidence is often weak. For a given shock today, less migration may result compared to historical times because international borders and international laws limit migration. On the other hand, increased migration could occur because of lower transportation costs and greater availability of information.

11.5   THE ECONOMIC EFFECT OF MIGRATION

The last section has provided evidence on migration patterns in response to climate shocks. In this section we explore the economic effects of such migration, including evidence on the use of migration as a risk-coping strategy. This includes both internal migration and (less frequently) international migration.

11.5.1   Internal Migration

Internal migration is a frequent phenomenon in developing countries. It can take various forms. Circular and seasonal migrants return to their homes after a limited period of time, typically less than six months. Permanent migrants shift their work and residence completely to a new location (Findley, 1994). Economic growth and internal migration can be seen as complements. Migration fuels economic growth and economic growth, especially when it is spatially localized, fuels migration.

Through internal migration, households seek to diversify their portfolio of economic activities in order to ensure survival or to improve their standards of living (Ellis, 1998). Household members access new opportunities in distant labour markets. Diversification from rural to non-rural activities implies that income risks in different economic activities of the household are not correlated (De Brauw and Mueller, 2012). It has been predicted that climate change will increase income risk for rural households in developing countries. Diversification through internal migration may therefore in the future increase in importance as a risk management strategy by rural households in developing countries.

Households in Vietnam use seasonal migration to increase their living standards. Annualized expenditure grew by 5.2 percentage points due to increased migration (De Brauw and Harigaya, 2007). This was despite the fact that poor transportation infrastructure and limited off-farming employment opportunities reduced people's ability to use migration for diversification. In this case, the typical migrant was relatively well educated, relatively young and male.

An important barrier to migration is the lack of information on potential returns to labour in distant markets, although it is a constraint that can be overcome through learning and experience (Bryan et al., 2014). De Brauw and Harigaya (2007) highlight the importance of community networks for finding jobs in urban areas. Migration patterns are also shaped by institutional arrangement. Evidence from China indicates that the risk of expropriation – which increases as people leave land behind – deters rural-urban migration (Mullan et al., 2011). Land tenure security, in contrast, increases migration.

Liquidity constraints lead to poverty-related labour immobility (Phan and Coxhead, 2010). Evidence from Vietnam showed that the effect of migration on income inequality varied depending on the receiving province's characteristics. Migration to the provinces with growing industries and labour markets reduces income inequality, while migration to other regions does not (Phan and Coxhead, 2010).

11.5.2   International Migration

The purposes of migrating abroad are similar to the purposes of migrating internally: increased living standards and improved income stability. Income differentials between countries provide incentives to leave a country with relatively low income levels and move to a country with relatively high income levels.

The typical international migrant from developing countries has above average education and income levels. The international transfer of human capital that occurs when relatively well-educated individuals move from developing to developed countries has been termed 'brain drain' (Beine et al., 2008, p. 631).

International outmigration of talented people can have a number of negative but also some positive consequences at the household and country level. On the negative side, skilled migrants are net fiscal contributors and their departure therefore represents a loss for those left behind. Secondly, skilled and unskilled labour are complements in the production process. Loss of skilled labour may decrease productivity (and wages) of unskilled labour left behind and increase productivity (and wages) of skilled labour. As a result, inequality between skilled and unskilled labour may increase.

Finally, skilled labour attracts foreign direct investments and research and development (R&D) activities (Docquier and Rapoport, 2007).

However, international migration may also bring advantages to developing countries' economies. Having a household member abroad still benefits the sending household if she sends remittances. Remittances reduce income variability and the risk of complete income failure in the sending household. Remittances from the USA to Mexico or from Russia to Central Asia, for example, constitute an important part of gross domestic product (GDP) and increase investment in these migrants' country of origin. The ultimate impact of remittances on welfare also depends on household spending patterns. Remittances spent on durable goods, education or investment have a stronger effect on poverty alleviation and household welfare than remittances devoted to consumption.

Furthermore, the prospect of migration opportunities may also motivate people in developing countries to obtain better education. In developing economies, education is not valued as much as in developed economies. Wages for high-skilled workers are generally substantially higher in developed economies. If migration to a developed country is a real possibility, then people in developing countries may decide to invest in their education. In the end, not everyone is going to migrate, and the developing economy benefits from increased stocks of human capital (Beine et al., 2001; Mayr and Peri, 2008).

By going abroad migrants extend their own network. If they stay in touch with their home community, this also extends the network of those left behind. The importance of networks has been shown for business and investment decisions, and – not least – for future migration decisions (Docquier and Rapoport, 2007).

Finally, developing countries can benefit from migrants who decide to return. Until now, however, return migration is most common for migrants from the Middle East, Asia (except India) and the developed world. 'There is little indication of any return for immigrants from Africa' (Dustmann and Weiss, 2007, p. 7).

11.6 MIGRATION AS A TOOL FOR CLIMATE-RESILIENT DEVELOPMENT

Whether the economic consequences of migration are positive or negative and whether migration allows people to adapt efficiently to climate change depends on an array of socio-economic, political and institutional conditions. This section explores under what conditions migration will contribute to climate-resilient development.

Migration can have positive economic effects if migrants go to productivity-enhancing areas. It can have negative economic effects if migrants go to areas where their labour is not efficiently employed. Migration can be efficient and productivity-enhancing if certain preconditions are satisfied. These preconditions include efficient institutions, for example, land tenure security, sufficient information about potential migration destinations and about alternatives to migration, such as local adaptation. Violent conflict, misinformation or credit constraints, on the other hand, can lead migrants to destinations where they will be unable to be productive.

11.6.1   Developing Alternative Adaptation Options

Migration is not the only strategy to adapt to climate change. While migration can be a powerful tool for adaptation it is also very costly. The use of alternative adaptation strategies will therefore often be preferred, for example, local adaptation of the agricultural sector, rather than migration to cities. An integral part of using migration as an efficient adaptation strategy is a solid understanding of those alternatives. Migration becomes a viable choice when its costs and benefits compare favourably to those of other adaptation options.

Being aware of all alternatives gives people a choice between migrating away and less costly ways of adapting to new environmental conditions. The costs and benefits of migration choices need to be understood – including psychological and social costs. For example, the fact that migration is a highly gender-specific process – with most migrants being young men – systematically disturbs social processes such as family formation and adds to the social costs of migration.

11.6.2   Helping People Make Good Migration Choices

If people choose migration over other adaptation options, then it is in the interest of the policy maker and national economy that they make the most efficient choice. Public policy has a role to play in helping people make efficient migration choices.

Providing information: insufficient information on potential costs and benefits of migrating to certain destinations can lead to inefficient migration decisions. Migrants may incur the costs of migration but overestimate economic opportunities (Munshi, 2003; Bryan et al., 2014). Reliable information on migration destinations is key to making efficient migration decisions. In addition, taking into consideration all types of costs, be they economic, social or psychological, is an integral part of making an informed choice about migration. Currently, migrant networks play an important role in transmitting such information from those who have already migrated to their home communities (Munshi, 2003; De Brauw and Harigaya, 2007; Bryan et al., 2014).

Alleviating credit constraints: liquidity constraints lead to poverty-related labour immobility (Phan and Coxhead, 2010). In other words, people will not be able to migrate to the most suitable, productivity-enhancing locations if they are credit constrained and unable to cover costs of migrating to these destinations. Instead, they might move to less suitable, but closer areas. Hence, credit constraints can force people to take the 'wrong' migration decision because migrants incur up-front costs (transportation costs, costs from not working, set-up costs in destination location). These costs are especially high in areas with poor transportation infrastructure and in areas with limited access to credit.

Improving institutional quality: people may choose not to migrate even if they and their families would benefit from migration if inadequate institutions reduce their incentives to do so. Land tenure security can affect incentives to migrate, for example, if people are not able to sell their land in order to generate capital or are not confident reclaiming it upon return (Deiniger and Jin, 2006; Mullan et al., 2011). Improved land tenure security also increases people's choice of alternative adaptation options, for example, adaptation in local agriculture, since these tend to involve long-term investments that create costs in the short term and benefits in the long term. They will only be undertaken if an individual is confident they will reap the benefits in the long term (Besley, 1995).

Avoiding forced migration: stronger institutions are also key to minimize the risk of forced migration, where 'migrants are faced with death if they remain in their present place of residency' (Hugo, 1996, p. 107) and have little choice but to leave, irrespective of the consequences. Conflict may also increase credit constraints and force people to choose sub-optimal locations, for example, a neighbouring country regardless of its economic opportunities. In addition, absence from the labour market will likely result in deterioration of refugees' human capital.

Clarifying legal status: defining the legal status of people migrating due to environmental reasons. Until now, the legal situation of people migrating due to environmental reasons remains undefined. Environmental migrants do not have a legal status comparable to that of refugees, which would grant them legal protection to enter a country. Yet, the UN expects that climate change will lead to increased numbers of displaced people. The legal status of environmental migrants needs to be defined, for example, in a process led by the UN or the UN High Commissioner for Refugees (UNHCR), which might have the power to declare an 'environmental crisis' and give affected people certainty about their legal situation.

11.6.3 Managing Economy-wide Effects

Policy makers should be aware that people staying in areas affected by outmigration may be negatively affected if public goods and services are no longer provided. This may lead to growing economic disparities within countries and have direct negative effects on stayers. Supporting measures may be needed in areas affected by outward migration, but also in the receiving jurisdictions.

Supporting areas affected by outward migration: the effect of outward migration and 'brain drain' can be lessened by promoting links between migrants and their region of origin. Persisting links between migrants and those staying behind can mitigate potentially negative effects of migration, for example, if migrants send remittances back home or return to invest newly acquired capital or skills.

Managing further retreat, if necessary: it is possible that climate change will make certain areas all but uninhabitable. In such situations, voluntary migration may eventually give way to 'managed retreat' (defined as 'the progressive abandonment of land and structures in highly vulnerable areas and resettlement of inhabitants' (Mearns and Norton, 2010, p. 116). While reducing people's vulnerability to the adverse consequences of climate change, resettlement may increase their social and economic vulnerability. Resettlement is often a heavily politicized and delicate process. Not only the economic but also the psychological and social costs of people being resettled are very high, requiring careful processes and thorough consultation (see, for example, the World Bank's Operational Directive on involuntary resettlement (World Bank, 2013)).

Facilitating integration of migrants in the destination region: migration will also pose challenges to the receiving jurisdictions. Public policy can help alleviate these challenges by helping to manage the absorption process, especially in urban areas. The arrival of migrants poses important economic and social challenges to receiving communities. A receiving city's labour market and infrastructure might not have the capacities to accommodate rapidly increasing numbers of people. If arriving migrants encounter problems entering the labour market or do not have access to public goods this will lead to economic and social problems. It is therefore crucial to strengthen the absorptive capacity of migration destinations, in particular urban labour markets and public services.

Reducing climate risks in the destination region: there may also be a need to direct migration movements to areas of decreased environmental risk. An important part of internal migration involves moves from environmentally vulnerable areas to areas that are equally vulnerable, albeit for different reasons (Miller, 1982). For example, migrants might leave drought-prone agricultural areas to cities located in low-elevation coastal areas that are prone to increased flooding. It is important to identify such migration movements and take measures to manage them.

11.7 CONCLUSIONS

The empirical evidence shows that people in developing countries are likely to respond to climatic change by migrating internally. There is less evidence on the relationship between climate change and international migration.

The effect of climate change on migration depends crucially on socio-economic, political and institutional conditions. These conditions affect both vulnerability to climate change and how important climate change is in determining migration decisions.

People working in the agricultural sector are particularly affected by short-term climate shocks (droughts, flooding and so on) and long-term climate change. Their vulnerability, however, depends on their ability to adapt to these changes, for example, through the use of new crop varieties, as well as through non-agricultural activities, such as consumption smoothing through access to credit, insurance and social safety nets.

Migration has been a widespread response to climate variability and change in the past. There is strong evidence of this, for example, in the Sahel region of West Africa. Migration might also be an effective response to the climate risks of the future, but only under certain preconditions.

Access to information on the economic and social costs of migration, on the advantages and disadvantages of potential destination locations and the absence of credit constraints can help potential migrants make decisions that will improve their livelihoods.

Policy intervention is required to reduce potential negative impacts in both the sending and receiving region. Badly managed migration is associated with high economic, social and psychological costs. Sound policy makes the difference between migration as an effective adaptation tool and migration as a sign of failed adaptation and economic mismanagement.

REFERENCES

Abramitzky, R., Boustan, L.P. and Eriksson, K., 2013. 'Have the poor always been less likely to migrate? Evidence from inheritance practices during the age of mass migration', *Journal of Development Economics*, **102**, 2–14.

Aguilar, A. and Vicarelli, M., 2011. 'El Nino and Mexican children: medium-term effects of early-life weather shocks on cognitive and health outcomes', Mimeo, Harvard University.

Anderson, W., Johnson, N. and Koyama, M., 2013. 'Jewish persecutions and weather shocks: 1100–1800', GMU Working Paper in Economics No. 13-06.

Barreca, A., Clay, K., Deschenes, O., Greenstone, M. and Shapiro, J.S., 2013. 'Adapting to climate change: the remarkable decline in the U.S. temperature-mortality relationship over the 20th century', NBER Working Paper No. 18692.

Barrios, S., Bertinelli, L. and Strobl, E. 2006. 'Climatic change and rural-urban migration: the case of sub-Saharan Africa', CORE Discussion Paper No. 2006/46.

Barrios, S., Bertinelli, L. and Strobl, E., 2010. 'Trends in rainfall and economic growth in Africa: a neglected cause of the African growth tragedy', *The Review of Economics and Statistics*, **92**(2), 350–66.

Beine, M. and Parsons, C., 2013. 'Climatic factors as determinants of international migration', International Migration Institute and Oxford University Working Paper No. 70.

Beine, M., Docquier, F. and Rapoport, H. 2001. 'Brain drain and economic growth: theory and evidence', *Journal of Development Economics*, **64**(1), 275–89.

Beine, M., Docquier, F. and Rapoport, H., 2008. 'Brain drain and human capital formation in developing countries: winners and losers', *The Economic Journal*, **118**(528), 631–52.

Besley, T., 1995. 'Property rights and investment incentives: theory and evidence from Ghana', *Journal of Political Economy*, **103**(5), 903–37.

Borjas, G., 2014. *Immigration Economics*. Cambridge, MA: Harvard University Press.

Boustan, L. Platt, M., Kahn, E. and Rhode, P.W., 2012. 'Moving to higher ground: migration response to natural disasters in the early twentieth century', *American Economic Review: Papers & Proceedings*, **102**(3), 238–44.

Bryan, G., Chowdhury, S. and Mobarak, A., 2014. 'Underinvestment in a profitable technology: the case of seasonal migration in Bangladesh', *Econometrica*, **82**(5), 1671–748.

Burgess, R., Deschenes, O., Donaldson, D. and Greenstone, M., forthcoming. 'The unequal effects of weather and climate change: evidence from mortality in India', *Quarterly Journal of Economics*.

Burke, M., Hsiang, S. and Miguel, E., 2014. 'Climate and conflict', Mimeo, University of California at Berkeley.

Castaneda, I.S., Mulitza, S., Schefuss, E., Lopes dos Santos, R.A., Sinninghe Damste, J.S. and Schouten, S., 2009. 'Wet phases in the Sahara/Sahel region and human migration patterns in North Africa', *Proceedings of the National Academy of Sciences*, **106**(48), 20159–63.

Claussen, M., Brovkin, V., Ganopolski, A., Kubatzki, C. and Petoukhov, V., 2009. 'Climate change in Northern Africa: the past is not the future', *Climatic Change*, **57**, 99–118.

De Brauw, A. and Harigaya. T., 2007. 'Seasonal migration and improving living standards in Vietnam', *American Journal of Agricultural Economics*, **89**(2), 430–47.

De Brauw, A. and Mueller, V., 2012. 'Do limitations in land rights transferability influence mobility rates in Ethiopia?', *Journal of African Economies*, **21**(4), 548–79.

De Menocal, P.B., 2001. 'Cultural responses to climate change during the Late Holocene', *Science*, **292**(5517), 667–73.

Deiniger, K. and Jin, S., 2006. 'Tenure security and land-related investment: evidence from Ethiopia', *European Economic Review*, 50, 1245–77.

Dell, M., Jones, B.F. and Olken, B.A., 2012. 'Temperature shocks and economic growth: evidence from the last half century', *American Economic Journal: Macroeconomics*, **4**(3), 66–95.

Deryugina, T. and Hsiang, S., 2014. 'Does the environment still matter? Daily temperature and income in the United States', NBER Working Paper No. 20750.

Deschenes, O. and Greenstone, M., 2007. 'The economic impacts of climate change: evidence from agricultural output and random fluctuations in weather', *American Economic Review*, **97**(1), 354–85.

Deschenes, O. and Greenstone, M., 2012. 'The economic impacts of climate change: evidence from agricultural output and random fluctuations in weather: reply', *American Economic Review*, **102**(7), 3761–73.

Docquier, F. and Rapoport, H., 2007. 'Skilled migration: the perspective of developing countries', *IZA* Discussion Paper Series No. 2873.

Dustmann, C. and Okatenko, A., 2014. 'Out-migration, wealth constraints, and the quality of local amenities', *Journal of Development Economics*, **110**, 52–63.

Dustmann, C. and Weiss, Y., 2007. 'Return migration: theory and empirical evidence', CReAM Discussion Paper No. 02/07.

Ellis, F., 1998. 'Household strategies and rural livelihood diversification', *Journal of Development Studies*, **35**(1), 1–38.

Findley, S.E., 1994. 'Does drought increase migration? A study of migration from rural Mali during the 1983–1985 drought', *International Migration Review*, **28**(3), 539–53.

Gray, C.L. and Mueller, V., 2012. 'Natural disasters and population mobility in Bangladesh', *Proceedings of the National Academy of Sciences*, **109**(16), 6000–5.

Heal, G. and Park, J., 2013. 'Feeling the heat: temperature, physiology & the wealth of nations', NBER Working Paper No. 19725.

Henderson, V.H., Storeygard, A. and Deichmann, U., 2014. '50 years of urbanization in Africa – examining the role of climate change', World Bank Development Research Group Policy Research Working Paper No. 6925.

Henry, S., Beauchemin, C. and Schoumaker, B., 2004. 'The impact of rainfall on the first out-migration: a multi-level event-history analysis in Burkina Faso', *Population and Environment*, **25**, 5.

Hugo, G., 1996. 'Environmental concerns and international migration', *International Migration Review, Ethics, Migration, and Global Stewardship*, **30**(1), 105–31.

Jia, R., 2014. 'Weather shocks, sweet potatoes and peasant revolts in historical China', *Economic Journal*, **124**, 92–118.

Keane, D., 2004. 'Environmental causes and consequences of migration: a search for the meaning of environmental refugees', *Georgetown International Environmental Law Review*, **16**, 209–24.

Kelley, C., Mohtadi, S., Cane, M., Seager, R. and Kushnir, Y., 2015. 'Climate change in the Fertile Crescent and implications of the recent Syrian drought', *Proceedings of the Natural Academy of Sciences*. doi:10.1073/pnas.1421533112

Lubbers, R., 2004. 'Refugees and migrants: defining the difference', BBC News, 4 May 2004. Available at http://news.bbc.co.uk/go/pr/fr/-/1/hi/in_depth/3516112.stm (accessed 16 February 2016).

Marchiori L., Maystadt, J.-F. and Schumacher, I., 2011. 'The impact of weather anomalies on migration in sub-Saharan Africa', *Journal of Environmental Economics and Management*, **63**, 355–74.

Marris, E., 2014. 'Two-hundred-year drought doomed Indus Valley civilization', *Nature*. doi: 10.1038/nature.2014.14800

Mayr, K. and Peri, G., 2008. 'Return migration as a channel of brain gain', NBER Working Paper Series No. 14039.

McKenzie, D. and Rapoport, H., 2007. 'Network effects and the dynamics of migration and inequality: theory and evidence from Mexico', *Journal of Development Economics*, **84**(1), 1–24.

Mearns, R. and Norton, A., 2010. *Social Dimensions of Climate Change – Equity and Vulnerability in a Warming World*. Washington, DC: World Bank.

Miguel, E., Satyanath, S. and Sergenti, E., 2004. 'Economic shocks and civil conflict: an instrumental variables approach', *Journal of Political Economy*, **112**(4), 725–53.

Miller, J.C., 1982. 'The significance of drought, disease and famine in the agriculturally marginal zones of West-Central Africa', *Journal of African History*, **23**(1), 17–61.

Mueller, V., Gray, C. and Kosec, K., 2014. 'Heat stress increases long-term human migration in rural Pakistan', *Nature Climate Change*, **4**, 182–5.

Mullan, K., Grosjean, P. and Kontoleon, A., 2011. 'Land tenure arrangements and rural–urban migration in China', *World Development*, **39**(1), 123–33.

Munshi, K., 2003. 'Networks in the modern economy: Mexican migrants in the U.S. labor market', *Quarterly Journal of Economics*, **118**(2), 549–99.

Myers, N., 2002. 'Environmental refugees: a growing phenomenon of the 21st century', *Philosophical Transactions of the Royal Society B: Biological Sciences*, **357**(1420), 609–13.

Oster, E., 2004. 'Witchcraft, weather and economic growth in Renaissance Europe', *Journal of Economic Perspectives*, **18**(1), 215–28.

Phan, D. and Coxhead, I., 2010. 'Inter-provincial migration and inequality during Vietnam's transition', *Journal of Development Economics*, **91**, 100–12.

Piguet, E., Pecoud, A. and de Guchteneire, P., 2011. 'Migration and climate change: an overview', *Refugee Survey Quarterly*, 1–23.

Riehl, S., Pustovoytov, E., Weippert, H., Klett, S. and Hole, F., 2014. 'Drought stress variability in ancient Near Eastern agricultural systems evidenced by δ13C in barley grain', *Proceedings of the National Academy of Sciences*, **111**(34), 12348–53.

Robalino, J., Jimenez, J. and Chacon, A., 2015. 'The effect of hydro-meteorological emergencies on internal migration', *World Development*, **67**, 438–48.

World Bank, 2013. *Operational Manual – Involuntary Resettlement*. Available at http://web.worldbank.org/WBSITE/EXTERNAL/PROJECTS/EXTPOLICIES/EXTOPMANUAL/0,,contentMDK:20064610~menuPK:64701637~pagePK:64709096~piPK:64709108~theSitePK:502184~isCURL:Y,00.html (accessed 16 February 2016).

Index

adaptation to climate change
in agrarian economies 164–5, 169, 171, 173–4
assessment
analysis of methods 112–15
analysis of uncertainty 109–15
mainstreaming 101–2, 116
phasing and timing 102–3, 109–10, 116
policy-orientated approaches 101, 116
problems with classic approach to 99–101
baselines and additionality for 105–6
challenges
to assessment 114–15, 117
climate change over time 110
methodological 104–9, 116
prioritizing options 110
and responses 55
uncertainty 8, 100–101, 116–17
in climate-resilient cities 143, 145, 153–6, 158–60
and climate risk 53–4
constraints and barriers 57–8
creating environment for
community-based cooperative resource management 66
incentives and property rights 65–6
information 64–5
infrastructure 67–8
migration 68–9
spatial and industrial policy 66–7
structural transformation 69–70
discounting 106–7
economic development as best form of 3
'entry points' for action 7, 9
equity and distributional effects 107–8

evidence on options
early action to address long-term risks 134–5
early adaptation studies 128–9
early decisions with long lifetime 132–4
early low-regret options 103, 129–32
no-regret options 103, 113–14, 135, 137
practical implementation issues 135–7
exogenous trends affecting
location-based inequality 59–60
urbanization 60–61
implications
of pursuing climate-resilient development 9
of spatial development patterns 17
increased demand for 4
initiatives commonly associated with 54
and insurance instruments 62, 184–5, 188–9, 192, 194, 196–9
integrated
with development policy 9
proactive approach to 5
limitations of economic literature 1
and migration 8–9, 47, 68–9, 204, 206, 215–16, 218
move towards climate-resilient development 2–3, 9
objectives of 104–5
priority areas requiring 5, 7
responses
autonomous 53
and challenges 55
designing 7
and NPV 6
transformational 8
scale and transferability 108–9